BACKPACKER
THE OUTDOORS AT YOUR DOORSTEP

Trekking the Southern Appalachians

BACKPACKER

THE OUTDOORS AT YOUR DOORSTEP®

Trekking the
Southern
Appalachians

THE CAROLINAS, TENNESSEE, GEORGIA

Jack Igelman & Corey Hadden

THE MOUNTAINEERS BOOKS
is the nonprofit publishing arm of The Mountaineers Club, an organization founded in 1906 and dedicated to the exploration, preservation, and enjoyment of outdoor and wilderness areas.

1001 SW Klickitat Way, Suite 201, Seattle, WA 98134

BACKPACKER
THE OUTDOORS AT YOUR DOORSTEP
33 East Minor Street
Emmaus, PA 18099

Published simultaneously in Great Britain by Cordee, 3a DeMontfort Street, Leicester, England, LE1 7HD

Manufactured in China

Acquiring Editor: Cassandra Conyers
Project Editor: Laura Drury
Copy Editor: Brenda Pittsley
Cover and Book Design: The Mountaineers Books
Layout: Mayumi Thompson
Cartographer: Brian Metz/Green Rhino Graphics
Photographer: All photographs by Jack Igelman unless otherwise noted.

Cover photograph: *Trekker on the Appalachian Trail in the Roan Mountain area.* (Photo by Mark Carrol)
Back cover photograph: *Waterfall* (Photo by Ben Walters)
Frontispiece: *Log among flowers (*Photo by Ben Walters)
All shullphoto images are the exclusive copyrighted property of Harrison Shull. All rights reserved.

Library of Congress Cataloging-in-Publication Data
Igelman, Jack.
    Backpacker, trekking the southern Appalachians : the Carolinas, Tennessee, Georgia /
by Jack Igelman and Corey Hadden.— 1st ed.
        p. cm.
    Includes bibliographical references and index.
    ISBN 0-89886-966-8
    1. Hiking—Appalachian Region, Southern—Guidebooks. 2. Backpacking—Appalachian Region, Southern—Guidebooks. 3. Trails—Appalachian Region, Southern—Guidebooks. 4. Appalachian Region, Southern—Guidebooks. I. Title: Trekking the southern Appalachians. II. Hadden, Corey. III. Title.
    GV199.42.A65I44 2004
    796.51'0974—dc22
                                    2004025802

♻ Printed on recycled paper

Contents

Opposite: Storm over Pisgah National Forest (© shullphoto)

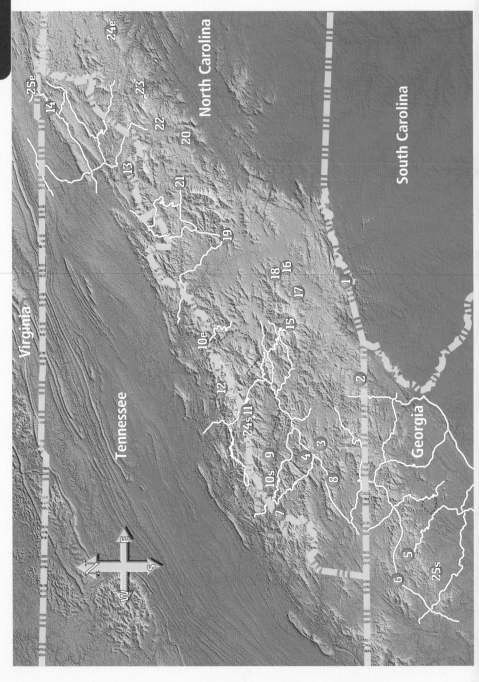

Legend

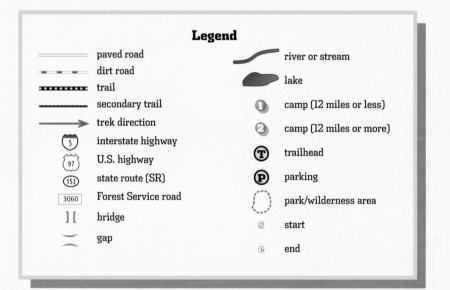

paved road	river or stream
dirt road	lake
trail	camp (12 miles or less)
secondary trail	camp (12 miles or more)
trek direction	trailhead
interstate highway	parking
U.S. highway	park/wilderness area
state route (SR)	start
Forest Service road	end
bridge	
gap	

Summary of Treks

Trek	Trek Highlights	Difficulty	Days	Miles	Shuttle	Elevation Gain	Nearest town
1	Cuts through the beautiful Jocassee Gorge region	Strenuous	4-7	52.4	Yes	16,100	Cleveland, NC/Cashiers, SC
2	Hike beside the wild and scenic Chattooga River; big mountain views.	Strenuous	3-6	55.2	Yes	12,900	Clayton, GA/Franklin,NC
3	Views of Great Smoky and Blue Ridge Mountains	Strenuous	3-5	46.9	Yes	14,300	Franklin,NC/Wesser, NC
4	Historic Appalachian Trail and stellar views from southern Appalachian balds	V. Strenuous	3-5	54.8	No	16,300	Wesser, NC
5	Rugged, remote, and the historic AT	V. Strenuous	3-5	53.2	No	17,400	Ellijay, GA
6	Beautiful waterfalls, country roads, and the Cohutta/Big Frog Wilderness	V. Strenuous	5-7	92.6	Yes	19,600	Ellijay, GA/Ducktown, TN
7	Ancient trees, rugged terrain, wilderness	Strenuous	4-6	56.5	No	18,400	Robbinsville, NC
8	Traverse the rugged high ridges across southwestern North Carolina's remote national forests.	Strenuous	2-4	39.8	Yes	13,600	Hayesville, NC/Franklin, NC
9	Hike through the largest roadless area in the East along the banks of Lake Fontana.	Easier	3	36.8	Yes	9200	Bryson City, NC/Fontana Village, NC
10	Traverse the highest ridges of the most massive mountains in the east on the historic Appalachian Trail.	V. Strenuous	4-6	71.8	Yes	21,600	Robbinsville, NC/Newport, TN
11	Follow beautiful Deep Creek, then climb over Clingman's Dome, second highest peak in the East with amazing views.	Strenuous	2-4	41.3	Yes	10,300	Cherokee, NC/Gatlinburg, TN
12	Look for old chimneys and homesteads before heading to the cooler high country and the Appalachian Trail.	Strenuous	3-5	53.8	No	16,800	Gatlinburg, TN
13	Brilliant views from grassy meadows	V. Strenuous	3-5	44	Yes	11,700	Erwin, TN/Roan Mountain, TN
14	Circumnavigate a serene valley on long ridge lines.	Easier	2-4	41	No	11,600	Damascus, VA
15	Seldom traveled section of the MST	Strenuous	3	35	Yes	8000	Waynesville, NC
16	Lots of water crossings on the South Mills River and Bradley Creek in the heart of the Pisgah forest	Easier	2-5	33.5	No	5700	Brevard, NC
17	Gorgeous views from mountain balds and granite domes	Strenuous	2-4	30	Yes	9700	Brevard, NC/Canton, NC
18	Walk the Pisgah ridge with dramatic views and varying terrain.	Strenuous	3-4	40	Yes	8200	Asheville, NC
19	Challenging ascent to the East's highest mountain	V. Strenuous	3	34	Yes	12,200	Asheville, NC
20	Hike across the Grand Canyon of the East, the Linville Gorge, en route to the highest mountain east of the Mississippi.	V. Strenuous	4-6	51.6	Yes	15,700	Jonas Ridge, NC/Marion, NC
21	Walk the crest of the Blacks with over 10 peaks above 6,000 feet	V. Strenuous	2-3	31.3	Yes	6900	Old Fort, NC/Burnsville, NC
22	Lots of river crossings and waterfalls before climbing up and over rugged Grandfather Mountain	Strenuous	4-6	46.8	Yes	11,600	Jonas Ridge, NC/Banner Elk, NC
23	Take in extraordinary views from Blue Ridge Parkway, dive into lush forests of the high country, and climb rugged highline over Grandfather Mountain.	Strenuous	2	40.5	Yes	7200	Blowing Rock, NC/Linville, NC
24	Thru-hike the rugged and beautiful western mountains and experience everything the southern mountains offer.	Strenuous	28	327.4	Yes	67,700	Cherokee, NC/Asheville, NC/Blowing Rock, NC
25	Thru-hike some or all of the most famous footpath in the world through the southern Appalachians.	Strenuous	6-8 wks	462	Yes	120,000	Ellijay, GA/Helen, GA/Franklin, NC/Wesser, NC/Newport, TN/Hot Springs, NC/Roan Mountain, TN/Damascus, VA

Introduction

Trekking in the southern Appalachian Mountains with only essentials on your back is like bringing times past into the present. Minus the high-tech gear, GPS units, and energy bars, traveling through the mountains is much as it was a century ago. The towering hardwoods, ancient rivers, and mountains are still here; so are the sounds of wind and rushing water and the sweet aromas of pine needles and wildflowers. And of course, the mode of transportation is the same: two feet.

Trekking is an escape from the technological clutter of the twenty-first century. In a hectic world, time for adventure and places for solitude can be hard to find; but in the forest, cell phone reception is poor and visa cards aren't accepted. Your feet are the ticket to cut loose from the fray.

So you say trekking doesn't deliver the kind of thrills attained climbing gnarly rock routes or paddling dicey rapids? Who can deny that a 30-minute lightning storm takes on new meaning viewed from a 6000-foot bald; trekking solo at dusk in a remote gorge stirs the imagination; or that fording a swollen creek in the dead of winter has bona fide consequences?

Trekking in the ancient Appalachians is also an immersion in millions of years of cultural, geologic, and biological history. Nowhere in North America is the biodiversity matched. Nowhere east of the

A small section of the Appalachian Trail

11

Rockies are the mountains higher and the gorges deeper. And nowhere on the continent are the mountains and rivers older.

While there is a timeless quality to the southern mountains, the corridors of wilderness have been decidedly squeezed. Experiencing the southern Appalachians by foot may ultimately help preserve these corridors. Some argue that tempting more visitors to the shrinking wilderness threatens to spoil its solitude. We counter that shielding this treasure from the public is more dangerous to the protection of the Appalachians than promoting their recreational value. Careless development and renegade legislation are far more serious threats than boosting the population of explorers.

The mission of this guide is to help you discover the rich history and striking beauty of the southern Appalachian Mountains. The treks described within this book are your invitation to adventure and to witness times past in the southern mountains.

The What, Why, and Where of Trekking

Foot travel in the mountains is an honest way to experience and admire the southern mountains. But make no mistake, the routes described in this book require a serious commitment of time, calories, and money. So before you journey, take a moment to mull over the bare bones of backpacking in the southern Appalachians.

Why we trek. You're tired, thirsty, and the three-day-old polypro tee shirt sealed to your body smells and feels like a dead rat. And there are still two days and 20 hard miles to go. At the moment, it may be advisable not to ask yourself why you're schlepping through the woods—although it's a worthy question to consider eventually, particularly before you invest a small fortune on gear.

Collectively, we can come up with dozens of reasons why we trek through the mountains. There is the sense of adventure, solitude, sunsets with dreamy colors, crystal-clear swimming holes, and unspoiled vistas. You may discover that what draws you are the physical challenges of 20-mile days, taking risks, or living self-reliantly. Perhaps you spend time in the mountains for more noble causes, such as research or environmental service.

Whatever the impulse to don a pack and visit the mountains by foot is entirely yours to consider, but your motive to journey through the mountains unquestionably will be occasionally challenged, sometimes reinforced, and always rewarded.

What is a trek? The treks in this guide share one element in common: they all exceed 30 miles. But the similarities end there. We believe that each trek has at least one unique element, whether it's length, a natural feature, or a cultural or historical legacy.

Whatever draws you to a particular trek in this book, prepare for long days, changes in weather, wrong turns, great views, and hopefully a few smiles. In all, a

Opposite: Purifying water on Hazel Creek in the Great Smokies

trek is an expedition through the mountains requiring self-reliance, skills in campcraft, a respect for the environment, and an emphasis on fitness.

Where to trek. The Appalachian range stretches like a spine for several thousand miles from Alabama to Newfoundland. This guide considers portions of four states in the southern region of the Appalachians: North and South Carolina, Tennessee, and Georgia. Understanding the regional names can be a bit confusing. To keep it simple, all of the treks in this guide are within the Appalachian Mountains. To be more precise, two great ranges flank the southern section of the Appalachians, the Blue Ridge range on the east and the Unaka Mountains to the west. But within the Blue Ridge and Unaka are subranges with familiar names, such as the Great Smoky Mountains within the Unaka or the Black Mountains within the Blue Ridge. While the Unaka and the Blue Ridge run generally from the southwest to the northeast, there are several equally impressive ranges that run perpendicular to and between the two major chains, such as the Balsams and the Nantahalas.

Occasionally, the routes travel through land protected by private boundaries such as the Grandfather Mountain preserve, but the majority of trails are within public boundaries including state parks, national forests, and land managed by the Department of the Interior, such as the Blue Ridge Parkway and the Great Smoky Mountains National Park.

Rather than arbitrarily link trails to exceed 30 miles, we chose treks that have geological, cultural, or biological significance. For example, the 70-mile section of the Appalachian Trail (AT) in the Great Smokies follows the crest of the range from end to end. And the 30-mile Art Loeb Trail in the Pisgah National Forest is dedicated to a local hiking pioneer and it seemed unjust to exclude the hike or contrive to augment its length.

In many cases, we included sections of larger trails covered by countless guidebooks. Two examples are the AT and the Foothills Trail in the Carolinas. These trails are often the only foot access to some of the most stunning areas of the region, such as Roan Mountain on the Tennessee/North Carolina line. In some cases, we offer a twist—for example, a variation to the traditional Foothills Trail. There are hundreds of multiday combinations of trails in these ancient mountains. No doubt you will discover remarkable treks not included in this guide.

Islands of Life

The Appalachian Mountains are blanketed with a dark shade of green in the summer months giving them a degree of uniformity when seen from a distance. But within the green canopy, the southern mountains are alive with a wildly diverse population of trees, plant life, and animals. While the mountains were formed 300 million years ago, the diversity of life blossomed after the planet's most recent ice age.

The southern Appalachians were not glaciated, but were affected by the last ice age. When the climate warmed and the glaciers retreated, northern plant communities and wildlife began to head north *and* upslope. So in addition to already lush low- and mid-elevation forests, plant communities found in the northern United States and Canada are also found on the higher peaks in the southern Appalachians, but not in between. In western North Carolina alone, more than 200 peaks reach above 5000 feet, and forty-three pass the 6000 mark, forming a "biological archipelago" reaching into the southeastern United States.

Trees and plants. The staggering diversity of life in the southern Appalachians is unparalleled in North America outside of the tropics. Lush carpets of moss and lichens cover every exposed rock and boulder. Ferns, Solomon's seal, and woodnettle tickle your ankles. Overhead, dense thickets of rhododendron form long green tunnels that block the sun. Carolina silverbell, dogwood, and redbud splash spring's first color. And shooting skyward are the legendary giants: tulip poplar, red oak, basswood, Carolina hemlock, white pine, and red maple. Consider that in the southern Appalachians there are more species of trees than on the entire continent of Europe.

Several treks in this guide slice through the legacy of the last global cooling. Just by slogging your pack another 5 miles to the crest of the Daniel Boone Boy Scout Camp and Trail on Grandfather Mountain, or to the Appalachian Trail on Clingmans Dome, a dramatic change in tree species provides evidence of the ecological effect of the last ice age on the trees and plants of the southern Appalachians. At lower elevations, hike through typical mixed hardwood forests of poplar, magnolia, witch hazel, and red oak, among other species. Farther along are northern hardwood forests similar to woods in New York or Connecticut. And near the upper reaches of the mountain stand spruces and firs, relics of the boreal forest's southern expansion during the last ice age.

Wildlife. Botanical diversity in the southern mountains has spawned an enormous diversity of insects, which in turn creates an enormous diversity of wildlife. Flip over any decaying log or rock and you'll likely find one of the region's twenty-seven colorful species of salamander, which tend to favor wet or moist areas. During the day, be aware of the region's more conspicuous snakes: black rat snakes up to 8 feet long, ring-necked snakes, timber rattlesnakes, and copperheads. Rattlers and copperheads are the only poisonous snakes in the area and, as with all wildlife, should be treated with respect.

Moving around the food chain are all sorts of mammals, including mice, flying squirrels, skunks, raccoons, bobcats, deer, wild hogs, and bears, to name a few. Enjoy all wildlife from a distance without disrupting the animal's behavior. If the animal changes its behavior because of your presence, then you are too close. Back off and quietly move along. Remember that wild animals are working much harder than you just to survive. Show ultimate respect for wildlife by not feeding them, packing out all of your food scraps and garbage, and hanging your food in camp.

A fawn (Photo by Randy Moore)

Birds. If you have little experience holding a pair of binoculars steady or, for that matter, trying to follow something the size of an avocado seed racing through the leaves of a tulip poplar at 30 mph more than 75 feet above your head, you may have a tough time actually seeing some of the snazzier birds of the forest. So enjoy their singing even if you can't find the soloists.

But before you discount the flurry of glittering-things-with-wings and the inevitable headache that comes from straining to see some bird's underside high up in the canopy, get to know your neighbors closer at hand. The southern Appalachians are alive with all sorts of lower-flying creatures, including the Carolina chickadee, tufted titmouse, Carolina wren, white-breasted nuthatch, brown creeper, dark-eyed junco, eastern towhee, northern cardinal, and the regal pileated woodpecker, which is bigger than your cat with a wingspan as wide as your pack is tall.

Diurnal raptors are among the most visible birds. They include the broad-winged hawk, with a black and white banded tail and a high piercing whistle; the peregrine falcon, unmistakable with its pointed wings and powerful flight, usually seen around cliffs and rocky outcrops where it prefers to nest; and two of the accipiters, either the Cooper's or the sharp-shinned hawk, long tailed for quick maneuvers in thick woods where they prey on the colorful birds you worked so hard to catch a glimpse of.

There are other songsters and birds to stumble upon, like wild turkey and ruffed grouse, and when you do, their sudden and explosive burst of flight will snap you out of a daze. Also listen for the unmistakable, eerie whinny of the eastern screech owl; the "who-cooks-for-you, who-cooks-for-you-all" call of the barred owl; and at the highest elevations, the steady stream of short, hollow whistles of the northern saw-whet owl.

Indigo bunting (Damon Hearne/Slabcreek Photography)

Environmental Stewardship

Traveling through the mountains has an impact no matter how delicately you step. We believe a solid environmental ethic begins with a dedicated low-impact campcraft routine and progresses to an awareness of natural and human forces shaping the future of the southern forest.

Trek lightly. No matter how lightly you tread, trekking in the mountains has an impact. We urge you to adopt an environmental ethic and campcraft practice that borders on the obsessive. The fragile balance of the Appalachian ecosystem depends on it.

For this reason, we advocate going above and beyond simply treading lightly. Consider doing the following:

- Bring a trash bag and fill it.
- Plan well and bring food that produces minimal organic and packaging waste.
- Observe local regulations and restrictions, such as campfire bans, no camping zones, and trail closures or reroutes, especially where closures protect threatened or endangered plants and wildlife.
- Appreciate all flowers and other natural and cultural artifacts as they are. It's a federal offense to collect anything on public land without a permit.
- Restore damaged campsites by repairing or eliminating sprawling fire rings, resurfacing the camp with fresh leaves, and picking up garbage.
- Camp only in established sites.
- Use stoves rather than campfires.
- Bring a trowel and bury your waste in a cat hole at least 200 feet from water, campsites, and trails. Covering your waste with leaves is not sufficient.
- Volunteer on a trail or cleanup crew. Plan your trek to coincide with a local hiking club's work day. Come out for National Trails Day, held nationwide in early June.

The bigger picture. While you will experience solitude and beauty, you will also encounter disturbing signs of human impact to the forest: beer cans, candy wrappers, old tires, human waste, campsites so disheveled and muddy that not a thread of grass dares to sprout, and behemoth fire rings big enough to cook a pig.

Like many wild places across the nation, the southern Appalachians are seriously threatened. Nowhere is the threat more evident than in Great Smoky Mountains National Park. Last year, the park managed 9 million tourists, more than double the number at Yosemite, the next most visited national park in the country.

The issues of sprawl and growth are at the doorstep of these mountains and fully at home in the rest of the southern Appalachians. Overcrowding in the park and at other popular destinations is spawning new development, wrongheaded legislation, and new roads. Habitat loss and fragmentation due to road building and sprawl is the single greatest threat to wildlife anywhere. For instance, the proposed North Shore Road in the park will have a devastating effect on the largest roadless tract in the East (See Trek 9, Lakeshore Trail).

Non-native pests, invasive species, and disease are decimating southern forest communities, too—somber news for a landscape known for its trees. Once the undisputed king of the forest with diameters regularly exceeding 10 feet, the American chestnut is now nothing more than a diminutive understory tree, sprouting in vain again and again from the ancient roots of former giants, its growth stopped dead in its tracks when the tree reaches a few inches in diameter. The culprit is an exotic fungus brought to the United States aboard overseas freighters in the early 1900s.

The endearing hemlock, whose often-pure stands cast darkness on deep mountain coves in the middle of the day, is also under attack by an exotic insect, the hemlock woolly adelgid, which literally sucks the life out of the tree. Hemlocks provide an irreplaceable role in forest communities. Their dense canopy provides shelter to wildlife by moderating temperatures in cold winter months and on hot summer days, in addition to supplying food and nesting sites for many species. It also plays an important role in maintaining cool stream temperatures, and preventing erosion.

Air pollution, coming primarily from coal-burning power plants in the Ohio Valley and automobiles, is another threat to the mountains here. According to some estimates, on a typical summer day visibility is 80 percent worse than it was fifty years ago. Instead of waves of blue ridges, a musty haze makes the mountains appear like a grainy photo.

We encourage users of this book to adopt an ethic that will ultimately protect the southern Appalachians. Stay abreast of state and national environmental legislation; support local, regional, and national organizations, and legislators that favor protection; and encourage others to act.

Trekking Fundamentals and Essentials

The following suggestions address the basic fundamentals of trekking the southern Appalachians. We suggest a lightweight approach to traveling in the mountains, but make sure you cover all of the essentials.

Pack weight and physical conditioning. To paraphrase the famous author and woodsman Horace Kephart (see Trek 9, Lakeshore Trail), one of the blessings of trekking in the wilderness is that it reminds us of how little we need to be perfectly happy. Taking only the bare essentials is the way to go. Although perfecting the art of what not to pack takes creativity and experience.

There are too many methods for reducing weight in your backpack to mention them all—for example, there are innumerable lightweight products on the market, such as titanium tent stakes, as well as plenty of obscure strategies, like using lithium batteries rather than alkaline because they are 50 percent lighter. We advise scrutinizing your pack after every trek to determine which pieces of gear you can leave home the next time. Also, be creative and find items that serve two purposes, like using an extra pair of socks for gloves or a bit of duct tape for repairs and to treat blisters.

So how much should your pack weigh? We have absolutely no idea. Some experts suggest aiming for 25 to 35 percent of your body weight. An acceptable pack weight depends on your weight, height, fitness level, and the length of your expedition. If you're into numbers, step on a scale with your loaded pack, but with experience you'll come to know when your pack is within an acceptable range.

The weight of your pack doesn't matter if you are unfit, however. Don't underestimate the demands of walking with a pack on your back. The best way to stay fit is to hit the trail as often as possible. If you are new to hiking, slowly add bulk to your pack and seek hikes of varying terrain. If you live miles from any trail, develop an exercise routine that blends strength training with aerobic activity. Run two to four times per week, accelerating your heart rate to help prepare for uphill hiking. Have a routine of leg exercises to strengthen your legs. And don't neglect your upper body—consider a regime of pull-ups, push-ups, dips, and other exercises that don't require a gym. If you have access to a health club, definitely get off the couch and use it.

Layers and clothing. It is possible to fill your backpack with a few thousand dollars worth of high-tech clothes. On the other hand, you may have exactly what you need in your wardrobe already. Who knew that the musty old wool sweater or shabby fleece vest would actually come in handy one day? Whether you choose to bring along crisp new outfits from the outdoor shop or instead rustle together a mishmash of wear from the closet, there are a few principles to keep in mind.

Anyone who has spent time in the woods in a rainstorm knows that cotton has about as much utility as an electric hairdryer on the trail. Cotton is nice in the hot summer because it stays cool against your skin. In cooler seasons, though, cotton items are a total disaster. In lieu of cotton, bring fabrics, such as polypropylene or Capilene, that wick moisture from your body and are quick drying.

The concept of layering is what will keep you warm and dry in the cold and rain and cool when it's hot and humid. Layering means wearing several relatively thin, light items of clothing, rather than one or two thick, heavy layers. In the southern Appalachians consider three layers: an insulating layer like a long-sleeved Capilene shirt, a middle layer such as a fleece jacket, and an outer layer such as a Gore-Tex suit to protect you from snow, wind, and rain.

While Dad's old wool sweater will keep you warm, it's heavy and tends to dry slowly. The innovations in outdoor wear have advantages that make them worth the investment if you plan to keep trekking. Make no mistake, you can drop a large chunk of change on gear, but you can also keep costs down if you're new to outdoor adventure. Consider secondhand shops, the classifieds, discount websites, or friends with too much gear.

Choosing a hiking shoe. Without a solid, proper-fitting pair of boots you may as well stay home in front of the TV—it'll be a lot more fun. Take the time and do the research to find a pair that's just right. It's definitely subjective, but a few guidelines follow to help you evaluate your current pair or to shop for a new pair.

It's your choice as to how beefy your boot is. Having a sturdy and comfortable boot is ideal for multiday treks because you'll probably have a relatively large pack and cover several miles per day. I wear a lighter boot in warm weather and beefy leather in the winter. Deciding on the stiffness and durability of a boot also depends on your size and the terrain. We recommend a leather or waterproof boot.

Ask a qualified sales clerk or experienced hiker to check your foot for idiosyncrasies and to recommend an ideal shoe. When shopping for a new pair of boots, make sure

Take time for foot care.

you try them on with the socks you plan to hike in. Check that the boot doesn't slip in the heel and that your toes have plenty of room to wiggle in front. Some recommend you try boots on in the afternoon on the theory that your feet expand after you've been upright all day. You also can try slipping your bare foot into the boot (when the salesperson isn't looking, of course) to really get a feel for the grooves and contours of the boot's interior. Definitely take time to walk around in your boot and consider the ankle support as well as the stiffness of the soles and the protection on the side. And before you hike in a new boot, make sure you put on some street miles to break them in.

Taking care of your boots is also a worthy habit to practice. Use leather treatment for boots to keep the material soft and avoid drying them in front of fires and other heat sources, as the heat tends to dry the material.

Food. Using a learn-by-doing cooking approach with Outward Bound students has rewarded us with bowls of the foulest concoctions imaginable: crunchy pasta, cream of wheat with mortar-like consistency, and other unmentionable dishes. Don't underestimate the power of having good food in the woods. Not only is food your source of energy, but also a source of happiness. Bring plenty, have variety, and take time to cook a proper meal.

Come on and peek into our food bag. In it you'll see pasta, rice, dried beans, grits (after all, we are in the South), fresh vegetables, cheese, tortillas, pita bread, peanut butter, snack bars, fresh and dried fruit, gorp, and granola. We suggest carrying dehydrated foods to stay light. My favorite camp meal is rice, beans, tortillas, cheese, and a dab of salsa. With just a few simple ingredients you can come up with a smorgasbord of simple, but tasty dishes. We prefer one-pot meals to minimize cleaning, but grand feasts are always in high order.

Consider bringing a simple spice kit too. Include fresh garlic, olive oil, salt, pepper, hot sauce, cinnamon, curry powder, and oregano. Just a bit of seasoning can add a world of difference to even the blandest dish. Remember to check your stove and fuel before you go, and pack a simple repair kit to suit your stove, along with an extra lighter or matches.

Cleaning up after a meal also deserves a bit of attention. Stay clear of water sources and don't bury food extras. Consider using a handful of leaves to scrub your pot and dishes and pack out the leaves caked with food. Whatever your scrubbing and cleaning technique, make sure you leave no trace. It goes without saying that you should pack out all food that you came with. It's hard to keep track of every crumb, chocolate chip, or sunflower seed that spills over in a feeding frenzy, so we encourage a careful sweep after every meal and snack.

To discourage critters from eating your food, hang your food bag. Raccoons, field mice, and skunks are waiting in the shadows to nibble on your granola and dive into the peanut butter once you're fast asleep. Designated campsites in the Great Smoky Mountains National Park have full-on bearproof food-hanging systems, but in most places you are on your own.

Water. Staying properly hydrated with a backpack is a struggle. Experts suggest an average of 4 quarts of water per day. No doubt that figure soars on 15-mile days and in the summer when the humidity peaks. We recommend carrying 2 quarts of water and refilling as needed. In each chapter we identify water sources and indicate stretches of dry hiking. Bear in mind that weather conditions can affect the reliability of springs and streams.

Make sure you purify water. The consequences of not doing so are too grim to mention (see *Giardia* in your medical guide). There are numerous ways to purify water, such as filters, boiling, and iodine. If using iodine tablets or liquid, be familiar with the recommended doses and routines to safely treat your water. We encourage choosing minor water sources over larger bodies of water—for example, a small feeder creek rather than a wide river.

Use your routefinding tools. Using this book alone to guide you through the woods is an incomplete strategy. Providing intimate details of a 40-mile trek with every subtle twist for each route would make for a mundane read and eliminate an element of adventure. Some of the treks are well marked and it would be hard to lose your way. Others trails have significant navigational challenges. Further, the thick canopy of trees in the southern mountains has a dizzying effect and can disorient and challenge even the best navigators.

Our navigational tools consist of a quality topographic map and compass. While we don't discourage use of an altimeter and GPS, we admit that we are not technologically savvy enough to take advantage of them ourselves. And from a budget standpoint, nothing beats a $10 compass.

Eastern box turtle (Damon Hearne/Slabcreek Photography)

Make sure you understand the basic fundamentals of map and compass navigation (or how to use a GPS unit) before you set foot on trail. Know how to orient your map properly—many ignore the difference between true north and magnetic north in the southeast since the difference is marginal—roughly 4 degrees. Also become familiar with contour lines on a topographic map. Make sure you can identify the difference between a ridge and drainage and between peaks and valleys.

Hygiene. One of the most liberating aspects of spending time in the backcountry is the opportunity to leave the aftershave, deodorant, and shampoo behind. You may beg to differ—especially after a steamy day in the mountains. However, powder-room accoutrements are hardly necessary in the forest. Our wash kit consists of the utter basics: camp soap for washing hands, toothpaste and toothbrush, and sunscreen. A small washcloth or bandanna also comes in handy. Other extras like foot powder, nail clippers, and lotion are a matter of preference. Rather than bringing your entire tube of toothpaste, consider transferring a bit to a small container, like a film canister, and share with your mates to help lighten their load.

The level of personal hygiene is up to you, but a bare minimum is essential to stay healthy for several days in the backcountry, plus it's refreshing. Nothing beats a dip in a cool swimming hole or washing up at the end of the day. We highly suggest washing hands frequently and thoroughly, particularly before meals and after pit stops. Do keep any soap (even the camp-friendly kind) away from water sources. Foreign chemicals will upset a stream's ecological balance.

Also consider cleaning pots and dishes after every meal to keep critters and microscopic organisms at bay. Boiling water or a bit of bleach is all you need to sterilize your eating gear. And again, stay clear of water sources and pack out every morsel of food and trash.

Injuries and first aid. There are at least three things you should bring with you on a trek to address medical issues: a first-aid kit, some level of first-aid training, and good judgment. As for training, several organizations offer basic to advanced, specialized wilderness first-aid training. We recommend basic training at a minimum. A complete first-aid kit can be purchased or you can prepare your own. Be familiar with its contents and periodically check expiration dates. It's also advisable to carry a small first-aid book as a reference.

Gear checklist. The following gear checklist provides the basics for trekking light. Items marked with an asterisk (*) are on the Mountaineers' list of Ten Essentials you should always carry in the wilderness.

Boots (or lightweight hikers)
Backpack
Sleeping bag
Sleeping pad
Ground sheet
Tarp, tent, Megamid*

Toothbrush, toothpaste, dental floss
Soap (for hand sanitation)
Appropriate clothes and layers for conditions (carry extra clothing in case of emergency)*
Extra socks
Rain and wind gear
Long underwear top and bottom
Warm hat
Sun hat or bandanna
Camp sandals
Hanky
Headlamp*
Extra batteries
Map and compass*
First-aid kit*
Bowl and spoon
Pot
Stove
Fuel
Lighter, waterproof/windproof matches*
Repair kit*
Knife
Food (carry extra for emergencies)*
Spice kit
Sun screen,* lip balm
Camera, film
Plato's *Republic*
Water bottle (carry extra water for emergencies)*
Water filter or iodine

Smooth Trekking

Being ill prepared for unpredictable events can transform a multiday trek into a grim slog through the woods. Be ready for anything by keeping your skills sharp and preparing for twists that may impact your journey. The following is a list of considerations that will increase the likelihood of a smooth trek in the southern Appalachians.

Solo vs. group trekking. John Muir once wrote, "Only by going alone in silence can one truly get into the heart of the wilderness." Solo journeys have immense rewards. Solitude is a fine time to reflect, journal, and have peace. You set your own breaks and no snoring will bother you.

As glamorous as it sounds, however, hiking solo has its perils. It can be lonely, scary, and potentially more dangerous. We encourage hiking with a partner in order to be more effective in an emergency. But if you insist on going alone, we wish you a bon voyage. Just let someone at home know your itinerary and take care.

As wilderness trip leaders, we've had wonderful experiences hiking in groups. Great bonds are formed with unlikely people and there is a dynamic in numbers that can lead to life-changing experiences. But groups have challenges of their own—they tend to move at a slower pace, decisions can be a lengthy process, and worst of all, you'll have to share your gorp.

Probably, the size of your group will be small and among friends. Be aware of size restrictions in different land management areas such as wilderness areas. Take care to minimize your impact, from noise to keeping a tidy campsite. And bring enough snacks to share.

Be weather savvy. As warm damp air from the Gulf of Mexico slams into the mountains, the air is forced upward where it cools and forms rain or snow

Hank Igelman on trail

and everything in between. Up to 100 inches of precipitation a year falls in the wettest parts of the southern Appalachians near the headwaters of the Chattooga River in North Carolina. Nearly as wet are the higher elevations, which can see up to 80 inches of precipitation in a year. Middle- and lower-elevation valleys tend to see about half as much precipitation due to the rain shadow effect created by the surrounding mountains.

Much of the rain comes in torrential cloudbursts accompanied by intense lightning storms. In the summer at most elevations rain can be a welcome relief to a sweaty day on the trail. But at other times of the year, and especially at higher elevations, cold rain, even a light drizzle, can quickly drop the air temperature 5 to 15 degrees or more. Plan ahead and bring the right equipment: rain gear that works, extra dry clothes, and boots that will dry out quickly when wet. Bring high-energy snacks to keep your internal furnace cranking away if you get wet and chilled. If you hear the booming of thunder in the distance, get off the high ridges and peaks before the storm is upon you, and insulate yourself from ground current with your pack or sleeping pad if lightning is closer than a couple of miles.

Though the southern mountains aren't especially known for wind, many of the high ridges and peaks above 5000 feet are extremely exposed. Ask yourself why there are few trees on some of the highest peaks or why some of the trees have branches growing only on one side, looking somewhat like a flag. Grandfather Mountain and Mount Mitchell both have recorded wind speeds in excess of 100 mph. Though you will most likely encounter a beautiful and benign day in the mountains no matter what time of year you choose to travel, be aware of changing conditions and act accordingly.

Winter travel. One of the great aspects of the southern Appalachians is that trekking is a year-round sport. Warm winter days, even long stretches of warm weather are typical, but do keep in mind that snow in April is possible too, even down here in the sunny South. We argue that the most dangerous conditions that you will encounter in the southern mountains are temperatures in the 30s or 40s and heavy rain. Yuck! We'll take 20 degrees and snow over that anytime.

We highly encourage traveling these treks in the winter as well as the other seasons. There are fewer people, bare trees open up views obscured in the summer,

Snow on hemlock needles

and short days and inclement weather add a new element of adventure. In the winter, plan for freezing rain, snow, wind, and subfreezing temperatures. After all, the coldest temperature recorded in North Carolina was minus 34 degrees Fahrenheit on Mount Mitchell, and the high peaks occasionally experience gale force winds.

The treks in this book are nontechnical. Crampons and ice axes are not typically necessary, but keep in mind that icy conditions can be treacherous. Additions to your list of gear might include extra layers, a winter sleeping bag, gaiters, booties, and mittens. Bring extra food, hot drinks, and an emergency meal, too. As for additional winter skills, know the signs and symptoms of hypothermia and how to prevent, treat, and respond to it. And always drink copious quantities of water to keep your body functioning at a high level.

Stream crossings. On many of the treks in this guide, you will encounter plenty of water. If you like stream crossings try the Pisgah Loop or the Mountains-to-Sea Trail from Table Rock to Grandfather Mountain—you won't be disappointed. As always, use your judgment prior to crossing a stream, especially when the water is high because of rain or snow. Beware of slippery rocks and wear boots or a pair of water shoes or sandals to avoid sharp objects obscured in the water. Before entering the water, make sure you unbuckle your sternum and waist straps to exit your pack easily if you slip and fall.

Make your feet happy. Nothing beats a blister on the back of your Achilles tendon that rubs on your boot at each step. No matter your method of treatment, the blister persists until it's an oozing, infected scab that sends pain like fire up your leg. Okay, maybe a bit dramatic, but blisters really are unpleasant. In an unofficial survey, ten out of ten wilderness experts agree that preventive maintenance is the only way to stop blisters. Take time to stop and apply moleskin or duct tape to "hot spots" that suggest a blister is nigh. Some suggest a dab of petroleum jelly in places where you typically get blisters. If you do get a blister, keep your wound clean to prevent infection and avoid over-padding, which may rearrange your foot in the boot and cause more blisters.

Soggy feet are also a recipe for disaster when trekking. Keep an extra pair of dry socks (avoiding cotton, of course) for the evening and consider sleeping without socks to air your wet dogs out. Also consider bringing along a pair of sandals for stream crossings and camp.

Plan well. It goes without saying how critical it is to plan your expedition. At Outward Bound, time-tested systems and a well-stocked warehouse streamline the process of preparing for an expedition, yet instructors still take several days to plan every detail and pack gear. We don't suggest taking a sick day to plan for a weekend trek, save the day off for the trail, but taking the time to plan all the details will have immeasurable pay offs.

The toughest challenge of preparing for a trek is taking everything you'll need. In preparing for the treks in this book, read the appropriate chapter and review a topographic map so you have a solid mental picture of the trek. Consider evacuation routes, campsites, water sources, a menu, and shuttle plans. Review a checklist of gear to bring on your back and then re-read the checklist and eliminate items you don't really need.

Trek at your ability level. Keep in mind that our itineraries are recommendations. Many of the treks have a variety of camping options to lengthen or shorten each day. A 10-mile day may be easy for you but torture for your partner. Be aware of your fitness level and the terrain before you go. While the Appalachians are mere hills compared to the mountains of the West, they aren't to be taken lightly.

Change your route. The twenty-five treks described in this book have many variations. Please take the liberty to do them in reverse, day-hike them, or change them in any way you like. The ease of access and plentitude of roads and trails in the southern Appalachians allow for countless variations.

We also advise being flexible while out on trail, especially when your safety is in jeopardy. If your route is too challenging, consider a shortcut to avoid a tough climb. Also, be aware of weather that could create dangerous situations. For example, you might consider avoiding high ridges in summer afternoons when thunderstorms are brewing, or turning back when winter storms become more serious than the woolly worm predicted.

Shuttles and parking. Often we suggest reliable shuttle services and parking options at the start and finish of each trek. Be aware that parking in remote locations has consequences. Empty your vehicle of all valuables and, if possible, park in areas with heavy traffic. Since overnight parking regulations vary from year to year, contact the proper land agency to register your vehicle and clarify parking regulations.

Evacuations. Before you venture out, be aware of escape routes to civilization on the map. Also, consider places along your route with access to a public phone. Keep in mind that mobile phones are unlikely to have reception when you need it most. In the event of an emergency, keep your cool and take time to forge a good plan.

How to Use This Book

Each chapter has several resources to help plan and navigate the trek. Chapters start with the trek length, a difficulty rating, elevation information, map suggestions, and logistical information. The logistical information is intended to help you plan by providing the phone numbers for land managers, suggestions for running shuttles, water availability, and parking considerations at trailheads.

Treks are rated as Easier, Strenuous, or Very strenuous. The degree of difficulty for each trek is based on the overall elevation gain, length and duration, degree of navigational difficulty, and challenges such as river crossings. The ratings are subjective, so

Opposite: Lone tree on Looking Glass Rock, Pisgah National Forest, NC

you should also review additional information in each chapter—for example, the elevation profile and miles per day.

For each route, we recommend an itinerary based on a reasonable number of hours spent hiking, given the trail's terrain and profile. Each day's length also depends on the availability of established campsites and water. Generally, we suggest a shorter or longer itinerary with campsites to adapt the trek to your fitness and ability level. We also include the elevation gain for each day, total elevation gain for the trek, and a graphical elevation profile for the entire length.

The trail descriptions are intended to help you navigate, and to orient the trek with a historic, geographic, or environmental context. Each day is described, along with camping options, water sources, history, current issues, and other information. While the trail descriptions provide a detailed account of the route, in the spirit of adventure and ease of reading some navigational details are not described in full. Each chapter has a 3-D overview of the route and identifies relevant topographic maps to the area, but you should be prepared to navigate with a topographic map and compass. We generally use United States Geological Survey (USGS) 7.5' quads and National Geographic Trails Illustrated maps that cover the southern Appalachians.

Each chapter concludes with a mileage summary of trail highlights, land features, and milestones. However, bear in mind that these highlights are not a comprehensive description of the route—use the mileage summary to supplement the trail description along with other navigational tools.

We hope this guide accompanies you on many safe adventures throughout these wonderful and beautiful mountains. We also hope that spending time in these ancient hills will inspire you to act on their behalf—whether it's picking up trash, writing a letter to a politician, or supporting a conservation group.

Plan well, trek lightly, and enjoy the southern Appalachians.

A Note About Safety

Safety is an important concern in all outdoor activities. No guidebook can alert you to every hazard or anticipate the limitations of every reader. Therefore, the descriptions of roads, trails, routes, and natural features in this book are not representations that a particular place or excursion will be safe for your party. When you follow any of the routes described in this book, you assume responsibility for your own safety. Under normal conditions, such excursions require the usual attention to traffic, road and trail conditions, weather, terrain, the capabilities of your party, and other factors. Keeping informed on current conditions and exercising common sense are the keys to a safe, enjoyable outing.

The Mountaineers Books

Foothills Trail—Jones Gap State Park to Whitewater Falls (SC/NC)

Difficulty:	Strenuous
Distance:	52.4 miles
Elevation gain:	16,100 feet
Best season:	November through April, when leafless trees open up views along the escarpment. A nice summer trek, too, thanks to the abundance of streams, waterfalls, and Lake Jocassee. Typically, the fall colors peak during the last two weeks of October.
Recommended itinerary:	4 days (10–15 miles per day)
Water availability:	Water is abundant throughout the hike.
Logistics:	The route begins at the Jones Gap State Park headquarters in South Carolina and finishes at the Whitewater Falls parking area managed by the Forest Service on North Carolina State Route 281. The trek can be hiked comfortably in four days and showcases the spectacular terrain of the Blue Ridge escarpment. From Jones Gap State Park, the route follows a trail that is considered part of the Foothills Trail system. As it is traditionally hiked, the Foothills Trail is 76 miles beginning at Table Rock State Park and finishing at Oconee State Park. This trek presents an alternative route on official Foothills Trail spurs.

Many twists and turns are not mentioned in the trek description, but be assured that the Foothills Trail is extremely well marked with blazes and signs. The Foothills Trail is blazed in white, its spurs blazed in blue. Nevertheless, don't leave your maps at home, since losing your way in remote segments of the trek can have serious consequences. There are many campsites along the route, although the Foothills Trail Conference encourages use of designated sites only. Contact the Foothills Trail Conference (*www.foothillstrail.org*) to arrange a shuttle. Register overnight vehicles at Jones Gap and pay a nominal user fee. No overnight parking is available at the Upper Whitewater Falls parking area, so plan a scheduled pick up or consider finishing the trek before Upper Whitewater Falls at the Bad Creek Hydrostation located on SC 130, one mile from the SC/NC line. A hiker parking lot is maintained by the Foothills Trail Conference. The gates are open from 6 AM to 6 PM, although vehicles can exit at any time.

Jurisdictions: The route travels through a patchwork of public and private land management agencies, including Jones Gap State Park (864-836-3647); Caesars Head State Park (864-836-6115); Gorges State Park (828-966-9099); the Highlands Ranger District (828-526-3765), Nantahala National Forest; Andrew Pickens Ranger District (864-638-9568), Sumter National Forest; the South Carolina Department of Natural Resources (803-734-3888); and Bad Creek Hydrostation (864-944-4000).

Maps: USGS Cleveland, Table Rock, Estatoe Gap, Reid, and Cashiers; Foothills Trail Conference (*www.foothillstrail.org*)

Trail location: Begin at Jones Gap State Park in South Carolina. From Cleveland, South Carolina, travel west on US Route 276/South Carolina Route 11 for 3 miles, and turn right onto River Falls Road. River Falls Road becomes Jones Gap Road. The park entrance is about 6 miles from US 276. The end of the trek at the Upper Whitewater Falls parking area is located off of North Carolina Route 281 9 miles from US Route 64 near Sapphire, NC. From SC 11, travel north on SC 130, which becomes NC 281 at the state line.

In the northwest corner of South Carolina, the red dirt and gentle rolling terrain of the piedmont plateau runs smack into a blue wall of mountains. Here, the demarcation between the Blue Ridge Mountains and the foothills is abrupt, with sheer faces of granite, cascading falls, sharp ridgelines, and narrow gorges. The Cherokee called the escarpment the "Great Blue Hills of God." The trek begins in the Middle Saluda River gorge and traverses along the escarpment on portions of the Foothills Trail system linking a network of public land holdings. The trail

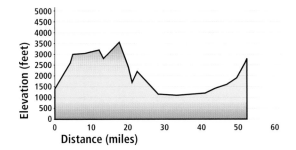

blazes through some of the most remarkable and remote sections of the Carolina mountains. Treasures along the trail include seldom-seen plant species like the Oconee bell, an uncommon wildflower that grows only in this region, a thriving black bear population, bald eagles, and waterfalls—including the highest waterfall east of the Mississippi.

DAY ONE 13+ miles 5200 feet

Begin hiking from the Jones Gap State Park trailhead (1400 feet). Follow the Jones Gap blue trail #1, a wide trail going due west and upstream. For the next 4.3 miles hike on a gentle grade along the Middle Saluda River (SC's first designated Wild and Scenic river) through a long narrow river gorge toward its headwaters. This section of trail, marked with a blue blaze, is considered a spur of the Foothills Trail and was originally graded by Solomon Jones in the 1840s. The 100-plus-mile trail system was established in 1981, in part by Duke Power (now Duke Energy), and is managed by the Foothills Trail Conference based in Greenville, South Carolina. The spur merges with the primary route of the Foothills Trail at mile 18 on Sassafras Mountain.

Alternative start: Consider beginning the Foothills Trail at its traditional eastern terminus at Table Rock State Park, in South Carolina off SC 11. From there, the trail skirts the massive granite walls of Table Rock and climbs over Pinnacle Mountain, then merges with the spur from Jones Gap State Park on Sassafras Mountain. The distance from Table Rock State Park to Sassafras Mountains is 8.8 miles.

Along the Middle Saluda section, consider a side trip up one of several spur trails to an array of steep creeks and waterfalls that cascade down the 1000-foot drop from the Tennessee Valley Divide marking the North/South Carolina border.

Eventually begin climbing up switchbacks through a section of the gorge known as the Winds. At mile 4.3 (2600 feet), the Jones Gap Trail forks right to US 276 inside Caesers Head State Park. Take the left fork on a short but steep connector trail known as the Tom Miller blue trail #2 toward the Raven Cliff Falls parking lot on US 276. There is a campsite at the fork. Camping is permitted in Jones Gap

Rosman

64

Nantahala National Forest

Sapphire

Horsepasture River

Toxaway River

Toxaway Creek

North Carolina
South Carolina

178

Bearcamp Creek

Thompson River

281

3

Flatrock
Mountain

Chimneytop
Mountain

Chimneytop
Gap

Whitewater River

Upper
Whitewater
Falls

T

2

Laurel Fork

North Carolina
South Carolina

Sumter
National Forest

Jim Timmerman
Natural Resources
Area

P

Bad Creek
Hydroelectric
Station

Lake Jocassee

Lake of Cassee

130

Lake Jocassee

11

Trek 1 52.4 miles

Brevard

64

276

North Carolina

South Carolina

Caesers Head
State Park

Jones Gap blue trail #1

P Jones Gap Rd

T

Jones Gap
State Park

River Falls
Road

Middle Saluda River

Gum
Gap

Slicking
Gap

Dolves
Mountain

Raven Cliff
Falls

276

Slicking
Mountain

Sassafras
Gap

Bigspring
Mountain

Whiteoak
Mountain

276 11

To
Cleveland, SC

Sassafras
Mountain

Table Rock
State Park

11

Elizabeth Pendleton on the Foothills Trail

State Park at designated campsites for a nominal fee—registration is required. Behind you to the north are excellent views of the gorge. In less than 1 mile, cross US 276 and enter land managed by Caesars Head State Park in South Carolina and follow the Gum Gap blue trail #13. The long, narrow corridor along the escarpment is known as the Mountain Bridge Wilderness.

Walk 1.5 miles to a fork. The Foothills spur trail follows the Gum Gap blue trail #13 to the right, and the Raven Cliff Falls red trail forks left to the impressive cascade. The round trip to the falls is less than 2 miles and worth the trip despite its popularity with day hikers. Geologically, the escarpment is the meeting of two tectonic plates and the dramatic change in elevation is responsible for the impressive scenery. From the fork, stay right toward Gum Gap, walking relatively level ground. To your left, the mountains drop precipitously to the piedmont as the trail curves above the deep drainage. About 1.5 miles from the fork pass the Natureland Trust pink trail #14. The pink trail meets a suspension bridge over Raven Cliff Falls in half a mile.

Soon exit the state park boundary, cross Matthews Creek, and continue walking up Julian Creek to Gum Gap at mile 8.3 (3050 feet) on the state line. At Gum Gap the trail bears left past the gate to travel southwest along the state line. Camping is not allowed on the south side of the trail between Gum Gap and Sassafras Gap, as it is within the watershed for the city of Greenville, South Carolina. From Gum Gap, the trail follows the eastern Continental Divide, also known as the Tennessee Valley Divide, and is an old road grade built by the Civilian Conservation Corps in the 1930s. The Corps played a large role in developing South Carolina's state park system, including nearby Table Rock State Park. Descend on a trail from Slicking Mountain and pass a water source, then stay left on a road track to Slicking Gap. A system of old grades and trail creates a slightly confusing route, but it is well marked.

After a mile, pass Dolves Mountain (3200 feet) and look for good views from a clearing to the north. Descend to Grunting Gap on an old road grade, then follow a trail over a knob, and then go left onto a logging road. At mile 13.2, consider camping near a dilapidated trailer at a wide curve in the road. The road goes downstream. At the curve, leave the road and follow a trail on your left over another small knob to a boggy area before Bigspring Mountain and an alternative campsite on an abandoned road grade. There is yet another campsite on a ridge 1.5 miles from the boggy area.

DAY TWO   14+ miles   2800 feet
The next day begins with an excellent walk up and down ridgelines once dominated by the American chestnut, now replaced by large oaks and tulip poplars. Begin heading up the trail over Bigspring Mountain (3160 feet), continue over Whiteoak Mountain (3300 feet), and then descend to Sassafras Gap. Ahead is Sassafras Mountain. Climb a steep trail approximately 800 feet to the summit, which is South Carolina's highest elevation (3554 feet). Arrive at a paved road and parking area just below the summit. Turn right on the road and regain the Foothills Trail, now marked with a white blaze, from the Sassafras kiosk, (which has an impressive winter view) and follow the trail downhill. Cross the road in 0.3 mile, continuing on the well-marked trail until again reaching the road in Chimneytop

Gap. Contour around Chimneytop Mountain in and out of several drainages—some dry and some wet.

Descend and arrive at US Route 178. Cross the highway on the bridge, then turn left and travel uphill on the gravel road. Soon you reach the Laurel Valley Trail access lot and enter the Jim Timmerman Natural Resources Area at Jocassee Gorges of the South Carolina Department of Natural Resources (DNR). Jim Timmerman was a former director of DNR and was instrumental in the state's acquisition of the area.

In the early part of the twentieth century, the Duke Power Company, predecessor to Duke Energy, began to acquire land, amounting to tens of thousands of acres, along the escarpment on the North/South Carolina border, known as the Jocassee Gorges. The steep topography of the area attracted the company as a potential location for future hydroelectric generation facilities.

In more recent years, Duke determined it would not utilize the majority of the land in the Jocassee Gorges and began to divest its holdings. Fortunately, the ecological and environmental value of the land was recognized and Duke committed to offering the states of North and South Carolina the first chance to buy and conserve it. By 1999, nearly 50,000 acres of land formerly owned by Duke was added to the public domain in the western Carolinas. Duke retains ownership and use of a section of land, but the bulk of the property, 32,000 acres in South Carolina, was turned over to public agencies.

From the kiosk at the Jim Timmerman parking area, leave the road, following the now familiar white blaze up stairs to a trail. The trail contours above the road, meeting it once, until climbing a ridge on Flatrock Mountain. Continue contouring around drainages and fingerlike ridges and in approximately 2 miles pass a campsite before crossing the access road and entering the Laurel Fork Heritage Preserve managed by the DNR. Go right up stairs, climb over a small knob, and then descend on a steep trail to the first of several major drainages that make up the Jocassee Gorges.

Arrive at the creek at mile 22.6 (2200 feet), and turn left heading downstream through dense rhododendron, doghobble, and Christmas fern. Also notice several old-growth poplars, hemlocks, and beeches. The following section crosses the creek several times on well-made bridges.

Soon after the fifth bridge, continue down many steps to a short spur trail leading to the base of a 30-foot waterfall and consider a break and cool splash of water. The trail eventually veers to the west, close to the creek and sometimes along an old road grade over aged bridges. The next 4 miles of trail is easy and pleasant hiking along the creek. The route weaves between trail and road and is well marked by signs and white blazes throughout. Finally, arrive at a spur trail on the left over a bridge and tonight's campsite above Laurel Fork Falls at mile 28 (1150 feet). At the base of the falls, the Laurel Fork flows into Lake Jocassee.

The Great Blue Wall

In 1971, Duke dammed the confluence of the Whitewater and Toxaway Rivers, filling a basin at the base of the escarpment to create Lake Jocassee. On a map, the main corridor of the lake resembles a buck's head, with several long narrow inlets forming its rack of antlers. Several rivers and creeks were flooded, including Laurel Fork Creek, the easternmost arm of the lake.

Once settled in camp, return to the main trail and go left to a kiosk. Fork left, and go 0.3 mile to the Jocassee shore—a good spot for a swim, but be aware that your wilderness experience may be interrupted by powerboats and jet skis. While Lake Jocassee was spared the flurry of development typical of manmade lakes in the South, bits and pieces of development and impact have appeared.

DAY THREE   15+ miles   4900 feet

Bear right at the kiosk, following the trail northwest and soon climbing a narrow ridge separating the Laurel Fork Creek drainage from the Toxaway River drainage. The trail meets a road grade, sometimes crossing and sometimes merging with it. The trail dives left toward the Toxaway River arm of the lake. Soon the trek crosses into North Carolina and the Gorges State Park boundary. In the Duke land deal, North Carolina took title to a 10,000-acre tract near the Jocassee Gorges headwaters, and 7100 of those acres became Gorges State Park in April 1999.

The trail meets the lake at a switchback and bears north up the lake past a campsite. Cross a bridge over Toxaway Creek at another campsite. To the right is a 5-mile trail to the Frozen Creek access on the east side of Gorges State Park—one of the few points of entry/exit by foot in the Jocassee Gorges. Continue to the granddaddy bridge of them all—a 225-foot suspension bridge over the Toxaway River at mile 33.3 (1100 feet). Camping is permitted in the Gorges State Park at designated sites only–new campsites are not permitted.

By now, you may suspect that so many finely engineered bridges in the backcountry could hardly be the work of a few poorly funded volunteer trail crews. In fact, Duke Energy played a large role in establishing the trail and designing and building many of the bridges. The Foothills Trail is well marked and easy to follow throughout the Jocassee Gorges region. Equally as impressive as the bridges are the scores of lumber sections carefully placed as stairs the entire way.

Past the bridge, walk south along the lakeshore and soon begin climbing again. The trail winds its way through uneven topography to Cobb Creek before exiting the state park underneath powerlines and into the Nantahala National Forest. Beyond Cobb Creek, continue over similar terrain to Bear Creek. At Bear Creek the trail follows the creek upriver past a designated campsite. Continue on trail and old road grades before arriving in the next major drainage and cross the Horsepasture River (1200 feet) on a bridge at mile 41. In less than 3 miles, arrive at a left turn to a campsite on Bearcamp Creek.

DAY FOUR   8+ miles   3200 feet

From camp, cross the creek on a bridge and go right upstream. Follow a rerouted section of the trail that is clearly marked. This section has plenty of water and solid hiking up and down rolling terrain on a combination of trails and old road grades. As usual, expect the trails to be well-maintained with well-marked intersections.

Reach Thompson River (1600 feet) at mile 46.9. Continue down a steep trail and cross Thompson River on a bridge. Turn right after the bridge, soon arriving at another creek. Follow the logging grade and eventually cross back into South Carolina and the Sumter National Forest. At mile 49, pass a spur trail to a designated campsite and arrive at the Whitewater Falls river corridor management area. To reach the Bad Creek access parking area, bear left and follow the Bad Creek spur trail 0.7 mile to the parking lot. Otherwise, turn right to follow signs toward Upper Whitewater Falls, staying on the east side of the Whitewater River and traveling upstream and eventually back into North Carolina.

The final 2 miles of the trek is five-star hiking to a grand finish. Walk upstream through dozens of old-growth hemlocks and a few behemoth beech trees. After a mile, cross Corbin Creek, then the Whitewater River on a bridge over gigantic boulders threaded by water rushing down the precipitous escarpment and shadowed by the steep forested walls of the gorge. Begin a steep climb up several hundred feet of switchbacks to a marked spur trail to the Upper Whitewater Falls Overlook at mile 51.9. Turn right and leave the Foothills Trail to join several tourists at the Upper Whitewater Falls Overlook and gawk at the highest falls east of the Rockies. Climb the stairs and follow the paved path to the parking area on NC 281 (2800 feet) at mile 52.4.

Opposite: Upper Whitewater Falls

Alternative finish: Rather than finish at Upper Whitewater Falls, stay left on the Foothills Trail. The Foothills Trail continues another 30 miles to Oconee State Park in South Carolina. The rest of the trail is worth considering as it descends into the Chattooga River gorge on the South Carolina/Georgia state line. From Jones Gap State Park to Oconee State Park is more than 80 miles of trail.

Trail Summary and Mileage Estimates

0	Jones Gap State Park (1400 feet), follow blue blazes west on Jones Gap Trail
4.3	Tom Miller Trail junction (2600 feet), go left onto Tom Miller Trail
5	US Route 276 (3000 feet), cross road and take the Gum Gap/Rainbow Trail
6.5	Junction with Raven Cliff Falls Trail (3020 feet), bear right at fork on Gum Gap Trail
8.3	Gum Gap (3050 feet), bear left to the southwest
12.2	Overlook at Dolves Mountain (3200 feet), continue on the Foothills Trail
13.4	Campsite in boggy area (2800 feet)
17.7	Sassafras Mountain (3554 feet), follow white-blazed Foothills Trail from kiosk
20.2	Chimneytop Gap (2400 feet), cross road and continue on trail
21.2	US Route 178, cross highway, then go left and uphill on gravel road (1700 feet)
22.6	Laurel Fork Creek (2200 feet), go left at creek
28.3	Laurel Fork Falls campsite (1150 feet), go left to site, trail continues straight
28.7	Kiosk at trail fork. Bear right onto Foothills Trail (1150 feet)
33.3	Toxaway River (1100 feet), cross 225-foot bridge, then go left
41	Horsepasture River (1200 feet), cross bridge
43.7	Bearcamp Creek and campsite on left (1420 feet)
46.9	Thompson River (1600 feet), cross on bridge and turn right
49.6	Whitewater River (1900 feet), right on Foothills Trail
51.9	Upper Whitewater Falls Overlook spur trail (2600 feet), go right
52.4	Upper Whitewater Falls parking area (2800 feet)

Suggested Camps Based on Different Trekking Itineraries

Night	<10 mpd	10 mpd	>10 mpd
One	4.3 miles - Tom Miller trailhead	13.4 miles - Near Bigspring Mountain	13.4 miles - Near Bigspring Mountain
Two	13. 4 miles - Near Bigspring Mountain	22 miles - Near Flatrock Mountain	28.3 miles - Laurel Fork Falls
Three	22 miles - Near Flatrock Mountain	33.1 miles - Toxaway Creek	43.7 miles - Bearcamp Creek
Four	28.3 miles - Laurel Fork Falls	43.7 miles - Bearcamp Creek	
Five	33 miles - Toxaway Creek campsite		
Six	43.7 miles - Bearcamp Creek		

Bartram Trail South (GA/NC)

Difficulty: Strenuous

Distance: 55.2 miles

Elevation gain: 12,900 feet

Best season: Year-round—summer is lush and steamy, fall colors peak in mid-October, winter has stunning vistas, and spring flowers are abundant from late March through May.

Recommended itinerary: 5 days (10–15 miles per day)

Water availability: Generally adequate, although some campsites may not be near water. Carry 2 to 3 quarts of water when leaving Dicks Creek, as it is nearly 9 miles until the next reliable source near Warwoman Dell. Seasonal streams may be flowing near Rainy Mountain. Beyond Martin Creek, the route follows ridge tops, crossing seasonal streams infrequently, so plan on leaving with at least 2 quarts and fill up at every opportunity. The Chattooga River and Warwoman Creek collect runoff from nearby roads and agriculture, so in these areas use water from springs and small tributaries instead.

Logistics: It is about an hour drive between the two trailheads. Happy Trails Shuttle Service (706-282-7672) will drop off your vehicle at the end of the hike or transport you to the Wallace Branch trailhead if you intend to link this trek with the Bartram Trail west of Franklin (see Trek 3, Bartram Trail North). The Bartram Trail in Georgia is blazed with plastic yellow diamonds, which become yellow painted or metal rectangles in North Carolina shortly after crossing Hale Ridge Road.

Jurisdictions: Tallulah Ranger District (706-782-3320), Chattahoochee National Forest; and Highlands Ranger District (828-526-3765), Nantahala National Forest

Maps: USGS Satolah, Whetstone, Rainy Mountain, Rabun Bald, and Scaly Mountain

Trail location: From Clayton, Georgia, head east on Warwoman Road (County Road S884) to Georgia Route 28 and turn right. Drive south for 2.2 miles and look for a parking area on the left, just before a bridge crossing the Chattooga River and the Georgia/South Carolina state line. The Bartram Trail enters the woods across the road through a small opening in the trees.

To get to trek's end, Buckeye Creek trailhead, return to Clayton and head north on US Route 441 for approximately 12 miles to Otto, North Carolina, and turn right onto Tessentee Road (North Carolina Route 1636). In about 4 miles, look for a hairpin bend and turn left off the pavement onto Buckeye Creek Road (North Carolina Route 1640) and proceed for about 0.5 mile to a small parking area.

In 1775, restless and nearly bankrupt, Quaker naturalist William Bartram wandered through the primordial mountains and vales of the southern Appalachians surveying the region's rich plant and animal life. Retrace his path along historic routes used by the Cherokee for thousands of years and, some say, Spanish explorer Hernando De Soto in 1540. As you leave the steamy lowlands for the mountains of the Blue Ridge, climb along the Tennessee Valley Divide, where water falls east to the Atlantic Ocean, or west to the Gulf of Mexico. At trek's end, consider winding your way along 14 miles of back roads beside the Little Tennessee River to the beginning of Trek 3, Bartram Trail North, and resume the explorer's travels through the heart of Cherokee country.

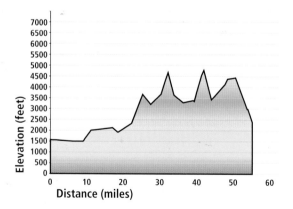

DAY ONE   9 miles   1000 feet

With Russell Bridge and South Carolina to your left, drop into the woods and enjoy the gentle path. Within a few minutes from the start, cross a long bridge over the West Fork and bear left through moist woods, listening for the sounds of swift water and memories of dueling banjos from the main branch of the Wild and Scenic Chattooga River. Skip over Holden Branch via an oft-submerged footbridge and parallel the Chattooga in the shade of giant white pine.

Early spring along the Bartram Trail (Photo by Corey Hadden)

N E S W

64

28

Highlands

Nantahala

National

Forest

106

64

28

Cullasaja River

Peggy Knob

Whiterock Gap

Nantahala

Fishhawk Mountain

National Forest

Scaly Mountain

Osage Mountain

Beegum Gap

1636

Wolf Rock

T 1640

The Pinnacle

Tessentee Creek

1636

106

246

North Carolina

Georgia

441

Otto

Little Tennessee River

441

North Carolina

Georgia

Georgia

South Carolina

T

28

28

Warwoman Road

Chattooga

River

Sumter

National

Forest

Chattahoochee

National

Forest

Chattooga River Trail

Rabun
Bald

Flint
Knob

Flat
Top

Warwoman Road

Warwoman Creek

Rattlesnake
Knob

Rock
Mountain

Rainy
Mountain

76

2

Becky
Branch
Falls

Warwoman
Dell

Courthouse
Gap

Little Tennessee River

441

Clayton

High on the hill to your right (northwest), find Holden Cemetery with marked graves of Confederate soldiers and stone foundations from old homesteads. Quickly come to Adline Branch and an orange-blazed path, and begin climbing away from the river. Stay on the Bartram Trail as it travels up and down for several miles through stands of mixed hardwoods and mountain laurel, passing two unmarked side trails along the way. Descend to Warwoman Creek, cross a stout bridge upstream from where William Bartram forded the Chattooga, and bear left, paralleling the creek as you cross Earls Ford Road. After a brief climb back into the hills, drop down to the banks of the Chattooga and follow the easy trail behind trees that let you play hide and seek with passing whitewater boaters, possibly the only people you'll see for the next few days, as the Bartram Trail is one of the least-traveled long trails in the southeast.

Nearing the end of your first day on the trail, climb up and over several small ridges and find a flat camping area near one of two creeks offering no hint that in a few feet their waters crash 75 feet down to the Chattooga below. A side trail heads down to the river beside Dicks Creek Falls.

DAY TWO   11 miles   2500 feet

Day two leads you away from the Chattooga and into the drier upland forest of the foothills and mountains. A few minutes out of camp, stay right as you pass the junction with the Chattooga River Trail and cross Sandy Ford Road. Follow the trail as it gradually climbs for several miles through Speed Gap (2020 feet) and Bob Gap (2050 feet). Contouring around the northern edge of Rainy Mountain (2945 feet), keep a look out for seasonal streams and fill up, as it is still 3+ miles to a reliable source near Warwoman Dell. Like a roller coaster, the trail continues up and down until shortly after Green Gap (2140 feet), where it quickly drops 200 feet into the dell.

Through the picnic area, look for the trail on the left, and follow it a short way to Warwoman Road. Carefully cross and begin to climb once again, passing Becky Branch Falls on a slick footbridge, ducking in and out of dark coves on your way to Martin Creek, your camp for the night. As the trail bends north, a small gorge of churning water greets you, as it did William Bartram after a long day. Just ahead you'll see what Bartram saw: "rushing from rocky precipices . . . under the shade of the pensile hills, the unparalleled cascade of Falling Creek, rolling and leaping off the rocks, which uniting below, spread a broad, glittering sheet of crystal waters. . . . " Pitch your tarp here beside a series of stunning waterfalls shrouded in rhododendrons and settle in with a copy of *Travels*, Bartram's cultural and natural history of the southeast recorded during a three-year trek through the region in the mid-1770s.

Opposite: Bartram's "unparalleled cascade" (Photo by Corey Hadden)

DAY THREE   14 miles   4400 feet

When you look at today's route, the first thing you'll probably notice is the quick climb to Courthouse Gap, nestled between two knobs at 2340 feet. Trace your finger north along the trail and count the many gaps and knobs between you and camp near Beegum Gap. Bartram knew better than to ride a horse up that kind of terrain, and instead headed southwest from Courthouse Gap to meet the Cherokee near the headwaters of the Little Tennessee River. As a result, he never caught water in his mouth from the seeping cliffs on the south side of Raven Knob or savored the breathtaking view of misty mountains from the summit of Rabun Bald (4696 feet), the second highest mountain in Georgia.

Climb the steep grade northwest out of Courthouse Gap aiming for Rock Mountain (3690 feet), 2 miles away. Descend quickly into Windy Gap, and then up again toward Blacks Creek and Rattlesnake Knobs, being sure to top off at any on-trail water sources. The pattern changes beyond Wilson Gap as the climbs become longer and steep, but the scenery only gets grander as you gain nearly 1000 feet en route to the open woods that crown Flat Top (4142 feet). Lose a few hundred feet as you descend into Saltrock Gap (3700 feet), and begin the drill once more as you gain another 1000 feet up to the lookout tower on Rabun Bald, bearing right at Flint Gap where a side trail leads west to Flint Knob. The view from here is worth every thigh-burning step and is among the few places in the southeast with a 360-degree view of the surrounding mountains. Beegum Gap, the night's camp, is another 1.5 miles down the trail to the north. Water can be found about 10 minutes beyond camp.

DAY FOUR   14 miles   3900 feet

The fourth day begins by diving straight into the thickest, darkest tangle of woods yet. Along the way, you'll cross countless creeks and springs emanating from the heart of the Blue Ridge Mountains. Miles later, recover from the tangle, or lament its passing, and climb the highest ridges toward your last camp at White Rock Gap (4150 feet).

From camp, follow the trail as it twists around roots and rocks for 2.5 miles to Hale Ridge Road. Turn right and walk the gravel road for 100 feet to the official trailhead for the North Carolina section of the Bartram Trail, and turn left. The Georgia/North Carolina state line is a few feet down the trail and unsigned, except for the rectangular orange blazes that begin to replace the yellow diamonds. The trail contours for several miles in and out of dark coves, crosses new footbridges built in 2003, and passes side trails heading down Hurrah Ridge and West Fork of Overflow Creek. Carefully cross North Carolina Route 106, just left of Osage Overlook and find a set of steps leading into the woods.

The trail is initially steep, crossing several rocky creeks before switching back and forth up the flanks of Scaly Mountain, the highest point in the trek at 4804

Yellow trillium (Damon Hearne/Slabcreek Photography)

feet. A side trail enters from the right where the Bartram Trail cuts west for the last time before traversing the long rocky summit, which in midsummer is dressed in nothing but blueberries, mountain laurel, and flame azalea. With a water bottle full of berries, drop off the Tennessee Valley Divide and meet up with Tessentee Creek, the last reliable water source until trek's end. Bear right on the old road (Forest Road 4620) and begin climbing once again, at first with the road, then up a series of switchbacks to your right that are easy to miss as the road continues on. Rest briefly while contouring past Peggy Knob and Hickory Gap and set your sights on the main ridge of Fishhawk Mountain, towering more than 2000 feet above the valley floor. Seasonal water may be found in Stephens Creek, a 10-minute walk downhill from camp at Whiterock Gap.

DAY FIVE 8 miles 1100 feet

Begin the day with a quick trip to the summit and exposed face of Whiterock, accessed via a short path found 0.5 mile down the Bartram Trail on the left. The distant views of hazy blue mountains and valleys reveal terrain that Bartram, De Soto, and Cherokees explored long ago. The Appalachian Trail hobbles along the spine of the nearest ridge on its way to intersecting the northern extension of the Bartram Trail, which begins to the west of Franklin (see Trek 3, Bartram Trail North).

Two last climbs lead past the twin summits of Fishhawk Mountain, and then the trail steadily descends to Wolf Rock on switchbacks and narrow ridges. Follow switchbacks down past Cedar Cliff to old roads, turning right and then right again before arriving at the Buckeye Creek trailhead.

Trail Summary and Mileage Estimates

0	Bartram trailhead at Russell Bridge (1580 feet)
0.4	West Fork of the Chattooga River (1570 feet), bear left after bridge
1.4	Holden Branch (1570 feet), cross on footbridge and follow Chattooga
2.7	Side trail and Adline Branch (1550 feet), stay straight on Bartram Trail
6.1	Warwoman Creek (1510 feet), cross bridge and bear left
6.4	Earls Ford Road (1510 feet), cross road and regain Bartram Trail
9	Side trail to Dicks Creek Falls (1510 feet), turn left for falls (0.25-mile round trip)
9.3	Chattooga River Trail (1570 feet), stay on Bartram Trail
9.4	Sandy Ford Road (1610 feet), cross road and regain Bartram Trail on opposite side
11.2	Speed Gap (2020 feet), skirt dead end of old road
12.8	Bob Gap (2050 feet), cross road and regain Bartram Trail on opposite side
17.1	Green Gap (2140 feet), bear left on Bartram Trail
18.5	Warwoman Dell (1940 feet), bear right onto road, then left onto Bartram Trail
18.7	Warwoman Road (1940 feet), cross road and regain Bartram Trail on opposite side
22.3	Courthouse Gap (2340 feet), stay straight, northwest, on Bartram Trail
25.3	Rock Mountain (3690 feet)
27.5	Wilson Gap (3220 feet), follow dirt road for 0.5 mile and look for trail on left
30.3	Saltrock Gap (3700 feet), bear right on Bartram Trail
31.4	Flint Gap (4300 feet), bear right on Bartram Trail
32.2	Rabun Bald (4696 feet), head north on Bartram Trail
33.8	Beegum Gap (3660 feet)
36.3	Hale Ridge Road (3300 feet), turn right onto road and then left onto Bartram Trail
36.4	Georgia/North Carolina state line, rectangular orange blazes replace diamonds
39	Side trail down Hurrah Ridge (3400 feet), stay left on Bartram Trail
39.3	Side trail down West Fork (3360 feet), stay left on Bartram Trail
39.9	North Carolina 106 (3760 feet), cross road and regain Bartram Trail
41.3	Side trail (4580 feet), stay left on Bartram Trail
41.9	Scaly Mountain (4804 feet)
44	Forest Road 4620 (3440 feet), bear right onto road and look for Bartram Trail on right
47.7	Whiterock Gap (4150 feet), stay straight on Bartram Trail
48.4	Side trail to Whiterock (4400 feet), 0.6 mile round trip
50.6	Wolf Rock (4460 feet)
53.8	Old road (3000 feet), turn right onto road
54	Old road (3000 feet), turn right onto road
55.2	Buckeye Creek trailhead (2400 feet)

Suggested Camps Based on Different Trekking Itineraries

Night	10 mpd	10–15 mpd	15–20 mpd
One	9 miles - Dicks Creek	9 miles - Dicks Creek	16 miles - Rainy Mountain
Two	20 miles - Martin Creek	20 miles - Martin Creek	34 miles - Beegum Gap
Three	30+ miles - Saltrock Gap (dry)	34 miles - Beegum Gap	
Four	39+ miles - West Fork	48 miles - Whiterock Gap	
Five	48+ miles - Whiterock Gap		

Bartram Trail North (NC)

Difficulty: Strenuous

Distance: 46.9 miles

Elevation gain: 14,300 feet

Best season: Year-round, though midwinter conditions can be severe at higher elevations.

Recommended itinerary: 3 days (15–20 miles per day)

Water availability: Reliable sources are often several miles apart, except where the trail follows Ledbetter Creek from the Nantahala River to Bellcollar Gap. Be sure to top off at every opportunity. However, avoid collecting water from the Nantahala River as it receives heavy runoff from agriculture, nearby roads, and motorboats on Nantahala Lake.

Logistics: The orange-blazed Bartram Trail ends at Cheoah Bald, 6 miles from the nearest trailhead. From Cheoah Bald, follow the white blazes of the Appalachian Trail to the end of the trek at Stecoah Gap and North Carolina Route 143. It is about an hour and a half drive between trailheads, so plan on a shuttle vehicle. South of Cheoah Bald, the outdated USGS Hewitt quadrangle shows Trail 67, Bartram Trail, heading southwest into the Snowbird Mountains from US Route 129, just west of the intersection of US Route 19 and North Carolina Route 1310. The correct route is noted here within the description of the trek, and an accurate map is available from the North Carolina Bartram Trail Society.

Jurisdictions: Wayah Ranger District (828-524-6441) and Cheoah Ranger District (828-479-6431), Nantahala National Forest

Maps: The North Carolina Bartram Trail Society publishes a series of excellent and inexpensive maps based on USGS quads that cover the majority of the trek (*www.ncbartramtrail.org*). National Geographic Trails Illustrated 785, *Nantahala & Cullasaja Gorges*, offers a broad overview of the entire route, as well as several nearby treks. USGS Franklin, Wayah Bald, Topton, and Hewitt.

Trail location: From the junction of US Routes 64/441 in Franklin, North Carolina, head west on US 64 for 1 mile to Sloan Road, and turn right. Follow it to the end, passing Wayah Ranger Station on the right. Turn left onto Old Murphy Road and bear right immediately onto Pressley Road and continue to the Wallace Branch trailhead at the end of the road.

To reach the trailhead at Stecoah Gap, return to Old Murphy Road and turn left toward Franklin. On the west edge of downtown, turn left onto Porter Street, then right onto West Main Street, and then left onto North Carolina Route 28. Continue for 38 miles to North Carolina Route 143, merging briefly with US Route 19 along the way. Turn left onto North Carolina 143 and look for the trailhead and parking area on the left in 1.7 miles.

If the southern portion of the Bartram Trail is on the front porch of the Nantahala National Forest, then the northern reach visits both the attic and the basement, traversing several of the highest balds of the Nantahala and Cheoah Mountains and crossing the Nantahala River, tucked at the bottom of a gorge so dark and deep that its Cherokee name translates to "noonday sun." Enjoy stunning views throughout this trek, as naturalist William Bartram did in 1775 when he ascended the summit of Wine Spring Bald and "beheld with rapture and astonishment, a sublimely awful scene of power and magnificence, a world of mountains piled upon mountains."

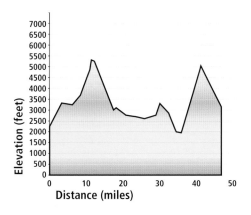

DAY ONE   16 miles   5900 feet

From the Wallace Branch trailhead west of downtown Franklin, begin climbing immediately through a dry oak forest to the crest of Trimont Ridge, just 1.6 miles away. Once on top, angle southwest around Bruce Knob and regain the main spine of the

Stecoah
Gap

Cheoah
Bald

Appalachian Trail

Ledbetter Creek

Nantahala River

143

28

28

28 19

19

19

2

422

129

1310

129

19

Rattlesnake
Knob

1401

Nantahala
Dam

Nantahala Lake

Nantahala

1310

Rock
Bald

Jarrett
Bald

Nantahala

28

Little Tennessee River

28

Nantahala

National

Forest

Nantahala

National

Forest

Appalachian Trail

Trimont Ridge

Franklin

T

Nantahala

Mountains

441

1310

Wayah
Bald

Wine
Spring
Bald

64

Appalachian
Trail

River

ridge as you head for Wayah Bald, the highest point along this section of the Bartram Trail. Dig deep to push up several steep knobs and step delicately down into narrow gaps, pausing occasionally to rest calves and knees and enjoy the lush summer growth or long-range winter views. If you've settled into a rhythm and have plenty of water, keep hiking past the first Locust Tree Gap. Otherwise, stop and refill at a spring 0.1 mile down the drainage to the north. In an hour, cross Forest Road 713 at Harrison Gap (3260 feet).

In the fall, bear hunters release packs of dogs eager for the chase and sometimes your food. I've encountered dozens of these gentle dogs over the years and have never had a problem with them other than the guilt I feel looking at their long faces, bony ribs, and wagging tails. Whatever your politics regarding bear hunting and half-starved dogs, keep an eye on your food as these dogs are quick! At the second Locust Tree Gap, pass through the first of two overgrown clearings maintained by the Forest Service as habitat for game animals such as grouse, turkey, and deer.

Wayah Bald observation tower
(Photo by Corey Hadden)

Beyond the second clearing, the trail begins its final climb to Wayah Bald. In 0.4 mile pass an old mica mine at a sharp bend in the trail. A rusty metal fence protects the unaware from stumbling over the lip of the mine, but a trail to the left leads to its base and views deep into the crevasse where aging logs brace against walls leaning under the weight of the mountain. Flakes of the sparkling mineral can be found here and throughout the region among the Precambrian schists, gneisses, and granites that form the foundation of the southern Appalachians.

Past the mine, the trail levels and meanders through woods dominated by ferns, rhododendrons, and tall oaks. Dozens of American chestnut saplings sprout in vain from ancient roots along the trail. The saplings don't make it past adolescence—their lives are cut short by the chestnut blight, which kills the trees when they are just 1 or 2 inches in diameter. Walk over a strong flowing creek, top off your bottles, and join the Appalachian Trail, bearing left to the summit of Wayah Bald (5342 feet). A lookout tower has stunning views in all directions. It's unknown whether William

Bartram topped Wayah Bald, but it's believed the "elevated peak" where he observed "mountains piled upon mountains" in his book, *Travels*, is Wine Spring Bald, down a short side trail, 0.7 mile from here.

Shortly past the turnoff for Wine Spring Bald, bid farewell to the Appalachian Trail for now and turn right onto the Bartram Trail. Continue to a small dry camp just past Jarrett Bald, 16 miles from the beginning of the trek at Wallace Branch. Be sure to collect water along the way, as the next reliable source is about 2 miles and 1700 feet down the mountain where Wine Spring Creek flows into Nantahala Lake.

DAY TWO   20 miles   5200 feet

The rocky trail twists through dark green hemlock forests until switchbacks even out the descent before nearly plunging to the banks of Nantahala Lake (3020 feet). Turn right onto North Carolina Route 1310, and contour 0.7 mile around the lake until you reach the Lakeside Campground and store. Turn left down a gravel driveway just past the store, cross a creek, and begin to climb, looking for the orange-blazed trail to the left after a sharp bend in the driveway. Back in the woods, gradually climb and contour around the lake, crossing two gravel roads on your way to the Nantahala River. Take in dramatic views of the lake and dam as you pass

Bike path along the Nantahala River (Photo by Corey Hadden)

through woods dominated by oaks with intermittent stands of striped and mountain maple and the occasional rhododendron tunnel.

Splash across the Nantahala River via a concrete ford to the left, and bear right onto the first gravel road, which is the High Water Trail. Walk the road and turn right onto an unmarked gravel road and parallel the river for 2 miles to Cloudwalker Cove Road. At the intersection, turn right, pass beneath the penstock, and come to North Carolina Route 1401. Cross the road and head right to the entrance of Appletree Group Campground, re-entering the woods to the right of the information kiosk. Back in the trees, parallel the Nantahala River on the edge of the campground listening for the sound of rushing water and the rattle of a kingfisher darting in and out of trees looking for calm water and a place to fish.

In Poplar Cove, the trail turns from the water and heads west into the moist hills, contouring past Piercy Creek and London Bald Trails. North of Rattlesnake Knob, listen for barred owls late in the afternoon, and if you're lucky, the yipping of coyotes, common but secretive residents of the southern Appalachians. Drop down short switchbacks past the Nantahala Power Company surge tank, continue to follow the gravel road downhill to North Carolina 1310, and turn right. Bear left after the bridge, and follow the Mountains-to-Sea bike path along the Nantahala River to Forest Road 422. Turn left, and come to US 19 and tracks for the Great Smoky Mountains Railroad. Camp near Ledbetter Creek is less than a mile through the woods.

DAY THREE 11 miles 3100 feet

Get an early start for the grand finale of the trek, a steady climb of 3000 feet to the summit of Cheoah Bald through Appalachian cove forest dominated by tulip poplar, rhododendron, and mossy boulders. Take a moderate pace on the ascent beside cascading Ledbetter Creek—which you eventually cross six times—and cool your feet in the shallow pools beneath its cascades. Shortly after the last crossing, head uphill and across Forest Road 259 on your way to Bellcollar Gap. Plod on through

Nantahala Lake (Photo by Corey Hadden)

late summer growth to a second encounter with the Appalachian Trail. Turn right onto the white- and orange-blazed trails and follow the well-worn path to Cheoah Bald's open summit at 5062 feet, gazing back on the piles of mountains traversed on the trek's 40-plus miles. Return to the Appalachian/Bartram Trail junction. Bear right, and follow white blazes to the trailhead at Stecoah Gap, 6 easy miles north on the Appalachian Trail.

Trail Summary and Mileage Estimates

0	Bartram Trail (2260 feet) at Wallace Branch trailhead
3.3	Locust Tree Gap (3340 feet), stay straight on Bartram Trail
6.2	Harrison Gap (3260 feet), cross Forest Road 713 and regain Bartram Trail
8.4	Locust Tree Gap (3700 feet), bear left onto grassy woods road
11	Appalachian Trail (4880 feet), bear left
11.4	Wayah Bald (5342 feet), follow paved footpath to trail on right
12.2	Bartram Trail (5280 feet), bear right onto Bartram Trail
17.4	Nantahala Lake (3020 feet), right onto NC 1310
18.1	Lakeside Campground and store (3120 feet), bear left onto Bartram Trail
20.7	Nantahala River (2780 feet), cross river and bear right onto gravel road (High Water Trail)
23	Cloudwalker Cove Road (2720 feet), right onto gravel road and pass under penstock
23.1	North Carolina 1401 (2720 feet), cross road and go right
23.2	Appletree Group Campground (2720 feet), bear right onto Bartram Trail
25.8	Poplar Cove Creek (2620 feet)
28.9	Piercy Creek Trail (2780 feet), bear left on Bartram Trail
30	London Bald Trail (3320 feet), bear right on Bartram Trail
32.4	Surge tank (2880 feet), follow gravel road
34.4	NC 1310 (2020 feet), turn right onto NC 1310
34.5	Mountains-to-Sea bike path (2000 feet), turn left onto trail and cross footbridge
35.7	Forest Road 422 (1960 feet), turn left on road and cross bridges
35.8	US 19 (1960 feet), cross road and railroad tracks
41	Appalachian Trail (4920 feet), bear right onto Bartram/Appalachian Trail
41.2	Cheoah Bald (5062 feet)
46.9	Stecoah Gap (3165 feet)

Suggested Camps Based on Different Trekking Itineraries

Night	10 mpd	10–15 mpd	15–20 mpd
One	11 miles - Appalachian/Bartram junction north of Wayah Bald	12 miles - Wine Spring Bald	16 miles - past Jarrett Bald (dry)
Two	20 miles - north of Nantahala Dam	25 miles - east of Appletree Group Campground	36 miles - Ledbetter Creek
Three	30+ miles - bivy north of London Bald Trail (dry)		40 miles - upper Ledbetter Creek
Four	40 miles - upper Ledbetter Creek	40 miles - upper Ledbetter Creek	

Bartram/Appalachian Loop (NC)

Difficulty: Very strenuous

Distance: 54.8 miles

Elevation gain: 16,300 feet

Best season: Year-round, though winter nights can be below freezing at higher elevations. Summer is high season for whitewater boating on the Nantahala River and recreational activities on adjacent national forest land. If you hope to find solitude during the summer, any trek that includes the famed Appalachian Trail may not be the best choice. Instead consider one of the other treks, many of which offer scenery that exceeds that found along the Appalachian Trail, but without the popularity. At other times of year, you can have virtually any trail in the southern Appalachians, including the Appalachian Trail, to yourself.

Recommended itinerary: 3 days (15–20 miles per day)

Water availability: Reliable water sources are often several miles apart as this trail frequently follows high ridges. Plan on making short side trips downhill when you need water. Avoid collecting water from the Nantahala River as it receives heavy runoff from agriculture and roads.

Logistics: As a loop hike, this trek presents no challenging logistics. The Appalachian Trail is blazed with white rectangles and the Bartram Trail is blazed with orange. The USGS 7.5' Hewitt quadrangle does not show the correct location of the Bartram Trail south of Cheoah Bald, but it is described accurately here.

Jurisdictions: Wayah Ranger District (828-524-6441) and Cheoah Ranger District (828-479-6431), Nantahala National Forest

Maps: The North Carolina Bartram Trail Society offers a series of excellent and inexpensive maps that cover sections 5–7 of the Bartram Trail (*www.ncbartramtrail.org*). National Geographic Trails Illustrated 784, *Fontana & Hiwassee Lakes*, or 785, *Nantahala & Cullasaja Gorges*. Each covers the entire trek, as well as several nearby treks, but their small scale renders them unsuitable for navigation once on trail. Also, USGS Wesser, Hewitt, Topton, and Wayah Bald.

Trail location: The trailhead is located in Wesser, North Carolina, behind the guest parking lot at the Nantahala Outdoor Center, midway between Bryson City and Andrews on US Route 19/74. Wesser is about 90 minutes southwest of Asheville.

Scrambling out of rugged valleys and across high mountain balds, this sublime trek smack in the heart of Cherokee country, both historic and present-day, offers the best of two worlds: the camaraderie of the celebrated Appalachian Trail and the solitude of the seldom-traveled Bartram Trail. The former was the nation's first designated national scenic trail while the latter traces the supposed route of eighteenth-century naturalist William Bartram through the lush cove and hardwood forests that dominate the southern Appalachians.

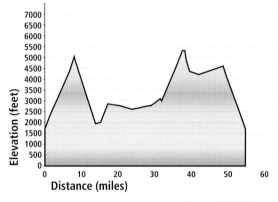

DAY ONE   20+ miles   7500 feet

Leaving the circus atmosphere at the Nantahala Outdoor Center behind, head northwest into the woods, being careful not to trip as you step over the tracks of the Great Smoky Mountains Railroad. Immediately begin climbing and contouring around Flint Ridge and in 1.5 miles pass over Watia Road in Wright Gap (2380 feet). Continue the rapid ascent in the open woods through Grassy Gap to the base of the Jump-up, a tumble of boulders and switchbacks that rise nearly a thousand feet in about a mile. Once on top of the main ridge, fill up your bottles at Sassafras Gap before heading to an early lunch a gentle 2.5 miles away at Cheoah Bald (5062 feet). Shrubby and often treeless, balds represent unique ecological communities in the southern mountains—and the reason for their distinction is still hotly debated among ecologists and naturalists. Possible answers include

Little Tennessee River

19

N E S W

Wesser Creek Trail

Wesser Bald

Appalachian Trail

Nantahala Outdoor Center

Lowing Bald

Nantahala National Forest

Trail

Nantahala River

19

1310

Piercy

Appalachian Trail

Cheoah Bald

Bartram Trail

Rattlesnake Knob

Stecoah Gap

129

Copper Ridge
Bald

Wayah
Bald

2

Appalachian   Trail

Rocky
Bald

Bartram   Trail

1310

Otter Mountain

Wine Spring Creek

Jarrett
Bald

1310

Poplar
Cove

Nantahala   Lake

Bartram   Trail

1

reek

London Bald Trail

1401

London
Bald

Nantahala River (Photo by Corey Hadden)

fires created by lightning and persistent grazing of livestock by the Cherokee and early settlers.

Explore the open summit and enjoy the dramatic view of the Nantahala Gorge. After lunch, discover a side trail leading to a breathtaking view of the Great Smoky Mountains and Fontana Lake. Refreshed and energized, head west from the summit and bear left onto the Bartram Trail aiming for Ledbetter Creek with its countless cascades and rich diversity of trees. Descend through boulders and bedrock and splash across the stream several times for the next 5.5 miles to the railroad tracks once again and US 19 (1960 feet). Carefully cross to Forest Road 422 and make your way over two bridges that span the Nantahala River, and turn right onto the Mountains-to-Sea bike path. Follow the paved trail through moist bottomlands beside the river and come to North Carolina Route 1310. Across the road and to the right just past the Nantahala Power Company installation, the Bartram Trail climbs back into the woods along an old access road that becomes a footpath 2 miles later on the far side of the power company's surge tank. Camp comes after a steep climb up the flanks of Rattlesnake Knob (4052 feet), in the vicinity of Piercy Creek.

DAY TWO   19 miles   4900 feet

Day two includes a stroll along the muddy banks of the Nantahala River, a brief reality check for those who believe development is only a suburban issue, and a traverse over the highest balds of the trek. Begin by crossing Piercy Creek, and contour in and out of steep-sided coves that offer glimpses through the forest canopy at the full length of the Nantahala Gorge. Drop steadily down old logging grades that switch back and forth through Poplar Cove to the banks of the Nantahala River. Walk upstream under towering hemlocks toward the Appletree Group Campground where the footpath merges with a gravel road. Look for blazes that lead you back into the woods along the river for a short time before dumping you at the campground's entrance on North Carolina Route 1401. Turn right onto the paved road, then left in about 300 feet onto Cloudwalker Cove Road. Cross the bridge, pass under the penstock, and turn left onto High Water Trail, a gravel road bordering several new homes that have sprung up in the last few years.

Here in Macon County, more than half of new-home permits are issued to out-of-staters, understandably seeking a little slice of mountain heaven. But, besides casting their shadow on the Bartram Trail, which passes by their mailboxes, such development casts a larger shadow on the integrity of the forest, which is being sliced and diced along its edges, and dissected by countless roads that cut through its middle.

Furious or indifferent, turn left at the end of the road (to avoid another house to the right!) and shortly arrive at Nantahala Dam Road. Turn left and cross the ford, and in 50 feet rejoice in the fact that the Bartram Trail leads up into the woods once more, toward a glorious 75-foot cascade. Climb and contour high above the reticulated shoreline of Nantahala Lake, and come to North Carolina 1310 by the Lakeside campground and store. Turn right and walk the road around the lake for 0.7 mile to the Bartram Trail, which dives into the woods 100 yards past the rushing waters of Wine Spring Creek.

Bartram and Appalachian Trails on Wayah Bald
(Photo by Corey Hadden)

The climb to Wayah Bald is rugged and steep, gaining more than 1500 feet in the first 2 miles. The strain on your calves and thighs gradually eases past Jarrett Bald (4890 feet) when the trail drops a few hundred feet into Sawmill Gap and crosses Forest Road 711. But the brief respite from the uphill slog only means more climbing to come. Rejoin the Appalachian Trail west of Wine Spring Bald and stay left, making easy work of the last 0.75 mile to the lookout tower on Wayah Bald, surrounded in early summer by blossoms of the flame azalea, mountain laurel, and rhododendron. Camp is an easy 0.5-mile jog down the trail to the Bartram Trail turnoff.

DAY THREE 16 miles 3900 feet

With a lighter pack, no serious elevation gains, and slightly fewer miles, the last day of trekking may seem like a day hike compared to the previous two days. However, don't underestimate the effects of the undulating trail on your legs, which have already seen two 20-mile days, and decide to sleep in. After breakfast, bid farewell to the Bartram Trail and stay left on the Appalachian Trail, marching up and down for endless miles through Licklog, Burningtown, and numerous unnamed gaps en route to Wesser Bald (4627 feet), the last of the high balds encountered on this trek. Bear left past the Wesser Creek Trail, and follow the main ridge as it narrows before steeply dropping to the trailhead at trek's end, across the river from where it began nearly 55 miles ago.

Looking east from Wayah Bald (Photo by Corey Hadden)

Trail Summary and Mileage Estimates

0	Appalachian Trail trailhead (1720 feet), head northwest
1.5	Wright Gap (2380 feet), stay straight on Appalachian Trail
6.8	Sassafras Gap (4380 feet)
8.1	Cheoah Bald (5062 feet)
8.3	Bartram Trail (4920 feet), bear left and follow orange blazes
13.9	US 19 and Forest Road 422 (1960 feet), cross road and follow Forest Road 422 across river
14	Mountains-to-Sea bike path (1960 feet), turn right and follow paved trail
15.2	NC 1310 (2020 feet), turn right onto NC 1310
15.3	Trailhead parking (2020 feet), turn left into woods on old access road
17.3	Surge tank (2880 feet), regain trail past tank
20.8	Piercy Creek Trail (2780 feet), bear right onto Bartram Trail and cross creek
23.9	Poplar Cove (2620 feet)
26.3	Appletree Group Campground (2700 feet), turn left onto old road
26.5	NC 1401 (2720 feet), turn right onto NC 1401
26.6	Cloudwalker Cove Road (2720 feet), turn left onto gravel road and cross bridge
26.7	High Water Trail (2720 feet), turn left onto gravel road/trail just past penstock
28.9	Nantahala Dam Road (2800 feet), turn left onto gravel road
29	Nantahala River (2780 feet), cross river over concrete ford and re-enter woods on Bartram Trail
31.6	NC 1310 (3120 feet), turn right onto NC 1310
32	Bartram Trail (3020 feet), turn left into woods
35.7	Sawmill Gap (4500 feet), bear left onto Forest Road 711, then right onto gravel road
37.5	Appalachian Trail (5280 feet), bear left onto Appalachian/Bartram Trail
37.6	Wine Spring Bald summit trail (5340 feet), stay straight on Bartram/Appalachian Trail
38.3	Wayah Bald (5342 feet)
38.7	Bartram Trail (4880 feet), stay left on Appalachian Trail
39.6	Licklog Gap (4380 feet)
42.1	Burningtown Gap (4236 feet)
48.7	Wesser Bald (4627 feet)
49.6	Wesser Creek Trail 26 (4140 feet), bear left on Appalachian Trail
54.8	Appalachian Trail trailhead (1720 feet)

Suggested Camps Based on Different Trekking Itineraries

Night	10 mpd	10–15 mpd	15–20 mpd
One	7 miles - Sassafras Gap	13+ miles - Ledbetter Creek	20+ miles - near Piercy Creek
Two	20 miles - Piercy Creek	25 miles - south of Walnut Cove	39 miles - Appalachian/ Bartram Trails junction.
Three	30 miles - north of Nantahala Dam	40 miles - Licklog Gap	
Four	40 miles - Licklog Gap		

Duncan Ridge Loop (GA)

Difficulty:	Very Strenuous
Distance:	53.2 miles
Elevation gain:	17,400 feet
Best season:	Year-round, though lush summer growth can obscure some sections of trail, and winter can bring freezing temperatures and snow at higher elevations.
Recommended itinerary:	4 days (10–15 miles per day)
Water availability:	On-trail water sources are few and far between, though water can be found downhill from most gaps if you descend far enough, often several hundred feet. Known water sources are described in the text.
Logistics:	From Three Forks, the Duncan Ridge Loop follows the white diamonds of the Benton MacKaye Trail (BMT) and the white rectangular blazes of the Appalachian Trail for approximately 1 mile until the two diverge near Long Creek Falls. Here, the Duncan Ridge Trail (DRT) joins the Benton MacKaye until the two trails part ways near the top of Rhodes Mountain. The Duncan Ridge Trail sees little regular maintenance, rendering it more challenging to find, let alone follow. It is marked by blue rectangular blazes, which are often faint and hard to see. Side trails leading to water also may be found. Expect the trail to be in poor shape—overgrown with fallen trees and extremely steep climbs and descents—compared to the Appalachian Trail and BMT. Trekking poles are highly recommended.
Jurisdictions:	Toccoa Ranger District (706-632-3031), Chattahoochee National Forest; and Brasstown Ranger District (706-745-6928)
Maps:	USGS Noontootla, Wilscot, Mulky Gap, Coosa Bald, Neels Gap, and Suches. The Appalachian Trail Conference map, *Springer Mountain to Bly Gap/Georgia*, could replace the Neels Gap and Suches maps. However, be aware

that while these maps indicate the location of each trail followed in this trek, inaccuracies do exist and several reroutes have occurred, especially around high-use areas along the Appalachian Trail. Compare the text and trek overview with the maps you plan to use.

Trail location: From Ellijay, Georgia, drive east on Georgia Route 52 for approximately 6.5 miles and turn left onto Big Creek Road. Follow Big Creek Road and then Double Head Gap Road (from where Big Creek turns left) for 15.3 miles to Forest Road 58, on the right. Drive approximately 6 miles on Forest Road 58, bearing right at a fork in the road, to the trailhead parking just past Long Creek where the Appalachian Trail and BMT emerge from the woods.

The prominent knobs on Duncan Ridge stick out like vertebra on the spine of a sleeping dragon. The trail that rides its back has been called Georgia's most strenuous footpath, and its rugged reputation is well-earned: steep climbs and kamikaze descents are the norm. Others say the strain comes from the psycho-

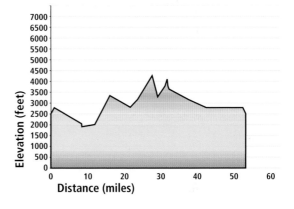

logical toll from inexhaustible summer growth and endless winter blowdowns. Starting at Three Forks, spend the first day warming up on the well-maintained BMT. Then on day two, leap onto the dragon's back and ride it for the next day and a half to the base of Blood Mountain, where the Appalachian Trail will be waiting to comfort you with its gentle grades and familiar blazes.

DAY ONE   15 miles   4900 feet

Leaving Three Forks, step forward onto the old forest road and ascend gradually beside Long Creek beneath rhododendron, hemlock, and mixed pines. In 0.8 mile, a side trail leads left to Long Creek Falls, where water slides and drops more than 30 feet, creating a refreshing spray. Just a few steps beyond this turnoff, the Benton MacKaye Trail merges with the Duncan Ridge Trail and turns left on a bridge over Long Creek, the last water source for the next 7.5 miles, and begins to climb; the Appalachian Trail bears right, not to be seen for another two days.

60

Benton MacKaye Trail

Skeenah Creek Road

Duncan Ridge Trail

Rhodes Mountain

Licklog Mountain

Wallalah Mountain

Toonowee Mountain

FS 4

60

Toccoa

River

Benton MacKaye/Duncan Ridge Trail

Rocky Mountain

FS 58

Appalachian Trail

Appalachian Trail

Three Forks

Benton MacKaye Trail

FS 42

Springer Mountain

FS 77

Etowah River

Mulky Gap

Clements Mountain

Duncan Ridge Trail

FS 39

2

Coosa Bald

180

Wolfpen Gap

Chattahoochee

National

Forest

Slaughter Mountain

Blood Mountain

Pilot Mountain

Appalachian Trail

Blood

Mountain

Wilderness

180

60

Woody Lake

Woody Gap

N

W E

S

3

60

Gooch Mountain

Suspension bridge over the Toccoa River (Photo by Corey Hadden)

The DRT is actually older than the BMT. Construction on the BMT didn't begin until 1980, whereas the Duncan Ridge Trail was completed in 1978 to form a multiple-day loop hike in conjunction with the Appalachian Trail. Soon after, the Georgia Appalachian Trail Club, which had served as chief caretaker for the Duncan Ridge Trail, withdrew from its partnership with the national forest and focused its energy solely on the Appalachian Trail. Recent projects on the Appalachian Trail include trail relocations away from high-use areas, new shelters, and tent pads, all of which help to reduce the impact that the multitudes of users have on the rich plant and animal communities. Like a foster child, the Duncan Ridge Trail has been under the care of the national forest, which has neither the time nor the resources to provide adequate maintenance. The result is a trail that isn't well maintained, so while you're out there take a few minutes to remove debris that may inhibit travel or undertake other small trail projects that may improve the route.

Once through the wildlife clearing above Long Creek, the easy-to-follow terrain snakes between ridge top and gap, often narrowly missing the summit, to the Toccoa River at mile 8.4. Consider lunch or an early camp near a small creek on the east side of the 260-foot suspension bridge that spans the river. After lunch, the trail gradually climbs nearby Toonowee Mountain—known locally as Tooni Mountain—on a series of wide-swinging switchbacks, crosses Georgia Route 60, and begins another mostly gentle climb, this time ascending the rocky flanks of Wallalah Mountain (3100 feet). Camp is the next knob over, on the broad crown of Licklog Mountain (3472 feet). Water may be found about 100 feet east of the gap between Licklog and Rhodes Mountain.

DAY TWO   11+ miles   4400 feet

Eleven miles at first may seem to be an innocent amount of mileage. Factor in more than 4000 feet of gain and loss, however, and you may reconsider. Add the search for water down tangled drainages, and midafternoon thunderstorms that turn every knob into a lightning rod, and suddenly the day looms larger than expected, and an early start is the only way to avoid an epic.

Make quick work of the ascent toward Rhodes Mountain, pausing in the slight gap beneath its summit to locate and follow the Duncan Ridge Trail straight up the ridge—don't take the BMT, which turns left. Winter views are sublime, but clearings from summer growth may be found on outcrops atop Rhodes Mountain. Repeating the pattern of the previous mile, descend to Rhodes Gap and begin another climb, but don't be fooled by the gentle grade, which becomes steep as you approach Gregory Knob. Pause in Sarvis Gap for water, which is found downhill, and south of the gap. Resume your slog up Fish Knob, then Clements Mountain, and Akin Mountain before dropping steeply into Mulky Gap at 6.6 miles. Water may be found a few hundred yards to the south down Forest Road 4.

Mulky Gap may have been ground zero for the 17-year cicada hatch in the north Georgia mountains in 2004. Living, dying, and shedding cicadas blanketed every leaf and limb surrounding the gap. Every square foot of trail and gravel road within a quarter mile was a crunchy

Summer lushness on Duncan Ridge Trail (Photo by Corey Hadden)

floor made entirely of cicadas. If the cicada invasion leaves you feeling queasy, know that Mulky Gap will be free of the little red-eyed creatures until 2021.

Beyond Mulky Gap, the trail is steep as it climbs nearly 800 feet up West Wildcat Knob, then repeats the task several more times as it climbs a series of knobs for the remainder of the day. In Bryant Gap, the DRT begins to parallel Forest Road 39 until its junction with Georgia 180. Camp in Whiteoak Stomp, beside Forest Road 39 at the base of Coosa Bald, or if you haven't had enough, press on to the magnificent stone shelter atop Blood Mountain, 6 miles and 3000 feet of additional gain.

DAY THREE   16 miles   5500 feet gain

The climb up Coosa Bald presents the steepest sustained section of trail yet—nearly 800 feet in 0.9 mile. If you can make it up without complaint, you are among a minority. The long summit covered with gnarled oaks, witch hazel, and young chestnuts offers no reward in summer, though winter and early spring provide a westward view of the ridge. The descent to Wildcat Gap is unforgiving: straight down grades of nearly 40 degrees and short bursts along a rugged, off-road vehicle trail.

In time, come to and cross Georgia Route 180 in Wolfpen Gap and begin your ascent of Slaughter Mountain with 800 feet steadily gained. The trail never finds the summit, but does reach a highpoint equal to that of Coosa Bald. Descend an easy grade on the recently rerouted trail beneath the northeast side of Slaughter Gap and pass the Coosa Backcountry Trail, which leads downhill and to the left. Contour past the gap and cut back to the right, over the ridge that leads to Blood Mountain. Ascend the ridge briefly and finally reach the easy grades of the Appalachian Trail as it rises to the apex of the trek on Blood Mountain (4458 feet), whose slickrock summit looks more like glacial polish than southern Appalachian exfoliation.

Descend and bear left (south) onto the Appalachian Trail. Reach the junction of the Slaughter Creek Trail shortly and turn right if you need water. Otherwise, stay left on the Appalachian Trail and make your way to Gooch Mountain Shelter, an easy stroll of 10.5 miles on well-maintained trail.

DAY FOUR   10 miles   2600 feet

The last day of trekking is a piece of cake compared to the previous three days. No major climbs or descents line the route, though an up and down rhythm is maintained all the way to the end. Beautiful woods provide the backdrop, abundant water sources quench your thirst, and a cemetery shortly before reaching familiar Long Creek Falls adds a spooky diversion. Soon reach the trailhead, exhausted perhaps, but proud that you didn't wake the dragon.

Opposite: Coosa Bald (Photo by Corey Hadden)

Trail Summary and Mileage Estimates

0	Forest Road 58 at Three Forks (2520 feet), head north on Benton MacKaye and Appalachian Trails
0.9	Appalachian and Duncan Ridge Trails (2800 feet), bear left on DRT
8.3	Forest Road 333 (2060 feet), cross road and regain BMT/DRT
8.4	Toccoa River (1920 feet), cross suspension bridge and remain on BMT/DRT
11.9	Georgia 60 (2020 feet), cross highway and regain BMT/DRT. Country store nearby
16	Benton MacKaye Trail (3360 feet), stay straight on DRT
21.6	Forest Road 4 at Mulky Gap (2820 feet), cross gravel road and regain DRT
23.6	Byrant Gap and FR 39 (3180 feet)
27.6	Coosa Bald (4280 feet)
29.1	Georgia 180 at Wolfpen Gap (3300 feet), cross highway and regain DRT
31.1	Coosa Backcountry Trail (3800 feet), stay right on DRT
31.7	Appalachian Trail (4120 feet), turn left for Blood Mountain, right for trek's end
31.9	Slaughter Creek Trail (3800 feet), turn left onto Appalachian Trail
32.2	Bird Gap, side trail to Woods Hole Shelter and Freeman Trail (3660 feet), stay straight on Appalachian Trail
37.5	Georgia 60 at Woody Gap (3180 feet), cross highway and regain Appalachian Trail
42.5	Side trail to Gooch Mountain Shelter (2800 feet)
52.4	Trail junction (2800 feet), turn left onto Appalachian Trail/BMT
53.2	Forest Road 58 at Three Forks (2520 feet)

Suggested Campsites Based on Different Trekking Itineraries

Night	<10 mpd	10–15 mpd	15–20 mpd
One	8+ miles - Toccoa River	15 miles - Licklog Mountain	15 miles - Licklog Mountain
Two	18+ miles - Sarvis Gap	26+ miles - Whiteoak Stomp	32+ miles - Blood Mountain Shelter
Three	26+ miles - Whiteoak Stomp	42+ miles - Gooch Mountain Shelter	
Four	33+ miles - Woods Hole		
Five	42+ miles - Gooch Mountain Shelter		

Note: The Hawk Mountain Shelter at mile 49.9 did not fit readily into one of the itineraries, but it has easy access to water and makes an excellent place to stay before coming out of the field. Most gaps found throughout the trek can accommodate at least one tarp or tent, though lush summer growth can obscure likely sites.

Benton MacKaye Trail (GA/TN)

Difficulty:	Very strenuous
Distance:	92.6 miles
Elevation gain:	19,600 feet
Best season:	Any season, although below-freezing temperatures may be experienced in the winter at higher elevations. Spring wildflowers peak mid-March to mid-May, and summer wildflowers are also quite spectacular. Fall colors peak at various times in October, depending on elevation.
Recommended itinerary:	5–7 days (13–18 miles per day)
Water availability:	Water is frequent along much of the trail, but dry stretches between safe and reliable sources may be 6 or more miles in length. Creeks and rivers that run through or near roads and homes are not recommended, though they may appear to be the only source. Where the trail passes homes or the occasional small business, stop in and ask to fill up—most people in the mountains will be happy to oblige.
Logistics:	An off-white diamond blazes the way for most of the trail's length. Current USGS maps, as well as other brands, show little if any of the Benton MacKaye Trail (BMT), and what is shown tends to be inaccurate. Along gravel roads, look for the blaze on telephone poles. On paved roads, look for blazes painted on the pavement or bridges, in addition to the familiar flimsy plastic Forest Service trail markers. To make navigating more interesting, the BMT is not blazed in its course through the rugged Cohutta and Big Frog Wilderness Areas. Here, the wilderness map available from either district ranger office plus good map and compass skills are requisites. This trek finishes approximately 65 miles by car from its beginning at Springer Mountain. Happy Trails Shuttle Service

(706-282-7672) can help with logistics.

Jurisdictions: Toccoa Ranger District (706-632-3031) and Armuchee-Cohutta Ranger District (706-695-6736), Chattahoochee National Forest (Georgia); Ocoee/Hiwassee Ranger District (423-338-5201); and Cherokee National Forest (Tennessee). Public and private roads and paths in isolated areas. No permits are required. Camping on private land without landowner permission is trespassing and unnecessary, except at Indian Rock Shelter, a "backcountry" shelter located on private land several miles west of the BMT's intersection with US Route 76. Questions regarding the BMT's traverse of private lands should be directed to the Benton MacKaye Trail Association (*www.bmta.org*).

Maps: USGS Noontootla, Wilscot, Mulky Gap, Blue Ridge, Cashes Valley, Dyer Gap, Hemp Top, Caney Creek, and Ducktown. A better map exists for the Cohutta and Big Frog Wilderness Areas, available from either the Armuchee-Cohutta or the Ocoee/Hiwassee Ranger District.

Trail location: To get to the trailhead near Springer Mountain from Ellijay, Georgia, drive east on Georgia Route 52 for approximately 6.5 miles, and then turn left onto Big Creek Road. Follow Big Creek Road and then Double Head Gap Road (from where Big Creek turns left) for 12.5 miles to Forest Road 42, on the right. In about 6.5 miles, pass the Appalachian Trail and immediately turn left into a parking area. The actual start of the Benton MacKaye Trail is 0.7 mile up the Appalachian Trail toward Springer Mountain.

The trek's end beside the Ocoee River in Tennessee is approximately 14 miles west of the Tennessee/North Carolina state line on US Route 64, beside the Ocoee Powerhouse No. 3. Thunder Rock Campground, on the other side of the river and behind the powerhouse off Forest Road 45, is a great place to stay the night before you begin hiking. A fee is collected for camping, but not for trailhead parking. To get to Ellijay from the Thunder Rock Campground, head east on US 64 for 9 miles to Tennessee Route 68 and turn right. TN 68 becomes Georgia Route 5 at the state line and goes on to merge with US Route 76 and Georgia Route 2 in Blue Ridge, Georgia. From Blue Ridge, Ellijay is a quick 14 miles down the highway.

The Benton MacKaye Trail is more than the southern Appalachians' other Appalachian Trail. Following the original route proposed for the Appalachian Trail by that trail's proponent, chief architect, and spiritual leader, Benton MacKaye, the BMT is essentially the parent of the nation's most famous footpath. Today the Appalachian Trail follows the prominent ridges along the eastern escarpment of the Blue Ridge until it traverses north and west across southwest North Carolina toward the Great Smoky Mountains. Yet the western crest in north Georgia and southeastern Tennessee was as wild as it gets—and it still is for the most part, despite the throngs of city dwellers, suburbanites, and retirees who carve out mountain hideaways seeking refuge from a more chaotic life.

Begin the trek in the dry oak forests atop Springer Mountain and end on the southern bank of the Ocoee River, where a perfect swimming hole awaits to soothe your aching muscles. Along the way, grunt up mountainsides and breathe easy along country roads, stand in awe of trees and ferns reminiscent of Tolkien's elfin world, and drench yourself in shoaling rivers and the spray of cascades.

Wall to wall ferns north of Springer Mountain (Photo by Corey Hadden)

76

Aska Road

Blue Ridge

5

76

76

5

5

CR 158

Rich
Mountain
Wilderness

Stanley Creek Road

Indian Rock
Shelter **3**

development
roads

76

5

To
Ellijay

Bushy Head Road

Fowler
Mountain

Flat Top Mountain **4**

FS 22

FS 64

Map 1

Map 2

Map 1

Trek 6 overview

Duncan Ridge Trail

Rhodes Mountain

Wallalah Mountain

60

Tipton Mountain
2

76

Shallowford Bridge

Blue Ridge Lake

Aska Road

76

Stanley Creek

Blue Ridge

5

76 5

76

5

CR 158

Indian Rock Shelter
3

development roads

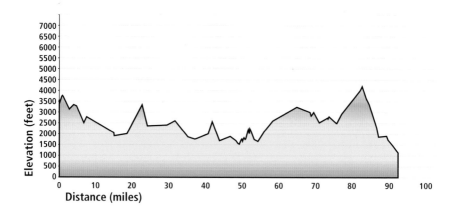

DAY ONE   15+ miles   2600 feet

The actual beginning to the Benton MacKaye Trail rests 0.7 mile south on the Appalachian Trail, up the steep and sometimes rocky trail that leads to the mecca of America's hiking community, Springer Mountain. Consider spending the night at the two-story shelter on Springer in order to get an earlier start for the challenging first day beginning at the grand junction of the eastern and western crests of the Blue Ridge.

Turn right onto the BMT and pass the plaque dedicating the trail to Mr. MacKaye (pronounced like "sky"). The trail descends gently, roughly paralleling the Appalachian Trail along a narrow ridge and turns sharply east traversing a fern-covered cove before dropping into the first of hundreds of many nameless gaps. In about a mile, an overgrown side trail leads to an outcrop of rock and a dramatic year-round view of the foothills and piedmont. Back on the BMT, cross Forest Road 42. Contour and climb through wet, north-facing coves lined with rhododendrons and step over several streams before crossing paths with the Appalachian Trail on the way to Three Forks, where three mountain streams merge, forming Noontootla Creek.

In the first few miles, the BMT meets up with or crosses the Appalachian Trail four times. One day, the BMT, which is still under development, will unfurl all the way to the Great Smoky Mountains, where it will reconnect with the Appalachian Trail to form a 500-mile loop.

At Three Forks, walk over the footbridge and cross gravel Forest Road 58 following the path now shared by the Appalachian Trail. Follow the old road grade as it gently rises for the next mile and dips in and out of the riparian zone through stands of white pine, hemlock, and a mix of hardwoods. At the end of that mile, look for a side trail to the left leading to Long Creek Falls and a perfect lunch spot in the spray of its 30-foot cascade. Refreshed, refueled, and back on the trail, bid farewell to the Appalachian Trail and pick up a new hiking partner, the blue-blazed

Opposite: Long Creek Falls (Photo by Corey Hadden)

Duncan Ridge Trail (DRT), which meets up with the Appalachian Trail in the other direction on the shoulder of Blood Mountain, forming a rugged 60-mile loop when combined with the Appalachian Trail (see Trek 5, Duncan Ridge Loop).

The BMT and DRT part ways just below the summit—the DRT tops out and eventually meets up with the Appalachian Trail on the shoulder of Blood Mountain, forming a rugged 53-mile loop (see Trek 5, Duncan Ridge Loop)—the BMT turns left at the junction to contour around the western side of Rhodes and descends more than 800 feet down to Skeenah Gap Road.

Follow the ridge up and down, occasionally dropping off its crest to pass from the side of one knob to another. The drier forest here is mostly a mix of oaks and pines, but the occasional stand of poplars and other cove species spill in where the trail passes through north-facing slopes. At mile 14.5, the trail begins its steep descent to the Toccoa River, losing more than 600 feet in elevation in the last half mile. Cross Forest Road 333 and quickly arrive at the locally famous "swinging bridge" spanning 260 feet across the minor rapids of the Toccoa River. Though its beauty may be inspiring, don't harvest your water from the Toccoa, whose upstream reach passes many roads and houses. A small creek can be found before you cross the bridge.

DAY TWO 15+ miles 5100 feet
The total elevation gain on day two is more than 5000 feet and rewarded with views from Wallalah, Licklog, and, at day's end, Tipton Mountain. Swing over the bridge and with as much water as you can carry—the next safe source isn't for another 7 miles—climb back and forth up the trail which gradually widens as it gains the dry crest of Toonowee Mountain.

At mile 3.5, cross paved Georgia Route 60, watching for cars, and re-enter the woods, passing over Little Skeenah Creek via a small footbridge. Over the next 2 miles, the path makes its first serious climb of the day—more than 1000 feet, with about half of it concentrated in the last 0.5 mile—as it twists its way up the rocky shoulder of Wallalah Mountain (3104 feet). Topping out, immediately set your sights on Licklog Mountain, a little more than 1 mile away and less than 400 feet higher, but attained only after a steep drop of more than 300 feet into the unnamed gap at its base.

A short distance north of Licklog's flat summit, a signed trail off to the right leads to a reliable spring. Beyond this, the next source of water is in Payne Gap in 4 miles. Not far from the spring, the trail climbs again, this time toward, but not quite reaching, the summit of Rhodes Mountain. The BMT and DRT part ways just below the summit—the DRT goes up and the BMT turns left at the junction to contour around the western side of Rhodes and descend more than 800 feet down to Skeenah Gap Road. At the forest's edge and slightly above the road, turn left and walk through overgrown roadside vegetation before the trail spits you onto the pavement.

For the next several miles, the wide path rolls over unnamed knobs and gaps—except Payne Gap which hosts camping and a reliable spring to the north, where a dense mix of young oaks, pines, and laurels dominate. The climb up Deadennen Mountain is easygoing, but the descent to GA 60 at Wilscot Gap is more abrupt. Recross GA 60 and begin the steady climb toward camp on the broad ridge north of Tipton Mountain. About 0.5 mile before camp, a side trail leads right to a reliable spring.

DAY THREE 19+ miles 3300 feet

Day three is as pleasant to experience firsthand as it is confusing to describe. Suffice it to say, the miles of walking a country road offer a refreshing departure from the deep woods. The first few miles are within the Chattahoochee National Forest, as are 6 isolated miles in the middle. In between and on the far side of the national forest island, the BMT follows public roads and traverses private land. Keep track of the white diamonds that blaze the way and routefinding will be a snap. Campsites near reliable water sources are limited to the headwaters of Laurel Creek, 15 miles away, and Indian Rock Shelter, 5 miles farther and today's destination.

From Tipton Mountain, descend the gentle grade to an unnamed gap with a seasonal spring to the right and contour around Bald Top en route to Brawley Mountain, which hosts one of the few remaining fire towers in the southern Appalachians. In Ledford Gap, join Forest Road 45 briefly, heading right, then in 100 feet, re-enter the woods to the right. The fire tower, which is closed to public access, is a vestige of an era when vast unpopulated tracts of wilderness were surveyed by one or two attendants, always on the lookout for signs of fire. Today, satellites and public tip-offs have all but replaced manned fire towers.

Slip past the tower and down the access road for 150 feet and turn right into the woods. The trail drops casually into Garland Gap at mile 3. Off-road vehicle traffic here precludes making this a nicer camp. Water may be found down the north slope. Climb and contour around Garland Mountain and quickly lose 800 feet over the next mile as the trail drops down to a three-way intersection of gravel roads at Wilscot. Cross the near road and head southwest along Shallowford Bridge Road for about 100 feet and re-enter the woods on the right, heading for Free Knob. The trail climbs for a gain of approximately 300 feet before settling in on the southern slopes of Free Knob, whose summit is never attained. Contour for a few hundred yards and descend back down to Shallowford Bridge Road and turn right to begin your country road adventure.

In 0.5 mile, pass a tubing outfitter and turn left over Shallowford Bridge. On the other side of the river, turn right onto paved Aska Road and walk for 0.4 miles to a left turn onto paved Stanley Creek Road. Follow the country road for 3.2 miles through woods and meadows and bear right into the forest at a small parking area just as you pass over Fall Branch. In a few hundred yards, another waterfall can be seen from an observation platform reached from a side trail leading to the right. Past the falls, the BMT picks up speed and another temporary partner, the Stanley Gap Trail, which shares the same tread for the next 2 miles, contouring and climbing around the eastern slope of Rocky Mountain. At the parting junction, bear left on the BMT, descend, and climb once again, this time to Scroggin Knob. From its top, drop more than 800 feet in a mile to Laurel Creek, which serves as an intermediate destination if daylight is running out. Otherwise, continue on to the road junction and turn left onto Laurel Creek Road, a four-wheel drive road, thus beginning round two of your scenic tour of southern Appalachian country roads.

Parallel Laurel Creek down the rough road, and bear right where it transitions to a maintained gravel road. Rise and fall with the road through fields and forest for another mile and turn left onto County Road 158, which quickly deteriorates into an overgrown two-track strewn with garbage. Just as suddenly as it dissolves, County Road 158 recomposes itself and makes a sharp right onto a maintained gravel road. Follow this route for 0.3 mile to the highway crossing at US 76. Cross the highway carefully. A few yards down the road to the left, turn right onto a small driveway, and in 20 feet, left at the fence. A trail parallels the fence on the highway for a few yards before ducking into an opening on the right.

The trail follows switchbacks up and over this unnamed mountain through dense stands of young pines before crossing to the wetter northwest slope and dropping down to another road and a covered bridge over Cherry Log Creek. Immediately past the bridge, cross the railroad tracks and bear left into the woods. In a few short yards the trail makes a sharp right turn and heads northwest up an unnamed tributary of Cherry Log Creek. Cross the creek several times over solid footbridges and merge onto a gravel road. Bear left at a fork in the road and in 0.2 mile turn right down Bills Lane, a driveway that blurs into the woods just past a house. Cross a creek and switchback up through the rhododendrons, and emerge on top of an earthen dam with a Lilliputian church to the left, observation platform and sitting area to the right.

Turn left onto the wooden deck and proceed to a gravel road and turn left. Round the bend in the road, stay straight at the fork, and turn right onto Indian Rock Road, dropping into the woods on the right in just a few yards. Cross another road, this one worn but not regularly used, and drop into the woods for the last time today. Camp is across the creek and to the left at the privately owned but publicly accessible Indian Rock Shelter.

DAY FOUR   14+ miles   3900 feet

Turning right out of the shelter's footpath, cross the creek to rejoin the gravel road past a large pond and through a second covered bridge. In the next 0.1 mile, stay straight at the first fork in the road, and enter the woods through a split rail fence where the road bears right. The old road parallels a small creek and passes JT's Trail, which heads left up a larger drainage.

Cross another gravel road and bear left above the road's edge just inside the woods for a few yards before turning right down the driveway of another mountain hideaway. Aim for the front door and just before you ring the bell, bear right into the woods and momentarily step between the house and a satellite dish. The path descends gradually past yet another home, and drops onto paved Mag Chapman Road in Tipton Gap. Stay right along the road and in 0.1 mile turn right onto the BMT, shared briefly with an off-road vehicle trail. Bear left almost immediately on a footpath inaccessible to machines and switchback up a steep slope to the top of the hill and begin descending the other side, taking care not to accidentally follow the ORV trails that bomb straight down the ridge.

In 0.1 mile, come to a confusing intersection of trails and old roads. Bear right, then left, following the white diamonds toward Sugar Creek, and the final stretch of paved road. Be sure to get the water you'll need for the next 5 miles from Sugar Creek, as the next good source isn't until Hudson Gap. Turn left onto the paved road, and in about 1 mile, turn right onto Bushy Head Road, which turns to gravel in 0.6 mile. Bushy Head Gap can be seen from the turn, wedged between high ridges.

Covered bridge past Indian Rock Shelter
(Photo by Corey Hadden)

At Bushy Head Gap, turn left and enter the woods. Navigating the 9.1 miles from Bushy Head Gap to camp in Halloway Gap is straightforward; the trail and all turns are obvious, letting you enjoy the wondrous lushness and views found in these hills. In Hudson Gap, cross Forest Road 793 and pick up some water, or wait until just past Hatley Gap, where a seasonal stream crosses the trail, and the ascent of Fowler Mountain begins in earnest. Atop Fowler Mountain, the trail bends to the right with the mountain itself, and eases its way up and down for another 1.9 miles to camp.

DAY FIVE 16+ miles 3200 feet

Enter the 45,000-acre Cohutta-Big Frog Wilderness and bid farewell to the white diamonds—you're on your own today. And, as always, be sure to leave camp with plenty of water. Though frequent on-trail sources can be found until mile 10, after Bear Branch there are no easily found sources until camp at Double Spring Gap.

Leaving camp, climb to Flat Top Mountain's expansive summit on an easygoing trail that follows the gentle contours of the land, even where the ridge itself begins to steepen. Along the crest of the mountain, step over numerous small streams bound for the South Fork of Jacks River. Descend through mature mixed hardwoods dominated by oak to Forest Road 64A and turn left, arriving at Dyer Gap and Forest Road 64 in 0.3 mile. Jog left onto Forest Road 64 for less than 0.1 mile and turn right into the woods. A great campsite can be found in 0.5 miles near the junction of the South Fork River Trail, which, if followed to the left for 0.25 mile, leads to another beautiful waterfall. Bear right onto the BMT/South Fork River Trail and pass beneath hemlocks and pines and through dark rhododendron tunnels.

In 1.5 miles, where the BMT begins to leave the river bottom, the South Fork River Trail turns left and briefly shares a few yards with the Pinhoti Trail. Climb back to the ridge top through mixed pines and oaks and turn left onto Forest Road 64 near Watson Gap.

In Watson Gap, head straight on Forest Road 22 for 0.3 mile and turn left into the woods. Ascend through mixed hardwoods until the trail drops down to a footbridge over Mill Branch. Parallel the creek for a bit, then climb up and over a shallow ridge and cross into the wilderness area before dropping into Peter Cove, whose small stream flows into Bear Branch—don't forget to fill your bottle as the going from here is dry until camp.

Join the Jacks River Trail for 0.1 mile, staying right, and bear left where the trails part ways. Climb in fits and spurts over rolling terrain to Spanish Oak Gap, where the BMT turns left and merges with the Hemp Top Trail for 3 miles to the top of its namesake. On Hemp Top, a young forest busily reclaims open space once occupied by a fire lookout. Camp is not far away at Double Spring Gap, about 1.5 miles up and down some minor knobs.

DAY SIX 11+ miles 1500

The final day of trekking, though shorter in distance and elevation gain, packs a mighty punch. Straight off from camp, the BMT gains more than half the day's elevation in the first 0.8 mile. And after you leave camp, the only reliable water source until trek's end shows up at midday, after the long descent to West Fork Rough Creek.

Leaving camp, dig deep and climb to the top of Licklog Ridge, take a breather, and turn left onto the Licklog Ridge Trail. The summit of Big Frog Mountain (4220 feet), clad in flame azaleas in mid-June, is an easy 0.5-mile climb.

Turn right onto Big Frog Trail and down undulating Fork Ridge, passing Big Creek Trail on the left in 0.9 mile. When Big Frog Trail turns left at the next junction, stay straight on the ridge top trail, which is Fork Ridge Trail. The trail steadily loses elevation for the next 2 miles to its end where the Rough Creek Trail accompanies the BMT down and to the left toward a usually dry crossing over the West Fork of Rough Creek. Here the BMT turns right onto the West Fork Trail.

In one last attempt to remain in the mountains, the trail climbs easily to the top of Chestnut Ridge, where it crosses Forest Road 221 and bears left onto an old Forest Service road. The going from here is easy. Just stay left at the Chestnut Mountain Loop and cross Forest Road 45. The banks of the Ocoee River will arrive all too soon.

Trail Summary and Mileage Estimates

0	Appalachian Trail at Forest Road 42 (3380 feet), head south on Appalachian Trail
0.7	BMT (3740 feet), stay right on Appalachian Trail for Springer shelter
0.9	Springer Mountain (3782 feet)
1.1	BMT (3740 feet), turn right onto trail
2.8	Forest Road 42 at Big Stamp Gap (3150 feet), cross road and regain BMT
4	Appalachian Trail (3360 feet), stay on BMT
4.8	Appalachian Trail (3300 feet), stay on BMT
6.7	Appalachian Trail (2560 feet), turn right onto shared BMT and Appalachian Trail
6.8	Forest Road 58 at Three Forks (2520 feet), cross and follow BMT and Appalachian Trail
7.6	Appalachian and Duncan Ridge Trails (2800 feet), bear left onto BMT/DRT
15.1	Forest Road 333 (2060 feet), cross and regain trail
15.2	Toccoa River (1920 feet), cross suspension bridge and remain on BMT/DRT
18.7	GA 60 (2020 feet), cross and regain BMT/DRT
22.8	DRT splits off (3360 feet), bear left onto BMT
24.2	Skeenah Gap Road (2380 feet), cross and ascend steps into woods on BMT
29.5	GA 60 (2420 feet), cross and regain BMT
31.7	Forest Road 45 (2620 feet), turn right onto Forest Road 45 for 100 feet, then right onto BMT
32.7	Brawley Mountain and fire tower, bear right onto Forest Road 45, then in 65 yards turn right onto BMT
35.2	Shallowford Bridge Road and Dial Road (1880 feet), cross Dial Road, follow Shallowford Bridge Road for 100 feet, then turn right onto BMT
36.6	Shallowford Bridge Road (1800 feet), turn right onto road
37.1	Shallowford Bridge (1774 feet), turn left over bridge
37.1	Aska Road (1774 feet), turn right onto road
37.5	Stanley Creek Road (1794 feet), turn left onto road
40.7	BMT at Fall Branch (2020 feet), turn right onto BMT
41.8	Stanley Gap Trail (2580 feet), stay right on BMT/Stanley Gap Trail
43.8	Stanley Gap Trail (3240 feet), stay left on BMT
46.7	Laurel Creek Road (1900 feet), turn left onto road

Trail Summary and Mileage Estimates (continued)

48.3	County Road 158 (1700 feet), turn left onto road
48.8	US 76 (1580 feet), cross highway, turn left along highway looking for break in fence line, and regain BMT in woods
49.2	Covered bridge and railroad crossing (1540 feet), cross tracks and bear left into woods between tracks and road
49.7	Sisson Road (1740 feet), bear left onto gravel road
49.9	Chapman Lake Trail (1780 feet), stay left on Sisson Road
50.1	Bills Lane (1680 feet), turn right into driveway
50.3	Cherry Lake dam and observation deck (1780 feet), turn left onto gravel road
50.5	Indian Rock Road (1840 feet), turn right onto road, then right into woods
50.8	Indian Rock Shelter (1760 feet)
50.9	Indian Rock Road (1770 feet), turn right onto gravel road
51	Covered bridge over Indian Rock Creek (1800 feet), turn left up driveway and enter woods
51.6	Gravel road (2180 feet), cross road and regain BMT
51.7	Gravel driveway (2220 feet), turn right down driveway, staying right at house
51.9	Mag Chapman Road at Tipton Gap (2060 feet), bear right onto paved road
52	BMT/ORV trail (2060 feet), bear right then left into woods
52.1	ORV crossing (2260 feet), cross ORV trail and bear left onto BMT
52.3	Six-way trail junction (2200 feet), bear right then left on BMT
53.3	Boardtown Road/Sugar Creek Road (1760 feet), turn left onto paved road
54.3	Bushy Head Road (1670 feet), turn right onto road
55.9	Bushy Head Gap (2100 feet), turn left onto BMT
58.4	Forest Road 793 at Hudson Gap (2620 feet), cross road and regain BMT
65	Halloway Gap (3260 feet), water north down hill
68.6	Forest Road 64A (3020 feet), bear left onto road
68.9	Forest Road 64 at Dyer Gap (2854 feet), turn left onto road
69	BMT (2870 feet), bear right into woods
69.6	South Fork River Trail (2620 feet), bear right onto BMT/South Fork River Trail
71.1	Pinhoti Trail/South Fork River Trail (2540 feet), bear right onto BMT
73.4	Forest Road 64 (2760 feet), turn left onto road
73.5	Forest Road 22 at Watson Gap (2720 feet), head straight on Forest Road 22
73.8	BMT (2820 feet), bear left onto BMT
75.8	Jacks River Trail enters (2510 feet), stay right on trail signed BMT/Jacks River Trail
75.9	Jacks River Trail departs (2510 feet), stay left on trail signed BMT
77.2	Hemp Top Trail at Spanish Oak Gap (2940 feet), bear left onto BMT/Hemp Top Trail
82.3	Licklog Ridge Trail (4040 feet), bear left onto BMT/Licklog Ridge Trail
82.8	Big Frog Mountain (4220 feet), turn right onto BMT/Big Frog Trail
83.9	Big Creek Trail (3660 feet), stay right on BMT/Big Frog Trail
84.7	Fork Ridge Trail (3380 feet), stay right on BMT/Fork Ridge Trail
86.7	Rough Creek Trail (2300 feet), turn left onto BMT/Rough Creek Trail

Trail Summary and Mileage Estimates (continued)

87.2	West Fork Trail (1880 feet), turn right onto BMT/West Fork Trail
89.4	Forest Road 221 (1920 feet), cross and follow BMT on old Forest Service road
89.8	Chestnut Mountain Loop (1740 feet), bear left onto BMT
91.1	Forest Road 45 and Thunder Rock Trail (1480 feet), stay left on BMT/Thunder Rock Trail
92.6	Bridge over Ocoee River (1150 feet)

Suggested Camps Based on Different Trekking Itineraries

Night   15--20 mpd

One	15+ miles - Toccoa River
Two	31 miles - Tipton Mountain
Three	50+ miles - Indian Rock Shelter
Four	65 miles - Halloway Gap
Five	80+ miles - Double Spring Gap

Note: Longer itineraries with shorter days are possible, though the irregular distances between campsites within reasonable reach of water preclude creating an itinerary with a consistent range of daily mileage different from the one described. However, the following campsites within reasonable reach of water (0.5 mile) are provided to help you plan an itinerary based on your interests, ability, and flexibility:

1 mile - Springer Mountain Shelter

3 miles - Big Stamp Gap

7 miles - Three Forks

12 miles - Bryson Gap

15+ miles - Toccoa River

21+ miles - Licklog Mountain, spring 0.4 mile north

26+ miles - Payne Gap, spring 600 feet north

31 miles - Tipton Mountain, spring ahead and behind 0.5 mile

46+ miles - Laurel Creek, southeast of Weaver Creek Road

50+ miles - Indian Rock Shelter

65 miles - Halloway Gap

69+ miles - Near South Fork Trail

71+ miles - Possible camping near Rich Cove, past Pinhoti Trail

80+ miles - Double Spring Gap

Joyce Kilmer Wilderness Loop (NC/TN)

Difficulty:	Strenuous
Distance:	56.5 miles
Elevation gain:	18,400 feet
Best season:	Year-round; late March and early April are best for spring ephemerals, and mid-October is ideal for fall colors. Winter can be mild or quite cold with night-time temperatures below freezing. Hunting for bear, deer, and boar are popular from mid-October to January 1.
Recommended itinerary:	4 days (10–15 miles per day, with time for exploration)
Water availability:	Plentiful along major creeks and their tributaries, but ridge tops are often dry, so plan accordingly.
Logistics:	From the trailhead to Naked Ground, the Slickrock Creek Trail has several water crossings. During periods of heavy rain, Slickrock Creek and the North and South Fork of Citico Creek may be dangerous and even impassable. Most trails are poorly marked, and locations on maps are approximate. The first several miles of Slickrock Creek Trail are some of the most heavily traveled in the Joyce Kilmer–Slickrock Wilderness Area, especially in the summer months when day hikers splash in its many pools. Parking may be limited, so arrive at the trailhead early to secure a parking spot. Numerous Forest Service campgrounds are scattered throughout the Nantahala and Cherokee National Forests for nearby camping the night before you enter the backcountry.
Jurisdictions:	Cheoah Ranger District (828-479-6431), Nantahala National Forest; and Tellico Ranger District (615-253-2520), Cherokee National Forest. Permits are not necessary for either wilderness area. Camping is not permitted in the Joyce Kilmer Memorial Forest.

Maps: U.S. Forest Service map *Joyce Kilmer–Slickrock Creek Wilderness and Citico Creek Wilderness*. Also, National Geographic Trails Illustrated 784, *Fontana & Hiwassee Lakes*, offers a broad overview of this and neighboring treks.

Trail location: From Robbinsville, North Carolina, drive US Route 129 north approximately 15 miles to an unmarked parking area on the left, just before the bridge over Calderwood Lake, west of Cheoah Dam. From Maryville, Tennessee, drive US 129 south approximately 35 miles to the bridge over Calderwood Lake. Immediately after the bridge, turn right into an unmarked parking area.

Killed by a sniper's bullet on a World War I battlefield in France, American poet Alfred Joyce Kilmer, author of *Trees*, never knew the haunting cathedral of poplar and hemlock that became his memorial eighteen years to the day after his death. Nowhere else in the eastern United States is there a forest so pristine and wild as the eminent Joyce Kilmer Memorial Forest, saved from the blades of thirsty logging companies in the early twentieth century due to its remote and inaccessible location.

Nestled in the southeastern corner of the combined Joyce Kilmer–Slickrock Creek and Citico Creek Wilderness Areas, the 3840-acre memorial spills off the Unicoi Crest, the high ridge that divides Tennessee and North Carolina. As you make your way to the memorial from the northern reach of the wilderness, explore adjacent valleys equally rugged but not so fortunate to have been spared the saw. Still, the forests have recovered and are home to some of the East's biggest trees, interspersed with tomorrow's giants. Witness the reality of nature's raw sense of justice when Slickrock Creek floods and brings down the mountains, literally tree by tree, obscuring trails and inundating stream crossings with massive debris piles and roiling water. This is as wild as it gets.

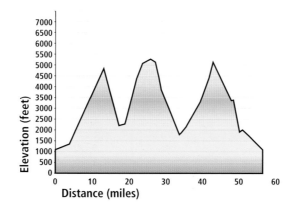

Cherokee

National

Forest

N
W   E
S

Slickroc'

Trail

Tennessee

North Carolina

Citico Creek
Wilderness

Joyce Kilmer–
Slickrock
Wilderness

3

Fodderstock

North Fork Citico Creek Trail

Brush Mountain

South Fork Citico Creek Trail

2

Bob
Stratton
Bald

Tennessee

North Carolina

165

28

Tennessee

Creek

Trail

North Carolina

Cheoah Lake

T

Cheoah
Dam

129

Hangover Lead

Nantahala

National

Forest

Joyce Kilmer–
Slickrock
Wilderness

Naked
Ground

Haoe   Lead   Trail

Jenkins Meadow Trail

Naked Ground Trail

Little Santeetlah Creek

Horse   Cove   Ridge

Joyce Kilmer
Memorial
Forest

1127

DAY ONE   13+ miles   6400 feet

The first day is an immersion deep into the heart of the Joyce Kilmer–Slickrock Wilderness. The goal is Naked Ground, an exposed and weather-beaten gap high on the main ridge that separates Slickrock Creek and Little Santeetlah Creek watersheds. Beginning on the Slickrock Creek Trail, a soupy two-track sandwiched between the rocky shore of Calderwood Lake and a wooded slope too steep to even duck into for nature's call, contour along and gradually climb in and out of cool north-facing coves. Shortly past the junction with Ike Branch Trail, keep your balance crossing small footbridges precariously perched on the sides of rock faces dripping with roots and lush summer growth. Round the end of Hangover Lead, enter the mouth of Slickrock Creek and the wilderness area.

During periods of heavy rain, the lower portion of Slickrock Creek presents a formidable challenge. Crossing the churning debris-laden water would be foolish. Often it's best to wait for the river to come down, or seek an alternate route. A few more yards and you'll find Lower Falls, beneath which swirls the most popular swimming hole in the area due to its proximity to the trailhead. Stop for a dip if it's not already crowded, then continue twisting and turning with the river past three trail junctions, several cascades, and numerous crossings until you see Big Stack Gap Branch Trail coming in from the right. Here the creek and the main trail turn sharply to the southeast.

Bear right past the junction with the Nichols Cove Trail, staying beside Slickrock Creek, now resembling one of the anonymous tributaries feeding its thirst. If you haven't stopped for lunch, do so before the 2500 feet of climbing to Naked Ground. Make your way to the first of many switchbacks that ultimately lead you through Slickrock Creek's headwaters to the high country. The ascent is tough, but climbing through selectively preserved old growth and stunning views nearing the top are worth every step.

Two forest giants (Damon Hearne/Slabcreek Photography)

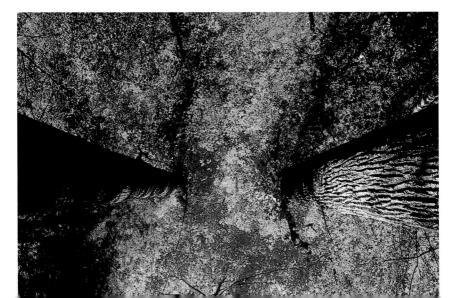

DAY TWO 15 miles 4900 feet

Start the day with an obligatory side trip through the East's most renowned stand of old growth. Taking only a day pack, head southeast down a long series of switchbacks via the Naked Ground Trail to the Joyce Kilmer Memorial Forest trailhead. Two-thirds of the way down, an alternate path crosses Little Santeetlah Creek to pass beneath some of the larger trees found outside of the Memorial Forest loop. From the trailhead, cross Little Santeetlah Creek and follow the 2-mile, figure-eight trail through one of the most spectacular stands of trees you'll ever see. Dominated by poplar and hemlock, some more than 400 years old, the memorial forest is also home to large basswood, maple, and oak, among others. Joyce Kilmer never knew these trees, but instead received inspiration for his most famous poem from a great white oak found on the Rutgers University campus where he was a student.

Joyce Kilmer Memorial Forest (Photo by Ben Walters)

After a tour of the memorial loop, return to the Naked Ground Trail and bear right onto the Jenkins Meadow connector. In half a mile, turn left onto the Jenkins Meadow Trail and begin climbing toward its namesake—though hardly a meadow now, it's so overgrown with briar and oak. Turning left, follow the narrow ridge west to the Haoe, second highest peak in the wilderness area, then north through a narrow gap and tunnels of rhododendron to the Hangover Lead Overlook, where the trail steps up to a small rocky perch that offers you the vastness of the southern Appalachians in one sweeping view.

Return to Naked Ground via the Haoe Lead Trail and head for Cherry Log Gap, your camp for the night, traveling up and over Bob Stratton Bald, the highest point in the wilderness at 5380 feet.

DAY THREE 19+ miles 4700 feet

Day three begins in a similar manner as yesterday with an obligatory side trip, this time down the North Fork Citico Trail and up the South Fork Citico Trail. Descend immediately from Cherry Log Gap down the North Fork Citico Trail through pockets of old-growth giants, surrounded by secondary growth—physically big but not fully matured. Both forks of Citico Creek offer the requisite cool water cascading in a cool, moist hardwood forest that one expects in the southern Appalachians. Savor the earthy aroma as you make your way down to the confluence and then return up to the high country.

At the crest of the Unicoi Mountains once again, this time at Cold Springs Gap, turn left onto Fodderstack Trail and climb toward Bob Stratton Bald. Retrace your steps of the previous day to Cherry Log Gap, nab your stuff, and ride the wave of knobs down the Unicoi Crest to Big Stack Gap to camp for the night. Water can be found a short jaunt down the Mill Branch Trail, which falls west out of the gap.

DAY FOUR   8+ miles   2400 feet

The last day of trekking is more like the first: set off with a full pack for the entire day of exploring creeks, coves, and the occasional ridgeline. Walk the easy mile from camp to Big Stack Gap Branch Trail and turn right, descending to Slickrock Creek, where you'll regain Slickrock Creek Trail heading southeast. Retrace your steps to Nichols Cove Trail and turn left, heading north. In 1.7 miles, near the junction of Yellowhammer Gap Trail, stone markers honor the short lives of twin girls whose family had a homestead in this cove. Bear right on Yellowhammer Gap Trail and follow the obvious, undulating path toward the gap of the same name. Just shy of the gap, the trail intersects Ike Branch Trail. Turn right, then left following the Ike Branch Trail through the gap and then begin the gentle descent along boulder-strewn Ike Branch back to the trailhead shortly after merging with Slickrock Creek Trail.

One of many fungi found in the southern Appalachians (Damon Hearne/Slabcreek Photography)

Trail Summary and Mileage Estimates

0	Slickrock Creek trailhead (1100 feet)
3.8	Ike Branch Trail (1360 feet), bear right on Slickrock Creek Trail
13.1	Naked Ground (4860 feet)
17.2	Joyce Kilmer Memorial Forest trailhead (2220 feet), turn right onto lower loop
18.8	Naked Ground Trail (2290 feet), turn left onto Naked Ground Trail
19	Jenkins Meadow connector (2400 feet), turn right onto connector
22	Haoe Lead Trail (4400 feet), bear left onto Haoe Lead Trail
23.6	Hangover Overlook and Deep Creek (5100 feet), bear right onto Hangover Overlook trail
25.8	Bob Stratton Bald Trail (5380 feet), head straight on Bob Stratton Bald Trail
27.1	Fodderstack Trail (5160 feet), turn right onto Fodderstack Trail
28.1	Cherry Log Gap (4420 feet), turn left onto North Fork Citico Trail
28.7	Cold Springs Gap Trail (3880 feet), stay right on North Fork Citico Trail
33.7	South Fork Citico Trail (1800 feet), turn left onto South Fork Citico Trail
34.2	Brush Mountain Trail (1880 feet), stay right on South Fork Citico Trail
35.5	Grassy Branch Trail (2150 feet), stay left on South Fork Citico Trail
39.4	Jeffrey Hell Trail (3310 feet), stay left on South Fork Citico Trail
41.8	Cold Springs Gap (4420 feet), turn left onto Fodderstack Trail
42.9	Stratton Bald Trail (5160 feet), stay left on Fodderstack Trail
47.9	Mill Branch Trail at Big Stack Gap (3380 feet), stay straight on Fodderstack Trail
48.5	Big Stack Gap Branch Trail (3400 feet), turn right onto Big Stack Gap Branch Trail
50.2	Slickrock Creek Trail (1920 feet), bear right onto Slickrock Creek Trail
51	Nichols Cove Trail (2020 feet), turn left onto Nichols Cove Trail
52.7	Yellowhammer Gap Trail (1750 feet), bear right onto Yellowhammer Gap Trail
56.5	Slickrock Creek trailhead (1100 feet)

Suggested Camps Based on Different Trekking Itineraries

Night	Slower (with one long day hike)	Faster (with two long day hikes)
One	8 miles - Big Fat Branch	13.1 miles - Naked Ground
Two	13.1 miles - Naked Ground	28.1 miles - Cherry Log Gap
Three	25.2 miles - Naked Ground (day hike)	47.9 miles - Big Stack Gap
Four	35.5 miles - Eagle Branch	
Five	45 miles - Glenn Gap (dry)	

Note: Many options exist for traveling shorter or longer distances within the wilderness area. A "slower" option covers the same terrain as the suggested itinerary, but includes only one day hike, to the Memorial Forest on day three; all other days require expeditioning with a full pack.

Fires Creek to Standing Indian (NC)

Difficulty:	Strenuous
Distance:	39.8 miles
Elevation gain:	13,600 feet
Best season:	Year-round, though mid-April is best for spring wildflowers and early-October is best for fall colors. Winter days may be mild or near freezing—long range views through leafless trees make this a beautiful season to be outside.
Recommended itinerary:	3 days (10–15 miles per day)
Water availability:	This trek follows high ridgelines for much of its length, making it necessary to carry 2–3 quarts of water and camp 15–20 minutes or more from a water source. The suggested itinerary, however, does not require dry camping.
Logistics:	Both the Rim Trail and the Chunky Gal Trail are marked with infrequent blue blazes; newer plastic blazes have been regularly placed along much of the route. The Appalachian Trail is marked with a white blaze. The trailheads are about an hour apart, making it necessary to leave a vehicle at each end or use a shuttle service (see the appendix for information on services). This trek connects with the Appalachian Trail, which can be hiked for days (or weeks) in either direction if a longer trek is desired, and can even form a grand loop of more than 100 miles via the Bartram, London Bald, Choga, and Old Wagon Road Trails.
Jurisdictions:	Tusquitee Ranger District (828-837-5152) and Wayah Ranger District (828-524-6441), Nantahala National Forest. No permits are necessary within the national forest or southern Nantahala Wilderness.
Maps:	USGS Hayesville, Andrews, Topton, Shooting Creek, and Rainbow Springs. National Geographic Trails

Illustrated 784, *Fontana & Hiawassee Lakes*, offers a general overview of the trek, as well as nearby treks.

Trail location: From Hayesville, North Carolina, follow US Route 64 west approximately 4.5 miles to North Carolina Route 1301, and turn right (North Carolina 1301 becomes State Route 1300 in about 2 miles). In approximately 4 miles, turn left onto Forest Road 340 and parallel Fires Creek for about 2 miles to the Rim Trail trailhead across the road from the Leatherwood Falls picnic area. To reach the Lower Ridge Trail trailhead near Kimsey Creek Campground, return to US 64 and drive east for approximately 26.5 miles to Wallace Gap Road. Turn right. In 2.5 miles at Wallace Gap, bear right onto Forest Road 67 and follow signs for the campground and trailhead parking.

The remote mountains of southwest North Carolina have been a refuge for many over the years. Most recently, fugitive Eric Rudolph, an accused serial bomber, hid from federal agents in Fires Creek for five years. In 1838, eight years after Congress passed the Indian Removal Act, thousands of Cherokee men, women, and children were forced to walk from their homes in the southern Appalachians to Oklahoma. The involuntary trek known as the Trail of Tears claimed thousands of lives.

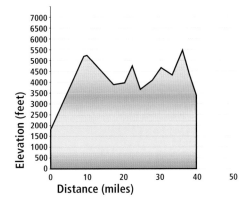

Unbeknownst to federal soldiers and state militia, several hundred Cherokee fled to these mountains and survived for decades until Congress recognized their sovereignty thirty years later. A remote location, abundant wildlife, and healthy plant communities are some of the reasons why this region has been sought by so many as a place to hide or explore. Expect dramatic vistas after quad-busting climbs up lonesome trails in the region's most isolated mountains.

DAY ONE   13+ miles   5500 feet

Begin with 2–3 quarts of water as this will be your only source until Bald Springs Branch, a 10-minute jaunt down a side trail past Johnson Bald, 8 steep miles up the trail. From Forest Road 340, climb immediately out of the thick rhododendrons that crowd the river bottoms in these mountains and climb steadily for 2

Bartram Trail

Appalachian

Trail

Nantahala Lake

1301

64

Nantahala River

Road

Gap

Wallace

Chunky Gal Trail

Kimsey
Creek
Campground

T

Boteler
Peak

Chunky

Gal

Mountain

2

FR 67

Standing
Indian

Appalachian

64

Appalachian Trail

Trail

North Carolina
Georgia

Misty morning in Nantahala National Forest (Photo by Corey Hadden)

miles and 1200 vertical feet up the Rim Trail to Graveyard High Top (3050 feet). As you ascend, winter offers refreshing views of the Valley River Mountains and Tarkiln Ridge, site of a winter camp allegedly used by Eric Rudolph. Over the next several miles, hop from one knob to the next along the skinny ridge passing numerous side trails that lead down to Fires Creek.

The ridge beneath your feet follows the backbone of the Tusquitee Mountains, which, along with the Valley River Mountains to the north, form a crater-like ring around Fires Creek. Unlike mountains found east of here, which are composed of impermeable schists, gneisses, and granites, these mountains are formed primarily of soft sedimentary rocks. The permeable nature of these rocks means less surface water, as it seeps easily into the porous strata. The result is fewer streams and more water for you to carry.

As you cross Potrock Bald, keep an eye out for round depressions in small boulders, believed to have been carved by the Cherokee hundreds of years ago as they prepared food or medicine. Approaching Tusquitee Bald, bear right onto Chunky Gal Trail, which passes over the bald at 5260 feet. From here it is possible to see Chunky Gal Mountain to the east, the Nantahala Mountains, and, near trek's end, Standing Indian, the highest point along the trek at 5499 feet. Head east from the summit over a small, unnamed knob and drop down a long series of switchbacks into the lushness of Big Tuni Creek. Camp is across Forest Road 440 at the Bob Allison Campground.

DAY TWO   14+ miles   5500 feet

Begin the day with some tricky navigation through the confusing braids of Big Tuni Creek. Once your bearings are straight, and with plenty of water, begin climbing and contouring in and out of coves to Boteler Peak, labeled as Shooting Creek Bald on some maps (5010 feet). Pass through Perry Gap (3800 feet), and, if you're thirsty and running low, briefly search for water down Forest Road 350. Nearing Boteler Peak, a side trail leads right through tree-lined fields to the summit, which has a small outcropping of rock but grand views to the north of yesterday's ridge walk. These fields, covered with grasses and shrubs, provide

Colorful fall leaves (Damon Hearne/Slabcreek Photography)

unique habitat in the high mountains for birds such as the eastern towhee, brown thrasher, and gray catbird—species that aren't typically found this deep in the forest. Conversely, edge habitat is often exploited by opportunistic species such as the brown-headed cowbird, which lays its eggs in the nests of defenseless songbirds, forcing them to be surrogate parents to the cowbird's offspring at the expense of their own.

Descend quickly down the trail as it follows and crosses old grassy roads down to Glade Gap, topping off your bottles before crossing US 64 and climbing steep tread up past Riley Knob. Camp beside the clear water of Buck Creek, down a fern-covered slope north of Grassy Gap.

DAY THREE   12 miles   2600 feet

Day three continues briefly along the skinny backbone of Chunky Gal Mountain before running smack into the Blue Ridge and the Appalachian Trail at elevation

4680 feet. Here, follow the Appalachian Trail north to Deep Gap through moist woods covered in spring with Soloman's seal, Indian cucumber, and several varieties of trillium. Make a quick trip for water down Kimsey Creek Trail to the north, then resume the uphill slog to the long summit of Standing Indian, shrouded in midsummer by blueberries ripe for the picking and panoramic views of the southern Nantahala Wilderness and the Tallulah River. In Cherokee mythology, Standing Indian was a brave warrior that stood watch over the valley towns for the evil monster that kidnapped a young child.

After lunch and a snooze, the trek turns away from the Appalachian Trail and Standing Indian on Lower Ridge Trail yet sustains its beauty as it follows a mostly descending path for a little less than 4 miles down to the trailhead near Kimsey Creek Campground.

Mountain Ash in late fall (Damon Hearne/
Slabcreek Photography)

Trail Summary and Mileage Estimates

0	Leatherwood Falls picnic area (1820 feet), turn left onto Forest Road 340
9.1	Potrock Bald (5215 feet)
9.9	Chunky Gal Trail (5260 feet), bear right onto Chunky Gal Trail
10	Tusquitee Bald (5260 feet)
17.3	Tusquitee Gap (3900 feet), cross SR 1307 and regain Chunky Gal Trail
20.3	Tate Gap (3980 feet), bear right on Chunky Gal Trail
22.4	Side trail to Boteler Peak (5010 feet), bear left on Chunky Gal Trail
24.6	Glade Gap (3679 feet), cross US 64 and regain Chunky Gal Trail
27.9	Grassy Gap (4100 feet)
30.3	Appalachian Trail (4680 feet), turn left onto Appalachian Trail
33.3	Deep Gap (4341 feet), cross Forest Road 71 and regain Appalachian Trail
36.1	Standing Indian (5499 feet), bear left onto Lower Ridge Trail
37.9	John Gap (4380 feet)
39.8	Kimsey Creek Campground (3400 feet)

Suggested Camps Based on Different Trekking Itineraries

Day	10 mpd	10–15 mpd	20 mpd
One	10+ miles - Gap between Tusquitee and Signal Balds	13+ miles - Bob Allison Campground	22+ miles - East of Boteler Peak
Two	18+ miles - East of Tusquitee Gap	28 miles - Buck Creek, north of Grassy Gap	
Three	30+ miles - South of Appalachian Trail junction		

Lakeshore Trail— Great Smoky Mountains National Park (NC)

Difficulty:	Easier
Distance:	36.8 miles
Elevation gain:	9200 feet
Best season:	Fall, spring, and winter. A good hike in the cooler months since the elevation of the hike does not exceed 3000 feet. Clearer views of the lake prevail when the trees are bare of leaves.
Recommended itinerary:	3 days (10–20 miles per day)
Water availability:	Lots and lots of water.
Logistics:	We recommend beginning at the Road to Nowhere for no better reason than hot public showers await you at the Fontana Dam Visitors Center on the other end. The visitors center (828-498-2234) is open May to November 1 and the showers are open year-round. Keep in mind that parking may be restricted if the nation is on "orange" terror alert. The Hike Inn runs a reliable shuttle service near Fontana Dam (828-479-3677 or *www.thehikeinn.com*). Unless you shuttle by boat, there are no convenient ways to make a shorter version of this trek. Park at the dam or continue across the dam to the end of the pavement. Reservations are not required for backcountry campsites along the Lakeshore Trail. Register for a free backcountry permit at any hour of the day at the Deep Creek Recreation Area near Bryson City or at the Fontana Marina, near Fontana Village, on a bulletin board at the entrance ramp.
Jurisdictions:	Great Smoky Mountains National Park (865-436-1231) Tennessee Valley Authority (865-632-8632)

Maps: USGS Fontana Dam, Tuskeegee, and Noland Creek. Some sections of the trail are unmarked on the quads. Also, National Geographic Trails Illustrated 229, *Great Smoky Mountains National Park.* Consider using both National Geographic and USGS, since USGS maps label historical features such as abandoned mines and communities, and cemeteries.

Trail location: To reach the trailhead, drive northwest from the center of Bryson City on Everett Street (it changes to Lakeview Drive, also known as the Road to Nowhere) for nearly 10 miles to its end at a tunnel. Bryson City is located on US Route 74. From Bryson City to Fontana Dam, take US 74 west, eventually forking right on North Carolina Route 28. Before Fontana Village, turn right onto NC 1245 (Fontana Dam Road) to the visitor center. Park at the visitor center or continue another 2 miles to the end of the pavement.

The historic Lakeshore Trail contours above Lake Fontana on the south end of the Great Smoky Mountains National Park in one of the park's most infrequently visited areas. The long narrow lake is shaped like a winding serpent with dozens of narrow legs that are flooded watersheds. The route passes remnants of old farms, bygone logging operations, cemeteries, abandoned automobiles, and beautiful sections of forest. The trail is like a history book passing through the

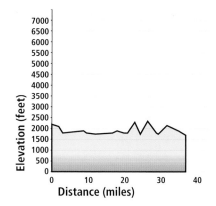

isolated coves and ridges of the Smokies where subsistence mountaineers once lived. Fontana Lake was completed in 1944 to spark the woeful Appalachian economy and to generate power for the war effort. The lake swallowed several communities and the park added to its domain 44,000 acres of private land isolated on the lake's north side. Between 1948 and 1970, the park service carved a portion of road to fulfill a promise to those displaced by the lake and park. Construction of the Road to Nowhere ceased because of the cost and environmental damage to the area—although threats to finish the road loom like a dark shadow. Considered the largest roadless section of mountain terrain east of the Rocky Mountains, this trek follows a course that was spared the bulldozers, although human impact is present.

Great Smoky Mountains

National Park

Eagle Creek

Hazel Creek

Pinnacle Ridge

Welch Ridge

Pilkey Creek

Proctor

2

Mill Branch

Fontana Dam

Fontana Dam Road

T P

28

Fontana Lake

Fontana Lake

74

Hazel Creek

Great Smoky Mountains

National Park

Forney Creek

Welch Ridge

North Fork Chambers Branch

West Fork

Kirkland Branch

Road to Nowhere

Ⓟ
Ⓣ

Fontana Lake

Fontana Lake

Fontana Lake

Bryson City

74

Bridge on the Lakeshore Trail

DAY ONE 11+ miles 2700 feet

The Road to Nowhere ends in a black hole that is a 350-foot tunnel. Tunnel-shy horses follow a 1.6-mile bypass, but hikers should experience the ambiance of the tunnel's interior cloaked in decades of graffiti. Gain the trail beyond the tunnel and contour through a lush forest of oaks, poplars, pines, and mountain laurel. The tunnel bypass merges with the main trail at a well-marked intersection. The trail mostly contours, though occasionally rising and falling over ridges. At the Whiteoak Trail junction, keep straight and walk past an old homesite lost among tall grass and trees. Past the homestead, cross a small stream and turn right on a road grade crossing a wood bridge over Gray Wolf Creek. Upstream, the road leads to Woody Cemetery. The Lakeshore Trail crosses the road heading uphill.

More than thirty cemeteries still maintained and visited by kinfolk pepper the Lakeshore Trail route. The agreement to relocate former residents included regular shuttles for families across the lake to visit the resting places. Most of the cemeteries are easy to find and occasionally labeled on USGS maps. Look for signs prohibiting horses at trail or road grade crossings. The trails typically lead to small plots on ridgelines. Some plots have a handful of graves, while others are a timeline for generations of settlers.

At mile 3, arrive at the Forney Creek Trail and the first of several campsites on the left. Turn left at the marked intersection. As with campsite number 74, many of the designated sites have seen plenty of visitors. Keep in mind that campers are restricted to designated backcountry campsites—probably a good idea since it wouldn't take long for new sites to look like pigsties. Speaking of pigs, there are a few in the area, as evidenced by their habit of rooting through the soil. At one point the feral pig population numbered in the thousands. While the population is controlled, pig sightings are common. All campsites have bear/pig-proof food-hanging systems and established fire rings.

From here, the trail contours around Pilot Mountain, moving in and out of small coves and drainages, crossing numerous creeks and wrapping around narrow, fingerlike ridges. The trail passes a major twist in the lake and crosses Welch Branch at mile 8.7, just past the confluence of two major flooded tributaries of the lake, the Tuckasegee River and the Little Tennessee River.

Keep on the look out for remnants of former lives. Hundreds of families were

Fontana Lake

displaced by the park's expansion. Many of the families took only what they could carry and left everything else behind. Around Welch Creek are several homesites complete with old stoves, wash buckets, rock walls, and solitary chimneys as lifeless as 2000-year-old Roman ruins. Pass campsite 98 at Chambers Branch, staying close to the lake for another 2 miles to a clearing right of the trail that is campsite 76 on Kirkland Branch.

DAY TWO   12+ miles   3300 feet
In the early 1900s, the timber industry moved full force into the Smokies. Large-scale operations decimated the southern forests at lightning speed. In the first thirty years of the twentieth century two-thirds of the land in the Smokies had been logged. In all, about 2 billion board feet were milled—enough to circle the earth 87,000 times. Companies like the Little River Lumber Company and Ritter Lumber Company were after the massive hardwoods to meet the burly demand of the growing country, while Champion Lumber preferred spruce and hemlock for their pulp. It was the destruction of the forest that eventually led to the park's protection. Most of the trees today are humble sizes, since logging continued until the 1940s. There is also significant damage to pine trees, thanks to the pine beetle, in sporadic sections of forest.

From campsite 76, contour above the narrow lake following its twists and turns. Beyond Pilkey Creek, cross Clark Branch and look left for campsite 77 on the site of a former home. The trail diverges away from the lake to contour around an unnamed knoll. Again the trail contours at roughly 1900 feet, occasionally rising and falling. At mile 20.8, the trail crosses Mill Branch—a short spur trail leads to campsite 81. Past Mill Branch climb to a ridge at mile 21.8 with a No Horses marker near a large white pine. To the left is Fairview Cemetery and the tombstone of a Civil War veteran. Back at the sign and white pine, turn right. Descend to Whiteside Creek in a quarter mile, then follow the old road grade uphill for one of the longer climbs on the Lakeshore Trail. Gain about 400 feet to Welch Ridge at a gap at 2300 feet.

Descend the old road grade for nearly 2 miles to Hazel Creek and the town of Proctor—the former residence of Ritter Lumber Company. The area was one of the most thoroughly logged areas of the park. At its height, the community had more than a thousand residents. Hard to believe, since the few remaining structures are practically swallowed up by vegetation. The Calhoun house across the creek is somewhat crudely maintained and the park service keeps several horses in the pasture. Campsite 86 is on the east side of the creek and has plenty of campsites. Although busy and impacted it's a good place to stop and explore. Downstream from camp, after a right-hand bend in the river, is a short spur trail to a spring for more reliable drinking water. The lakeshore is not much farther down the road.

Old coupe on the Lakeshore Trail

DAY THREE   12+ miles   3200 feet

In 1904, Horace Kephart arrived in western North Carolina. A local mountaineer agreed to meet Kephart with two of his mules and give him a look at the backwoods. They went to Hazel Creek, where he stayed for three years. An outdoorsman at heart, Kephart was a librarian in St. Louis who left his job and family to escape civilization for a spell. At first attracted to the remoteness of the mountains, he was eventually drawn to documenting the land and people of the Appalachians. The notes he gathered produced *Our Southern Highlanders*, a classic volume of southern literature that recorded nearly every aspect of mountaineer culture and life, including one of his favorites, bootlegging.

Kephart's homestead is up Hazel Creek along the former route of the Lakeshore Trail. The park service recently redirected the trail. The new, shorter version of the trail turns left on the west side of Hazel Creek past the old Proctor House and a few massive old oak trees. Head up Possum Hollow past Bradshaw Cemetery on the right (worth the stop—buried there is Moses Proctor, born in 1798 and the first settler along Hazel Creek.) This section of road has plenty of old homesites and flotsam of decades past. Eventually the trail climbs up Shehan Branch toward Pinnacle Ridge.

Reach an unnamed gap at 2350 feet before arriving at Ecoah Branch. Stay right on the old road grade descending to the branch, then climb again to Pinnacle Ridge. Contour around the ridge through Flint Gap and head down to

Horseshoe Bend on Eagle Creek at mile 28.7. Turn left and walk less than 1 mile to campsite 90 situated on a tip of the lake on the west side of the creek. Walk through the campsite and switchback away from the lake up Lost Cove Creek. Soon the trail switchbacks away from the creek, settling at about 2000 feet to wind above the lakeshore. The lake comes into view occasionally to the left. Near the end of the trail are the rusted out frames of several ancient coupes left dead in their tracks. From here, the hiking is casual to a parking lot at the Appalachian Trail trailhead. Stay on the pavement following Fontana Dam Road and walk another 2 miles to the Fontana Dam Visitor Center and hot showers courtesy of the Tennessee Valley Authority.

Trail Summary and Mileage Estimates

0	Road to Nowhere tunnel (2200 feet), gain trail beyond tunnel
1.9	Whiteoak Trail junction (2100 feet), go straight
3	Forney Creek Trail and campsite 74 (1800 feet), turn left at intersection
8.7	Welch Branch (1900 feet), cross creek
9.5	Spur Trail to campsite 98 at Chambers Branch (1800 feet)
11.9	Campsite 76 (1750 feet), continue on Lakeshore Trail
16.6	Campsite 77 (1800 feet), continue on Lakeshore Trail
17.9	Chesquaw Branch and Mitchell Cemetery (1900 feet), continue on Lakeshore Trail
19.8	Calhoun Branch (1800 feet), continue on Lakeshore Trail
20.8	Campsite 81 spur trail (1800 feet), pass trail, cross creek, and continue on Lakeshore Trail
21.8	Unnamed ridge, go right on Lakeshore Trail (left to Fairview Cemetery)
22.8	Welch Ridge (2300 feet)
24.3	Hazel Creek and town of Proctor (1750 feet), cross creek and turn left past old house
26.3	Unnamed gap (2350 feet), stay right on old road
28.7	Trail junction with Eagle Creek (1800 feet), turn left on Lakeshore Trail
29.2	Campsite 90 (1750 feet), turn right
31.6	Birchfield Branch (2150 feet), continue on Lakeshore Trail
34.8	Fontana Dam Road and Appalachian Trail (1900 feet), follow paved road
36.8	Fontana Dam Visitor Center (1700 feet)

Suggested Camps Based on Different Trekking Itineraries

Night	<10 mpd	10 mpd	>10 mpd
One	9.5 - Campsite 98	9.5 - Campsite 98	11.9 - Campsite 76
Two	16.6 - Campsite 77	20.8 - Campsite 81	24.3 - Campsite 86
Three	24.3 - Campsite 86	29.2 - Campsite 90	
Four	29.2 - Campsite 90		

Great Smoky Mountains Traverse (NC/TN)

Difficulty:	Very Strenuous
Distance:	71.8 miles
Elevation gain:	21,600 feet
Best season:	Spring and fall are best for wildflowers and fall colors, but can be crowded, as in the summer; winter can provide the most solitude, but solid snow and cold weather camping skills are a must.
Recommended itinerary:	5 days (15 miles per day)
Water availability:	Water is infrequent along the trail except at shelters, where most sources are reliable year-round. Small springs and seeps do exist in between, but are unreliable.
Logistics:	White rectangular blazes and well-marked trail junctions make the Appalachian Trail within the Great Smoky Mountains National Park easy to follow. All shelters require a backcountry permit and advance reservations. Additionally, the use of tents and tarps at shelters is prohibited unless the shelter is full, which is quite likely from early March through the end of May when the bulk of thru-hikers are passing through, and periodically during the summer and fall when other enthusiasts hit the trail. Pets are not allowed in the backcountry, but can be checked into a kennel before the start of the trek. The central portion of this trek exceeds 6000 feet and can see heavy snow in the winter months. Snowshoes may be required for some stretches of trail. The trailheads are approximately 100 miles apart, requiring a second vehicle for a drop off. The Hike Inn (828-479-3677) can arrange a shuttle. *www.thehikeinn.com*
Jurisdictions:	Great Smoky Mountains National Park (865-436-1231). A free backcountry permit is required for all

overnight trips within the park and all shelters require a reservation, unless you are a thru-hiker.

Maps: National Geographic Trails Illustrated 229, *Great Smoky Mountains National Park*

Trail location: The trailhead at Fontana Dam is located at the west end of Fontana Lake in North Carolina, about 50 miles southwest of Cherokee. From Cherokee, drive US Route 19 south for 25 miles to North Carolina Route 28. Bear right onto NC 28 and in about 25 miles, look for North Carolina Route 1245 (Fontana Dam Road) and signs for Fontana Dam.

The trailhead at Davenport Gap is about 1 hour from either Knoxville, Tennessee, or Asheville, North Carolina. To get there, take exit 451 off Interstate 40 and follow signs south toward Big Creek Campground for 2 miles. Turn right onto Mt. Sterling Road (North Carolina Route 284) and in less than 1 mile reach Davenport Gap.

The Appalachian Trail across the crest of the Great Smoky Mountains is the crown jewel of treks in the southern Appalachians, and perhaps among the most classic treks anywhere. To traverse the great ridge of the Great Smokies massif is to simultaneously experience the immense forces that build mountains and the delicate touch of nature's green thumb. Hike for more than 35 miles above 5000 feet through the boreal forest, timeless relic from the last ice age, presently under siege from a tiny insect that is sadly winning the battle. Reward yourself every day with classic views of smoky-blue mountains, meditative walks through old-growth, and storytelling over a hot meal with other wilderness lovers at any of the Appalachian Trail's handsomely crafted shelters.

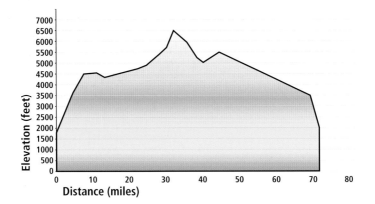

DAY ONE 13+ miles 5300 feet

The goal of Day One is to experience one or two of the national park's most magnificent vistas and make camp near a historic southern Appalachian bald. Cross Fontana Dam, highest in the East at 480 feet, and head up the road for 0.6 mile looking for the Appalachian Trail and its white rectangular blaze on the left just before the road ends. The trail climbs steeply up narrow ridges beneath Little Shuckstack, rising nearly 1500 feet in 2 miles, where it contours briefly north and west before gaining Twentymile Ridge. Heading northeast on the ridge, quickly find and take a short trail on the right leading to Shuckstack (4020 feet), and a view that will take your breath away, that is, if you have any left from the steep climb.

Back on the Appalachian Trail, drop into Sassafras Gap and junctions with Twentymile and Lost Cove Trails heading off to either side, and immediately begin the undulating climb up Twentymile Ridge toward the main crest of the Smokies at Doe Knob, passing Birch Spring, which will be your last water source for several miles. If, by the time you reach Doe Knob, daylight is on your side, consider the 5-mile round trip hike west to Gregory Bald, which offers another breathtaking view, this time of Cades Cove. If it's nearing the end of June, this trip is obligatory for Gregory Bald's stunning display of flame azaleas. The park service actively maintains the grassy nature of Gregory Bald, preserving the unique plant community and field where settlers once grazed their livestock during summer months.

From Doe Knob, the Appalachian Trail follows the main crest of the Smokies in the classic roller coaster fashion found throughout the southern Appalachians. Intermittent water sources can be found on either side of most gaps if you descend far enough. Otherwise, plan on topping off at Mollies Ridge Shelter before the final 2-mile push to the shelter just beyond Russell Field.

DAY TWO 16+ miles 5500 feet

An hour or so after leaving camp, pass through another grassy field at Spence Ridge, once used to graze cattle and sheep when summer temperatures soared in the valleys below, now slowly being reclaimed by trees and shrubs. The trail here becomes slightly more rugged as it climbs Rocky Top and Thunderhead Mountain. Though slightly lower than its neighbor upon whose shoulder it rests, Rocky Top (5441 feet) offers splendid views south of Fontana Lake and distant mountains. Pass over heath-covered Thunderhead Mountain at 5527 feet and quickly drop below 5000 feet in less than half a mile to an unnamed gap.

The trail rises and falls in this manner for much of its length through the park. The undulating terrain is caused by the insatiable appetite of streams slowly eating away at softer rock to form tight V-shaped valleys that eventually eat their way up to the highest ridges where gaps and sags form between knobs and peaks. As the angle of repose increases, unconsolidated rock from these peaks can slide downhill toward the gaps and streams, slowly or in sudden landslides. In the eastern United States, this

Map 1

Map 2

Trek 10 overview

Cades Cove

Tenhessee

Thunderhead
Mountain

Brier Knob

Mount
Squires

North Carolina

Russell
Field
Shelter

Great Smoky Mountains

National Park

Appalachian Trail

Gregory
Bald
Trail

Shuckstack

Welch Ridge

Fontana
Dam

Fontana Lake

28

Nantahala
National Forest

Map 1

Map 2

Trek 10 overview

N
W — E
S

321 73

Maddron Bald Tra

Greenbrier Pinnacle

Mount
Guyot

Potato Ridge

Tricorner Kno
Shelter 4

Mount
Chapman

Brushy
Mountain

Mount
Sequoyah

Tennessee

A p p a l a c h i a n   T r a i l

Mount
Le Conte

North Carolina

Great Smoky

Mountains

Hughes Ridge Trail

National Park

Mount
Kephart

Icewater
Spring
Shelter

Newfound
Gap

441

To
Cherokee, NC

**Cherokee
Indian
Reservation**

321

Cherokee

National

Forest

Pigeon

40

River

32

Tennessee

Mount
Cammerer

Davenport
Gap

T

North Carolina

Sunup
Knob

Pigeon

River

Snake Den Ridge

Cosby
Knob

Mount Sterling Ridge

Pisgah

National

Forest

Balsam

Mountain

Trail

Great Smoky

Mountains

National

Park

Map 2

process is slowed due to the extensive vegetation whose roots anchor the earth and rock. Ultimately, of course, the streams will win and fully erode the mountains away.

Past the gap, climb a small knob barely reaching 5000 feet and drop once again, this time to Beechnut Gap. Water may be found a few yards down the Tennessee slope. The trail remains easy for a few minutes before climbing, but never cresting, along the south side of Brier Knob, tree-covered at 5215 feet. Descend steeply to Starkey Gap and then, after another knob, Sugar Tree Gap. Note the "sugar trees" or sugar maples, perhaps more familiar to trail hounds from the northern Appalachians. In 1 mile, pass over Chestnut Bald and arrive at Derrick Knob Shelter where a nearby spring can refill your water bottles. Reaching Sams Gap (4760 feet), the Appalachian Trail bears right at its junction with the Greenbrier Ridge Trail, which heads down the Tennessee slope toward Indian Flat Falls, a 9-mile round trip adventure for those going fast and light.

Continue ahead to Cold Spring Knob and the Miry Ridge Trail junction and in about a mile climb and remain above the 5000-foot threshold for the next 35 miles, until late morning on the last day of trekking. The Appalachian Trail follows the main crest of the Smokies here, rolling along through beech gaps while straddling the Tennessee/North Carolina state line until it begins its final push to the summit of Silers Bald, highest point of the trek so far at 5607 feet. From its overgrown summit, side trails lead to vistas of rugged mountains and deep valleys. Camp is 1.5 miles away, down the switchbacks and through The Narrows to Double Spring Gap Shelter.

DAY THREE   13+ miles   3400 feet

The middle day of trekking can be a bittersweet experience, depending on your outlook. Highlights include walking through virgin forest and climbing Clingmans Dome (6643 feet), the highest mountain along the entire Appalachian Trail and bested only by Mount Mitchell's extra 41 feet for highest mountain in the eastern United States. The downside may be lack of solitude. Between Clingmans Dome, which can be reached by car and an easy walk most of the year, and Newfound Gap, where many park visitors achieve their "peak" experience of the park's highlands, you will likely encounter hordes of people. People watching can be fun, especially if you look and feel somewhat different from those you're spying. Anywhere the Appalachian Trail crosses paths with the general public, if you are wearing a backpack, you will attract attention and probably be asked by several people if you are through-hiking to Maine. If this sort of contact brings you down from your wilderness high, consider making the trek in the winter, which offers nearly complete solitude and a truly spectacular wilderness experience.

Leaving Double Spring Gap, begin the trek to Clingmans Dome with a gentle start, quickly passing the Goshen Prong Trail coming in from the left. In another 0.5 mile, pass above 6000 feet for the first time, and maintain a steady pace as the trail ducks in and out of virgin stands and small openings en route to Mount

Buckley, where an outcrop of rock offers an alternative reward if Clingmans' crowds sound less inviting. Continue up the trail to the summit of Clingmans Dome and a side trail to the observation tower, which resembles a UFO.

Back on the Appalachian Trail, pass through red spruce and skeletal Fraser firs on the undulating and sometimes rough descent to Newfound Gap, enjoying views along the way. The last water until camp near Icewater Spring, still 8 miles away, can be found near the Mount Collins Shelter, 0.5 mile down the Sugarland Mountain Trail, which comes in from the left. With 1.7 miles to go to Newfound Gap, the Appalachian Trail passes Road Prong Trail coming in from the left. A former Cherokee trail, it was improved during the Civil War with Cherokee labor to help supply Confederate soldiers with saltpeter from Alum Cave. Climb briefly up switchbacks through a cool stand of hemlocks and, gaining the ridge, step into a beech gap enclosure, fenced off to protect this rare

Midwinter on the Appalachian Trail (Photo by Corey Hadden)

plant community from the aggressive rooting of non-native wild boar. Finally, climb out of the woods into Newfound Gap (5046 feet) and brace for contact.

The Appalachian Trail retreats into the woods at the far side of the parking area, and easily climbs through a predominantly spruce and fir forest, here punctuated with yellow birch, on its way to camp at the Icewater Spring Shelter, 3.1 miles up the trail. Spread yourself out in the grassy yard and take a quick nap before making dinner and retiring to the stone shelter.

DAY FOUR   13+ miles   4400

The Appalachian Trail north and east of Newfound Gap is more rugged than its counterpart on the other side with several stout climbs and wildly exposed ridges. Be sure to begin the day with full water bottles as the next reliable on-trail spring is nearly 8 miles away near Pecks Corner Shelter. If you're desperate, a spring can be found north of False Gap near the site of an old shelter. Immediately after leaving Icewater Spring, contour along the North Carolina side of Mount Kephart, named

Shrubs and windblown trees on Charlies Bunion (Photo by Corey Hadden)

for Horace Kephart, park advocate and author of the classic *Our Southern Highlanders*. In a little more than a mile, bear left on a side trail that leads you to the grandest overlook yet, beneath Charlies Bunion; Charlie was one of Kephart's occasional hiking partners. Immediately, your gaze falls down to Porters Creek, more than 1500 feet below, and then rises to meet Brushy Mountain, Potato Ridge, and the distant hills rising from the Cumberland Plateau. The brown and gray slates and schists beneath your feet are part of the Anakeesta Formation, half a billion years old.

Drop into Dry Sluice Gap and pass the trail of the same name coming in from the right. Watch your step as you begin climbing the Sawteeth, a series of knobs and exposed edges with spectacular vistas opening to the west. Savor the views through here before digging in for the push to Pecks Corner Shelter, for water and lunch, just a bit farther along the Appalachian Trail with dramatic views of the mountains to come.

The afternoon's climbs up Eagle Rocks and Mounts Sequoyah and Chapman come like a one-two punch and a left hook out of nowhere. The last two each include 600 feet of sustained gain in less than half a mile. Camp is just shy of 6000 feet at Tricorner Knob, about a mile past the summit of Mount Chapman. Here, mighty Balsam Mountain, the largest subrange in the Great Smokies, intersects the Appalachian Trail.

DAY FIVE 15+ miles 3000 feet
The last and longest day of the trek traverses the most rugged and beautiful ridges in the Smokies before beginning the descent to Davenport Gap. Follow the familiar

white blazes up the well-graded trail around the western spur of Mount Guyot, named for nineteenth-century geographer Arnold Guyot, credited with mapping and accurately measuring the height of the highest peaks in the range. As it crosses Hell Ridge, so-named for the leaping flames of a devastating fire in the early 1900s, the trail begins to lose elevation, albeit in fits and spurts, until it finally drops below 5000 for the first time in three days.

Wrapping around the southeastern corner of Cosby Knob, fill up your bottles

Appalachian Trail in early spring (Photo by Corey Hadden)

at the shelter before entering virgin stands of northern hardwoods, replacing the spruce and fir forest that has dominated the high ridges since the other side of Clingmans Dome. Drop 500 feet into Low Gap and quickly gain nearly 800 feet as you circle around the west sides of Rocky Face Mountain and Sunup Knob, enjoying spectacular views in all directions.

In 1.5 miles, after the second of two unnamed knobs, a rugged side trail to the left leads 0.6 mile through heath-lined tunnels to a stone observation tower atop Mount Cammerer and one of the finest views in the park. Drop your pack and head to the tower for your last chance to recall the adventures you've had over the past few days. Or, if you find yourself wanting more, where you could be headed tomorrow.

Back at your pack, the Appalachian Trail bears left and continues the steady descent for 5 miles through remnant spruces, outcroppings of rock, and rhododendrons to the trailhead at Davenport Gap.

Trail Summary and Mileage Estimates

0	Fontana Dam Visitor Center (1800 feet), turn left on paved road over dam
1	Appalachian Trail (2090 feet), enter woods on Appalachian Trail
4.6	Sassafras Gap (3650 feet)
7.6	Doe Knob (4520 feet), bear right on Appalachian Trail
11.1	Mollies Ridge Shelter (4570 feet)
13.3	Russell Field Shelter (4360 feet), bear right on Appalachian Trail
22.4	Sams Gap (4760 feet), stay right on Appalachian Trail
24.8	Miry Ridge Trail (4920 feet), stay right on Appalachian Trail
28.4	Welch Ridge Trail (5440 feet), stay left on Appalachian Trail
30.3	Goshen Prong Trail (5740 feet), stay right on Appalachian Trail
32.2	Clingmans Dome Bypass Trail (6520 feet), stay left on Appalachian Trail
35.8	Sugarland Mountain Trail (5980 feet), stay right on Appalachian Trail
38.5	Road Prong Trail (5272 feet), stay straight on Appalachian Trail
40.2	Newfound Gap (5046 feet), cross parking area and go straight on Appalachian Trail
44.5	Charlies Bunion (5520 feet)
69.3	Lower Mount Cammerer Trail (3520 feet), stay right on Appalachian Trail
71.8	Davenport Gap (2020 feet)

Suggested Camps Based on Different Trekking Itineraries

Night	10–15 mpd	15 mpd	15–20 mpd
One	11+ miles - Mollies Ridge	13+ miles—Russell Field	16+ miles - Spence Field
Two	22+ miles - Derrick Knob	29+ miles - Double Spring Gap	36+ miles - Mount Collins
Three	36+ miles - Mount Collins	43+ miles - Icewater Spring	56+ miles - Tricorner Knob
Four	51+ miles - Pecks Corner	56+ miles - Tricorner Knob	
Five	63+ miles - Cosby Knob		

Great Smoky Mountains National Park— Oconaluftee River to Elkmont (NC/TN)

Difficulty: Strenuous

Distance: 41.3 miles

Elevation gain: 10,300 feet

Best season: Year-round, though mid-April is best for wildflowers and mid-October is best for fall colors. In winter, low and middle elevations tend to offer milder conditions and can offset the suffering one might encounter at higher elevations, which are prone to heavy snowfall and below-freezing temperatures.

Recommended itinerary: 3 days (10–15 miles per day)

Water availability: Reliable sources are generally several miles apart, with obvious exceptions where the route follows major creeks. Be sure to leave every on-trail water source with at least two full bottles.

Logistics: It is approximately 35 miles between trailheads and the park does not offer any public transportation or shuttle service. A park service campground in Elkmont offers a convenient place to spend the night before the first day of trekking. If you have your backcountry permit in hand, allow about 90 minutes for the drive to the Mingus Creek trailhead from Elkmont. Otherwise, plan an extra 30 minutes for a stop at the Sugarlands Visitor Center where a self-permitting station lets you fill out your own permit, assuming you have already obtained permission for sites requiring a reservation.

Jurisdictions: Great Smoky Mountains National Park (865-436-1231). A free backcountry permit is required for all overnight trips within the park, and all shelters and some campsites require an advance reservation. Sites along this trek that require an advance reservation include all shelters and sites 57 and 55.

Maps: National Geographic Trails Illustrated 229, *Great Smoky Mountains National Park*

Trail location: The Mingus Creek trailhead at the beginning of the trek is located approximately 1 mile north of the Oconaluftee Visitor Center in Great Smoky Mountains National Park, on the left side of US Route 441. To get to the Jakes Creek trailhead at the end of the trek in Elkmont, drive north on US Route 441 to the Sugarlands Visitor Center, approximately 28 miles, and turn left onto Little River Road, toward Elkmont and Cades Cove. In 5 miles, turn left on Elkmont Road and proceed approximately 3 miles to its end at the Jakes Creek trailhead. Setting your own shuttle by bike is feasible, though not recommended, even if you're up for the distance and elevation gain. A small shoulder on all heavily traveled park roads offers little space for cars to pass. If you insist on setting your shuttle by bike, consider hiking in the off-season, or doing the burly ride late at night or early in the morning.

Ecologically speaking, to hike from the Oconaluftee River up and over Clingmans Dome to Elkmont is analogous to traveling all the way to Canada and back again. Plant communities found along the trail will be similar to ones that would be encountered if you hiked all the way to Canada's boreal forest. Beginning in mixed deciduous woods along the Mingus Creek Trail, you'll pass first through cove hardwoods,

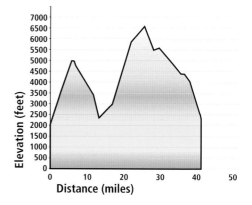

then northern hardwoods, and finally boreal forest communities. Along the way, savor cool hemlock groves and drier slopes covered with mixed oaks and pines. Near the Appalachian Trail at Clingmans Dome, you'll enter a world of conifers only found in the northern United States and Canada, and here. This trek celebrates the extraordinary biodiversity of the southern Appalachians and sections of two glorious footpaths, the Appalachian Trail and North Carolina's majestic rival, the Mountains-to-Sea Trail, stretching from Clingmans Dome to the Atlantic Ocean.

DAY ONE   14 miles   3600 feet
Shoulder your pack and set off from the trailhead parking area to follow an old dirt road beside Mingus Creek, hidden behind a dark wall of rhododendrons and doghobble, a luscious green plant with a zigzag stem. The trail is easy going for the next several miles as it passes through a small wildlife clearing surrounded by a mixed hardwood forest represented here by tulip poplar, red maple, white ash, and a mix of oaks. At 1.2 miles, a side trail leads 0.5 mile up Mingus Creek to a secluded cemetery. Otherwise, stay left on the main trail as it turns up Madcap Branch, the last on-trail water source until Deep Creek, more than 10 dry, mountainous miles away.

Once on the ridge to Newton Bald, pass Deeplow Gap Trail, coming in from the left, and follow the prominent ridge through the changing forest of poplars, oaks, pines, and laurels. Though distinct forest types do exist at relative elevations, lines between each community are often blurred due to localized differences in soil moisture, acidity, and nutrient level. At 5000 feet, amid a typical mix of northern hardwoods, Mingus Creek Trail ends and Newton Bald Trail begins. Take the left fork, passing 100 feet below the summit of Newton Bald, heath-covered and overgrown at 5170 feet.

Soon reach Newton Bald campsite 52 in a small gap and shortly beyond the junction with the Thomas Divide Trail. Make a sharp right turn, and after a slight descent, turn left onto the Sunkota Ridge Trail. Travel the ridge top for the next 5 miles, all the way down to Martins Gap (3430 feet). Small seeps may exist along the way in wet conditions.

After the long, dry descent, bear right onto the Martins Gap Trail for the final push to camp beside the clear, rushing water of Deep Creek, one of the park's most picturesque streams. Once at the river's edge, turn right onto the Deep Creek Trail, and travel up the creek for a few hundred yards to Burnt Spruce campsite 56. Rip off those boots and soak in cold mountain water, which at moments like this seems to exist just for you and your tired feet.

DAY TWO   15 miles   5400 feet
Deep Creek Trail makes four creek crossings in the next couple of miles, at least two of which are likely to get your feet wet. Keep boots and socks dry by taking them off and wearing sandals instead to protect your feet from sharp rocks and old fishing lures. Some folks like to wear old sneakers, though wet shoes never seem to dry in humid conditions.

Just beyond Poke Patch campsite 53, the Fork Ridge Trail can be seen across

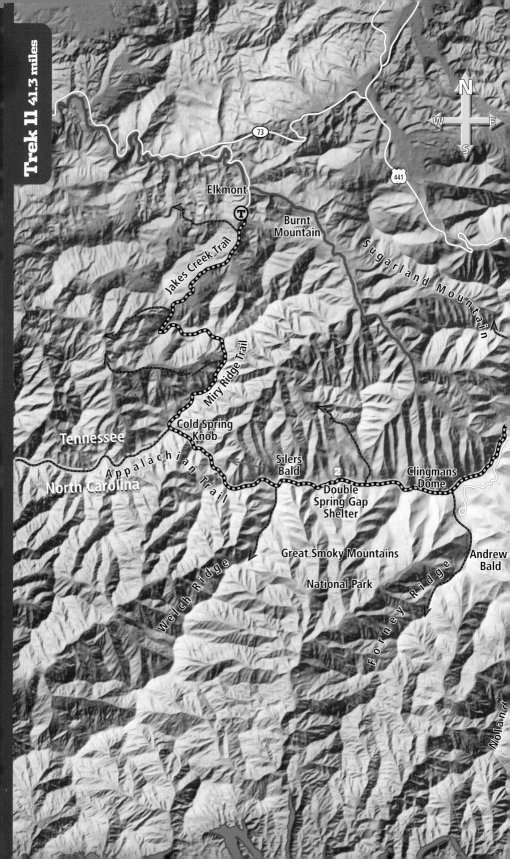

73

441

N
W   E
S

Elkmont

T

Burnt
Mountain

Jakes Creek Trail

Sugarland Mountain

Miry Ridge Trail

Cold Spring
Knob

Tennessee

Appalachian Trail

North Carolina

Silers
Bald

2

Double
Spring Gap
Shelter

Clingmans
Dome

Welch Ridge

Great Smoky Mountains

National Park

Forney Ridge

Andrew
Bald

Noland

Tennessee

North Carolina

Mount
Le Conte

Appalachian Trail

441

Clingmans Dome Road

Oconaluftee River

Deep Creek Trail

Rattlesnake
Knob

Newton
Bald

Cherokee
Indian
Reservation

Sunkota Ridge Trail

Mingus Creek Trail

Oconaluftee
Visitor
Center

T

Divide

Burnt
Spruce

Thomas Ridge

Blue Ridge Parkway

441

Cherokee Indian
Reservation

Cherokee

19

Deep Creek
Campground

the creek switching back through a small glade of ferns. Slip off your boots for one last wet crossing and begin climbing out of the juicy Deep Creek valley and set your sights on the highest peak in the park, in Tennessee, and on the entire Appalachian Trail: Clingmans Dome (6643 feet), 5 miles away and more than 3500 feet up. Most of the steep climbing is up Fork Ridge, and the final, more gradual ascent is along the Appalachian Trail. Toward the end of the climb enter the southern reaches of North America's boreal forest, here dominated by red spruce and skeletons of Fraser fir. The Fraser fir population has been practically wiped out by the balsam woolly adelgid, an insect accidentally introduced on the continent more than a hundred years ago.

Nearing Clingmans Dome, drop your pack and bear left on a short paved trail from a parking lot, and head for the summit and saucer-shaped observation tower for a 360-degree view of the surrounding mountains. The view from here is beautiful, without a doubt, but the Smokies, indeed all of the southern Appalachians, are in trouble. Significantly more air pollution is present today than in years past. On good days, it's still possible to see for a hundred miles, but on most days a yellowish haze made from ozone, sunlight, and automobile exhaust, in contrast to the naturally

Footbridge over Mingus Creek (Photo by Corey Hadden)

Fraser fir skeletons near Clingmans Dome (Damon Hearne/Slabcreek Photography)

occurring blue fog these mountains are famous for, can limit visibility to 20 or 30 miles; it's a bittersweet peak to climb.

Depressing as it may be, there is hope. If you have half a mind to act, the top of Clingmans Dome is a great place to begin composing a letter to your congressional representative demanding that the Clean Air Act be strengthened, or that more funding be allocated for research to control invasive species, which in the case of the adelgid, is largely funded by private donors.

Return to your pack and follow the Appalachian Trail, which rolls on for another mile before finally dropping below 6000 feet. Double Spring Gap Shelter sits high at 5507 feet 0.5 mile past the turnoff for Goshen Prong Trail.

DAY THREE 13 miles 1300 feet

The final day of the trek leads you back from Canada to the familiar hardwood forests at lower elevations. But first, walk through the Narrows to Silers Bald, which at 5607 feet, is one of the highest grassy balds in the southern mountains. Balds are a specialty of the southern Appalachians, although their existence is somewhat of a mystery. Southern mountains aren't high enough to penetrate tree line, yet dozens persist with grassy openings or shrubby summits covered with rhododendrons, laurels, and azaleas. One theory suggests that grazing herds on the high peaks kept young trees from

Tree frog (Damon Hearne/Slabcreek Photography)

overtaking pastureland. Others believe periodic fires started by lightning are the cause. Whatever the cause, balds increase the biodiversity of these mountains and offer the weary trekker a wide-open respite from the long green tunnel.

From the open summit of Silers Bald, the trail continues along narrow ridges and knobs to just beyond Buckeye Gap, where the Miry Ridge Trail enters from the right. Bid farewell to the Appalachian Trail, turn right onto the Miry Ridge Trail, and begin the gradual descent off the main crest of the Smokies on smooth tread.

Miry Ridge bulges from the side of the Smokies crest like a thorn in its side, staying close to, but slightly less than 5000 feet for most of its length until it smashes into Dripping Spring Mountain and Bent Arm. Where they converge, at an unremarkable knob at 4550 feet, the trail bends left traversing Dripping Spring Mountain before finally dropping nearly 700 feet in about a mile to Jakes Gap. Panther Creek Trail enters from the left and Jakes Creek Trail from the right. Bear right over the ridge down to Jakes Creek.

Back in the early 1900s, Jakes Creek was the dominion of the Little River Lumber Company whose mill in Elkmont was responsible for processing tens of thousands of board feet a day. From here, a railroad used for hauling the once great trees, mainly tulip poplar, extended far up Jakes Creek. In fact, the railroad climbed every creek in the Little River watershed, nearly up to Clingmans Dome. During periods of heavy rain, the muddy creek ran brown like chocolate milk, scouring its banks with the corpses of tulip poplar, spruce, and others in one long giant eruption. Today, Jakes Creek is still recovering. When it rains, the river now runs clear due to the natural filtering action of healthy soils and vegetation.

Passing the turnoff for Meigs Mountain Trail on the left and Cucumber Gap Trail on the right, Jakes Creek Trail bears left to trek's end, about 0.5 mile south of Elkmont.

Trail Summary and Mileage Estimates

0	Mingus Creek trailhead (2052 feet)
2.9	Deeplow Gap Trail (3620 feet), stay right on Mingus Creek Trail
5.7	Newton Bald Trail (5000 feet), turn left onto Newton Bald Trail
6.2	Newton Bald campsite 52 (5000 feet)
6.4	Thomas Divide Trail (4980 feet), turn right onto Thomas Divide Trail
6.8	Sunkota Ridge Trail (4780 feet), bear left onto Sunkota Ridge Trail
11.7	Martins Gap (3430 feet), bear right onto Martins Gap Trail
13.2	Bryson Place campsite 57 (2360 feet), turn right onto Deep Creek Trail
13.5	Burnt Spruce campsite 56 (2405 feet)
16.8	Poke Patch campsite 53 (3000 feet), bear left onto Fork Ridge Trail
21.9	Clingmans Dome Road (5880 feet), cross road and stay on Fork Ridge Trail
22	Appalachian Trail (5900 feet), turn left onto Appalachian Trail
25.6	Side trail to Clingmans Dome Trail (6610 feet)
27.6	Goshen Prong Trail (5740 feet), stay left on Appalachian Trail
28.1	Double Spring Gap Shelter (5507 feet)
29.6	Silers Bald (5607 feet)
33.1	Miry Ridge Trail (4920 feet), turn right onto Miry Ridge Trail
35.6	Lynn Camp Prong Trail (4410 feet), stay right on Miry Ridge Trail
36.6	Dripping Springs Mountain campsite 26 (4400 feet)
38.1	Jakes Creek Trail (4055 feet), turn right onto Jakes Creek Trail
40.9	Meigs Mountain Trail (2560 feet), stay right on Jakes Creek Trail
41	Cucumber Gap Trail (2540 feet), stay left on Jakes Creek Trail
41.3	Jakes Creek trailhead at Elkmont (2320 feet)

Suggested Camps Based on Different Trekking Itineraries

Night	10 mpd	10–15 mpd	20+ mpd
One	6+ miles - Newton Bald campsite 52	13.5 miles - Burnt Spruce Camp 56	22+ miles - Mount Collins Shelter
Two	17 miles - Poke Patch campsite 53	28+ miles - Double Spring Gap Shelter	
Three	28+ miles - Double Spring Gap Shelter		

Note: Several other campsites and shelters along this route can be used to tweak a given day's mileage by a couple of miles.

Great Smoky Mountains National Park—Old Settlers Trail/Appalachian Trail Loop (NC/TN)

Difficulty:	Strenuous
Distance:	53.8 miles
Elevation gain:	16,800 feet
Best season:	Spring and fall are best for wildflowers and fall colors. Trails can be crowded in the summer; winter can provide the most solitude, but solid snow and cold weather camping skills are a must.
Recommended itinerary:	4 days (10–15 miles per day)
Water availability:	Abundant throughout the trek at lower and middle elevations. Along the Appalachian Trail, all reliable sources are near shelters. On-trail springs, though reliable in wetter seasons, may run dry in summer.
Logistics:	A large parking area exists at Porters Creek trailhead, trek's end. To get to the beginning of the trek at Old Settlers trailhead, walk 1 mile northeast along the gravel road and turn right onto the bridge over the Middle Prong Little Pigeon River. The trailhead is on the left in 0.1 mile, immediately past a second bridge. All trails except for the Appalachian Trail, which is blazed with white rectangles, are unblazed, but most junctions are well signed. In winter, heavy snow and ice can be expected at higher elevations, requiring instep crampons and snowshoes. Most campsites within the park have cables rigged for hanging food to prevent bears and other critters from getting at your grub. It is expected that you will use these systems to keep your food safe and to protect the diets, health, and habits of local wildlife.

Jurisdictions: Great Smoky Mountains National Park (865-436-1231). A free backcountry permit is required for all overnight trips within the park, and all shelters and designated campsites require a reservation.

Maps: National Geographic Trails Illustrated 229, *Great Smoky Mountains National Park*

Trail location: From the US Routes 421/321 junction in Gatlinburg, Tennessee, proceed north on US 321 for approximately 6 miles to Greenbrier Road, and turn right. Stay right on Greenbrier Road for 4 miles to its end at Porters Creek trailhead.

Strike out through the northern foothills of the Great Smoky Mountains and sweat like the old settlers before seeking cool relief in the remnant boreal forest on the ridge of the most massive mountains in the southern Appalachians. Along the way, explore barns, chimneys, and rock walls built by hand at a time

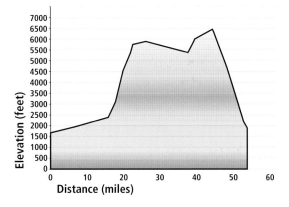

when everything took days and weeks of sweat and tears. Up high, if it's spring, share stories with a handful of thru-hikers bound for Maine at one of the several shelters found along the Appalachian Trail.

DAY ONE 8 miles 1700 feet

Amble down the gravel road beside Porters Creek and feel the cool pockets of air wafting up from the cold mountain stream. High in the trees, a song that sounds like a zipper with a hiccup signals one of spring's first migrants, the northern parula, a multicolored little warbler with a bright yellow throat. Cross right over the bridge above the Middle Prong Little Pigeon River, and look for the Old Settlers Trail on the left, just beyond a second bridge. Enter the woods and follow the gentle trail as it rolls along past several creeks and stone walls from the 1800s, many now covered with decades of moss and wildflowers. Explore any of the creeks that trace the contours of these soft hills. You'll discover many more homesites and chimneys, as dozens of families made their home here among the wooded valleys and coves.

Cove hardwoods dominate the moist lowland areas of the park, up to about 4500 feet before yielding to oak-dominated hardwoods, which prefer drier, sunnier

321

Old Settlers Trail

Settlers Camp

1

Greenbrier

321

Pigeon River

Greenbrier Road

Grapeyard Ridge

T

Middle Prong

T

Potato Ridge

Brushy Mountain

Porters Creek

Porters Mountain

Appalachian

Mount Le Conte

The Boulevard Trail

Mount Kephart

Icewater Spring Shelter

3

441

Tennessee

North Carolina

Newfound Gap

321

Cosby

Maddron Bald

Albright
Grove
Loop

Tennessee

Appalachian Trail

innacle

2

Otter Creek

Inadu
Knob

North Carolina

Mount
Guyot

Balsam Mountain Trail

Mount
Chapman

Mount
Sequoyah

Great Smoky

Mountains

National Park

rail

Hughes Ridge

N

W   E

S

Stream crossing on the Old Settlers Trail (Photo by Corey Hadden)

slopes. Along the way you'll pass through cool shaded groves of hemlock, dry hot ridges covered with thickets of mountain laurel, and soggy bottomlands where yellow ragwort and bluets dominate like the field of poppies near Oz. Camp near a towering old chimney, Settlers campsite 33.

DAY TWO   13+ miles   5900 feet

Get an early start on the day so there is time to explore a few settlers' camps, before turning your sights upslope toward higher ground and cooler climes. Recall the rolling trail from yesterday with its short, steep climbs and descents as you cross Redwine Creek, the first of many dry (hopefully) creek crossings you'll encounter on the way to the Tyson McCarter Barn, a picturesque lunch spot down a short side trail to a large well-preserved barn built in 1876. From here, it's a short distance to the first junction of the trek where Maddron Bald Trail enters from the right on what looks to be an old carriage road. Turn right and enjoy the gradual climb for a couple of miles over the smooth tread while it lasts; rougher trail lies ahead.

Cross a footbridge over Indian Camp Creek, which rages and tumbles down steep ravines on its way to joining the Pigeon River. Climb through a small stand of big hemlocks, a couple of arms' reach around, foreshadowing the giants to be found just

Opposite: Old stone wall beside the Old Settlers Trail (Photo by Corey Hadden)

around the corner along the Albright Grove Loop, a short side trail that showcases a remnant of the virgin old-growth forest that once spanned the southern Appalachians.

Enter the tranquil grove named for prominent conservationist and park advocate Horace Albright. Tiptoe among the tulip poplars, magnolias, and other giants that stand in sleepy silence. At first glance, these trees seem big, but not so big as to warrant a special trail just to show them off. As they stand together, it can be difficult to see that each one alone could be a showcase tree in any town square or university campus. And then you come to the *really* big ones. With trunks more than 20 feet around, these are the lords of the forest. Protect the vegetation that surrounds these behemoths and appreciate their grandeur from the trail where the view from base to canopy may lead to a crick in the neck, unless of course, you're looking at the colossal poplar that has had its crown knocked off.

Leave the grove and re-enter the world of sound and miniature trees again on the Maddron Bald Trail, staying right. Camp overlooks Otter Creek in a couple of miles and a stout climb of more than 1200 feet in and out of steep-sided coves.

DAY THREE 19+ miles 6600 feet
Be sure to leave Otter Creek with plenty of water as it may be more than 6 miles to the next reliable spring near Tricorner Knob Shelter. Climb immediately, but gradually, through thick rhododendrons, laurels, and hemlocks. Gain the narrow ridge leading to Maddron Bald and notice the dramatic change in forest type: You're now surrounded by spruce trees, boreal castaways left over from a colder era. Soon, an unmarked side trail to the left leads several yards through thick mountain laurel to the summit of the bald (5212 feet), which offers sublime views of the western foothills and the heart of Tennessee. The eastern towhee, a black-backed and rufous-sided bird slightly smaller than a robin, abounds in these shrub-dominated communities. Its song consists of two whistled notes and a sweet rattle sounding like "DRINK your TEEEEAAAAA!" Head up the trail to the next junction at Snake Den Ridge, and turn right before meeting up with the Appalachian Trail.

The Appalachian Trail through Great Smoky Mountains National Park can be a culturally and naturally enriching experience. Depending on the time of year, you may encounter eager thru-hikers, laurels and rhododendrons bursting in brilliant bloom, or 3 feet of snow on the ground.

Turn right onto the Appalachian Trail, and head south on the nation's first national scenic trail, so designated by Congress in 1968 after more than four decades of planning and constructing. For the next 16 miles, until camp at Icewater Spring Shelter, climb moderately steep knobs and narrow ridges through the remains of the once great spruce and fir forest, whose nearly complete destruction in the southern Appalachians is due to the balsam woolly adelgid, a small accidentally imported insect that literally sucks the life out of mature Fraser firs, leaving only their skeletons and a diminished forest community behind.

Charlies Bunion (Photo by Corey Hadden)

Shortly past Dry Sluice Gap, bear right on a short loop trail to Charlies Bunion, a tremendously exposed outcrop of slates and schists that appears to hold high court over Porters Creek and its tributaries, half a mile below. Reconnect with the Appalachian Trail just down the path from the overlook. In a little more than a mile come to the spring of Icewater Spring Shelter (5920 feet), and quench your thirst from its cold source. Find a space in the shelter to bed down, eat some good food, and enjoy the wide-open view of the night sky.

DAY FOUR   14+ miles   2600 feet
Wake up to one of the few places in the southern Appalachians with an unobstructed view of the sun as it rises over the Blue Ridge mountains. The last day of trekking cuts across one of the most spectacular trails and between two of the highest points in the park. Enjoy the grand finale of ridge top hiking in the park by turning right onto the Boulevard Trail, just 0.3 mile from last night's camp. Walk past overhanging views with drops of a thousand feet or more and gaze out at distant points west and north. Occasionally, small patches of snow can be found on the ground into late April, protected by cool seeps and shaded, north facing slopes. Near Myrtle Point (6480 feet), pass by a long shale outcrop and through a haunting stand of dead Fraser fir. Around the corner and up a slight incline, a side trail leads 0.2 mile to Myrtle Point, which offers a vast look at the rugged ridge the Appalachian Trail follows for most of its length through the park. Back on the main trail, it's a short climb to the trek's highest point on Mount Le Conte (6593 feet).

From here, amble down past the shelter, and turn right onto Trillium Gap Trail, which passes the Le Conte Lodge, a backcountry lodge with private cabins. In reverse order, the plant communities found on the way up begin to re-emerge as you gradually drop in elevation. At Trillium Gap, a side trail to Brushy Mountain (4911 feet) offers a last look at a bald heath community, much like the one found on Maddron Bald. Otherwise, turn right on Brushy Mountain Trail and continue the descent through mixed hardwoods and seeping springs, past brilliant spring wildflowers, to Porters Creek and the wide gravel path to the left that leads 1 mile to the Porters Creek trailhead, trek's end.

Trail Summary and Mileage Estimates

0	Old Settlers trailhead (1680 feet)
6.7	Settlers campsite 33 (1960 feet)
15.8	Maddron Bald Trail (2400 feet), turn right onto Maddron Bald Trail
17.8	Albright Grove Loop Trail (3120 feet), bear right onto Albright Grove Loop Trail
19.9	Otter Creek camp 29 (4560 feet)
21.9	Snake Den Ridge Trail (5360 feet), turn right onto Snake Den Ridge Trail
22.6	Appalachian Trail (5780 feet), turn right onto Appalachian Trail
26.2	Tricorner Knob Shelter (5920 feet)
37.6	Dry Sluice Gap Trail (5410 feet), stay right on Appalachian Trail
37.7	Side trail to Charlies Bunion (5400 feet)
39.3	Icewater Spring Shelter (5920 feet)
39.6	Boulevard Trail (6034 feet), turn right onto the Boulevard Trail
44.4	Side trail to Myrtle Point (6480 feet)
44.6	Mount Le Conte Shelter (6440 feet)
44.7	Trillium Gap Trail (6380 feet), turn right onto Trillium Gap Trail
48.3	Trillium Gap (4700 feet), turn right onto Brushy Mountain Trail
52.8	Porters Creek Trail (2200 feet), bear left onto Porters Creek Trail
53.8	Porters Creek trailhead (1900 feet)

Suggested Camps Based on Different Trekking Itineraries

Night	10–15 mpd (4 nights)	15–20 mpd (3 nights)	15–20 mpd (2 nights)
One	7 miles - Settlers campsite 33	7 miles - Settlers campsite 33	20 miles - Otter Creek campsite 29
Two	20 miles - Otter Creek campsite 29	20 miles - Otter Creek campsite 29	39+ miles - Icewater Spring Shelter
Three	32 miles - Peck's Corner Shelter	39+ miles - Icewater Spring Shelter	
Four	45 miles - Mount Le Conte Shelter		

Note: Consider other itineraries that include longer days (15+ miles) with shorter days (less than 10 miles) in order to maximize your time where you want to be. For example, hiking shorter days up high between shelters, rather than on Day One.

Appalachian Trail— Roan Highlands to the Nolichucky River (TN/NC)

Difficulty:	Very strenuous
Distance:	44 miles
Elevation gain:	11,700 feet
Best season:	Year-round. Late-April is the best for wildflowers and early-October is best for fall colors. Prepare for winter storms December through March since Roan Mountain and the high ridge along the North Carolina/Tennessee boundary tend to receive above-average snowfall.
Recommended itinerary:	4 days
Water availability:	Less obvious sources of water along the Appalachian Trail are marked with blue blazes. The ridges are typically void of water sources, so look for water in gaps or near shelters and campsites. Generally, prepare for dry sections of hiking over knobs and ridges.
Logistics:	While this route goes from east to west, thru-hikers refer to the trail direction as either north or south. The Appalachian Trail is marked with a white blaze. Look for blue blazes to identify spur trails to water and/or campsites. Avoid parking on US Route 19E as vandalism has been a problem.
Jurisdictions:	Appalachian/Toecane Ranger District (828-652-2144), Pisgah National Forest; and Nolichucky/Unaka Ranger District (423-638-4109), Cherokee National Forest
Maps:	Appalachian Trail Conference, map 2, *Moreland Gap to Sams Gap*
Trail location:	The northern terminus of the trail is located on US Route 19E in Tennessee about 1 mile from the Tennessee/North

Carolina state boundary. The southern end of the trek is along the Nolichucky River in Tennessee. From Interstate 26 near Erwin, Tennessee, take exit 15 and go east at the exit. Immediately turn right onto Temple Hill Road. In less than 1 mile, turn left onto River Road. Then turn left at the stop sign to cross the river. Take the first right onto Jones Branch Road, following the road to its end and park at the campground with permission.

The white blazes of the Appalachian Trail may be a hand line for the navigationally challenged, but 360-degree views from the grassy meadows of the Roan Highlands and Unaka Mountains will spin you in circles. Many seasoned thru-hikers consider this portion of the Appalachian Trail among its finest. Prepare for plenty of ups and downs on this spectacular 40-plus-mile section of trail that tops out on Roan Mountain—where the sights are dramatic no matter the time of year, whether the mountain is glazed with a crystal layer of rime ice in January, or pink patches of blooming rhododendron in June.

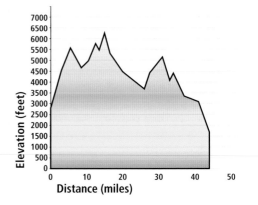

DAY ONE   10+ miles   3300 feet
From US 19E (2800 feet) reach the Apple House Shelter in a half-mile, and then head up a hill on an old mining road. The walking is easy to the shelter that was once used to store explosives for nearby iron ore mines. After a mile of walking, cross a four-wheeler track and reach rock steps beyond mile 2. Here the trail gets steep. Pass under a cliff and switchback to an overlook 50 yards to right.

At mile 3 arrive at Doll Flats (4560 feet) and begin to walk along the North Carolina/Tennessee state line. The Appalachian Trail leaves the woods crossing a grassy field with cows grazing to the east. Watch your step for cow piles on the trail from here to Big Hump. The trail is peppered with rocks and roots until reaching the grassy meadows at Big Hump.

At mile 5.5 arrive at Big Hump (5600 feet) with great views and a plaque commemorating Stan Murray. Murray was a former Appalachian Trail Conference chairman, conservationist, and local trail advocate. The route over Big Hump was part of a 65-mile trail relocation commandeered by Murray to include Roan

Mountain on the Appalachian Trail.

Descend to Bradley Gap, then cross Little Hump (5459 feet), taking care to follow less obvious blazes through the grassy meadow and regain the woods, eventually descending along an open field with good views toward North Carolina and easy walking to Yellow Mountain Gap at mile 8.5—named for the tulip poplar tree that blazes yellow in autumn. The gap intersects with Revolutionary War history: here the Overmountain men passed more than two hundred years earlier. In September 1780, a group of settlers marched over the gap from what's now Elizabethton, Tennessee, on their way to battle the red coats. The soldiers crossed in an early snowstorm and even-tually decimated the British in a battle at Kings Mountain, South Carolina, on October 7, 1780. The battled is consid-ered a turning point of the war.

At Yellow Mountain Gap are good views of a barn—the Overmountain Shelter—and Roaring Creek Valley. From the gap, the blue-blaze spur trail goes left less than a half-mile to the Overmountain Shelter, passing a spring along the way. The Overmountain Victory Trail, retracing the steps of the soldiers, also crosses at Yellow Mountain Gap. From Yellow Mountain Gap cross into the woods on the AT and climb over two knobs to the Stan Murray Shelter at mile 10.5 (5000 feet) in Low Gap. There is a spring 100 yards down the blue blazes to the left.

Snowy meadow above Yellow Mountain Gap

DAY TWO 9+ miles 3400 feet

From the shelter, begin a steep climb to Jane Bald, staying north of Grassy Ridge Bald. In less than 2 miles from the shelter arrive at a stretch of spectacular mountain balds. From Jane Bald (5800 feet) to Roan Mountain (6285 feet) the trail stays above 5000 feet, mostly through open meadow. At Jane Bald, bear right onto the Appala-chian Trail—to the left is a trail along Grassy Ridge. From here to Carvers Gap is excellent walking with several exposed camping possibilities until Round Bald, where no camping is permitted. Pass Engine Gap and continue over Round Bald, then descend to Carvers Gap at mile 13.5 (5500 feet).

Map 1

Tennessee

North Carolina

Clyde Smith
Shelter
2

143

143

226

Hughes
Gap

Beartown
Mountain

Ash
Gap

Round
Bald

Jane
Bald

Roan
Mountain

Carvers
Gap

Engine
Gap

N
W E
S

Erwin

26

Temple
Hill
Road

Exit
15

River Road

26

Jones Branch Road

Curley
Maple
Gap

Indian
Grave
Gap

N
W E
S

19E

T
P

Tennessee

North Carolina

19E

Doll
Flats

Big Hump

Yellow
Mountain
Gap

Little Hump
Mountain

1

Stan
Murray
Shelter

Map 1

Map 2

Trek 13 overview

107

Iron
Mountain
Gap

226

Tennessee

Unaka
Mountain

Low
Gap

Little Bald
Knob

North Carolina

eauty
Spot
Gap

Map 2

Rhododendron in bloom (Photo by Ben Walters)

At Carvers Gap, cross Tennessee Route 143/North Carolina Route 261. On the west side of Carvers Gap is parking and a paved road leading to the top of Roan Mountain. The mountain is among the most popular destinations in the region, especially in June when about 100,000 visitors visit for the blooming rhododendrons. In fact, Roan has been a well-known destination for many years: From 1885 to 1910 the summit of Roan was the site of the 300-room Cloudland Hotel, which was known as a retreat for hay fever suffers. John Muir was among the hotel's famous guests. The operation eventually folded, however, and the building was dismantled.

From Carvers Gap, the trail parallels the road for a short distance then crosses it and reenters the woods at the end of the guardrail. At mile 15, pass the blue blaze on the left leading to the shelter on the top of Roan Mountain—the highest shelter on the Appalachian Trail. Within a half mile the Appalachian Trail goes right, and to the left is the Cloudland Hotel site. Nearby is a picnic area and bathrooms. From here it's steep and rugged downhill to Ash Gap—where there is camping and springs. After a short climb to Beartown Mountain, continue descending to Hughes Gap. In all, descend more than 2000 feet in less than 3 miles from the top of Roan to Hughes Gap (4040 feet). At Hughes Gap, cross Hughes Gap Road, climb steadily to the top of Little Rock Knob at mile 19.5 (4900 feet), and then commence a steep downhill to a gap and spring. In less than a mile, follow the blue-blazed trail to the right to the Clyde Smith Shelter near a spring.

DAY THREE 13+ miles 3500 feet
From the shelter, it's easy walking to Greasy Creek Gap at mile 22 (4034 feet). From Greasy Creek, climb a knob and descend to a gap then over another knob. Continue over another knob and then on to Iron Mountain Gap at mile 26. At Iron Mountain Gap cross Tennessee Route 107/North Carolina Route 226. There

is a small campsite about 100 yards south on the right from Iron Mountain Gap. In a half-mile cross Forest Road 230, and climb to Little Bald Knob (4450 feet).

At mile 27.5, summit Little Bald Knob, then carry on to Cherry Gap, with several ups and downs over small knolls along the way. Climb from the gap and soon reach Cherry Gap Shelter with lots of campsites and a spring behind the shelter. Within a mile, reach Low Gap then begin a steep rocky climb to Unaka Mountain.

At mile 30.5, follow the sharp switchback to the left. Straight ahead is the old Appalachian Trail to Forest Road 230. Soon reach the summit of Unaka Mountain (5180 feet). Unaka Mountain is within the Upper Unaka region of the primary western band of mountains of the southern Appalachians collectively known as the Unaka Range. Generally speaking, the Unaka chain has three divisions running from north to south: the Upper Unaka, the Great Smokies, and the Lower Unaka.

From Unaka Mountain, descend to Deep Gap (4100 feet), also known as Beauty Spot Gap, in about 2 miles. At the gap, parallel the Forest Service road and look for a blue-blazed trail leading to a spring and campsite.

DAY FOUR 10+ miles 1500 feet gain

From the campsite, climb to Beauty Spot at mile 34—a grassy bald with top-notch views. From Beauty Spot Gap the trail stays near Forest Road 230. In about a mile, cross the Forest Service road at a couple of campsites and a small pull off for cars before arriving at Indian Grave Gap (3360 feet) at mile 37 and a

Winter vista from Roan Mountain

crossroads of several roads, including Tennessee Route 395 and Forest Road 230. Cross the Forest Service road and go right up steps and an initial steep climb. From Indian Grave Gap to Curley Maple Gap (3080 feet), the trail rolls up and down over small knobs. Cross a stream at mile 41 and arrive in Curley Maple Gap and the site of a shelter with a spring south of the trail. From the shelter, descend more than 1000 feet to the Nolichucky River, one of the region's premiere whitewater rivers. About a mile past the shelter, take a sharp turn onto an old logging road following and occasionally crossing Jones Branch. In less than 2 miles the road leaves the branch arriving at the Nolichucky Gorge campground and river outfitters at mile 44.

Trail Summary and Mileage Estimates

0	US 19E (2800 feet)
3	Doll Flats (4560 feet), continue on Appalachian Trail
5.5	Big Hump (5600 feet), continue on Appalachian Trail
8.5	Yellow Mountain Gap (4680 feet), continue on Appalachian Trail
10.5	Stan Murray Shelter (5000 feet)
12.5	Jane Bald (5800 feet), stay right at Grassy Ridge
13.5	Carvers Gap (5500 feet), cross TN 143/NC 261
15	Roan Mountain (6285 feet)
16.5	Ash Gap (5350 feet), continue on Appalachian Trail
20	Clyde Smith Shelter (4500 feet), look for blue blazes to shelter
26	Iron Mountain Gap (3700 feet), cross TN 107/NC 226
27.5	Little Bald Knob (4450 feet), continue on Appalachian Trail
31	Unaka Mountain (5180 feet), continue on Appalachian Trail
33	Deep Gap (4100 feet), continue on Appalachian Trail
34	Beauty Spot (4430 feet), continue on Appalachian Trail
37	Indian Grave Gap (3360 feet), cross TN 395 and Forest Road 230
41	Curley Maple Gap (3080 feet)
44	Nolichucky River (1700 feet)

Suggested Camps Based on Different Trekking Itineraries

Night	<10 mpd	10 mpd	>10 mpd
One	8.5 miles - Overmountain Shelter	10.5 miles - Stan Murray Shelter	20 miles - Clyde Smith Shelter
Two	16.2 miles - Ash Gap	20 miles - Clyde Smith Shelter	33.5 miles - Beauty Spot Gap
Three	26 miles - Iron Mountain Gap	33.5 miles - Beauty Spot Gap	
Four	33.5 miles - Beauty Spot Gap		

TREK 14

Shady Valley Loop (VA/TN)

Difficulty:	Easier
Distance:	41 miles
Elevation gain:	11,600 feet
Best season:	March through November
Recommended itinerary:	3 days (10–20 miles per day)
Water availability:	Water sources are springs of varying reliability. Along the Appalachian Trail on Holston Mountain, water is typically marked with signs and near shelters. In the Iron Mountains, water is more elusive and a pump is useful to draw water from lightly flowing springs. Springs are more likely to be wet in the spring and winter. In the summer and fall, be prepared for longer stretches of dry hiking. Consider stashing water at the trek's two intersections with US Route 421.
Logistics:	The loop begins in Damascus, Virginia, but the majority of hiking is in Tennessee. To avoid tempting thieves, park your car in town, a short distance from the trailhead. Damascus Methodist Church offers parking for up to a week with permission and operates a hostel (276-475-3441) on Creepers Way behind the church on the main street. "The Place" has hot showers and is open from April 1 to November 1—the price of admission is a donation. Damascus also has several lodging options and car camp spots nearby, such as the Backbone Rock Recreation Area, 4 miles south of Damascus on Tennessee Route 133. Damascus has a gear shop for maps and a grocery store for other last minute items.

No permits are necessary, but be aware that thru-hikers have priority to sleep in shelters on the Appalachian Trail. Also, bear in mind that the town population mushrooms for a weekend in May for the annual Trail Days celebration.

Jurisdictions: In Virginia, the Appalachian National Scenic Trail and Iron Mountain Trail are within Jefferson National Forest and the Mount Rogers National Recreation Area (800-628-7202). In Tennessee they are in the Cherokee National Forest (423-476-9700). A small section of trail is on public road.

Maps: National Geographic Trails Illustrated 783, *South Holston and Watauga Lakes*

Trail location: Damascus is 14 miles east of Interstate 81 and the town of Abingdon, Virginia. Follow US Route 58 from Abingdon to Damascus. Both the Appalachian Trail and the Iron Mountain Trail converge in Damascus. From town, clockwise hikers should follow US 58/Virginia SR 91 to the east. When the road makes a sharp turn left, go straight and cross Laurel Creek following Old Virginia 91. In a mile, look right for a gated road with an Iron Mountain Trail sign. Counterclockwise hikers can begin the Appalachian Trail at the Damascus Town Hall on the corner of Reynolds Street and Laurel Avenue (US 58). Follow the trail through town into the forest.

Nestled in northeast Tennessee, just south of the Virginia state line is Shady Valley. The long narrow valley is bordered by two relatively straight parallel ridgelines, Iron Mountains on the east and Holston Mountain to the west. Unlike the higher peaks and rugged terrain of the Great Smokies and the Blue Ridge, fertile valleys like Shady Valley, separated by long, wooded ridges, were forged by erosion and folding

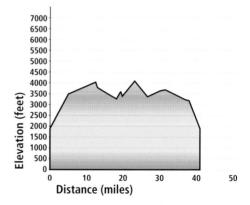

and fracturing about 250 million years ago when our continent collided with Africa. The long, relatively flat ridge crests of Iron Mountain and Holston Mountain are easy to navigate and pleasant to hike. Damascus (population 1000) is also an ideal point of entry. Known as Trail Town USA, the city has developed an industry around the Appalachian Trail and the Virginia Creeper Trail.

DAY ONE 12+ miles 5600 feet

Follow Old Virginia 91 out of Damascus to the trailhead at a gated road on the right.

Notice an ankle-high yellow mile marker. The sturdy markers begin at 18 and descend to the terminus of Iron Mountain Trail near Cross Mountain Road. Start up from the trailhead and climb steeply, sometimes switching back to a gap shrouded in rhododendron. Pass mile marker 1 and cross the Virginia/Tennessee state line. The next 17 miles stay close to the ridge top. Although the hiking is relatively moderate, the trail follows the spine of the ridge—rather than contouring—up and down numerous knolls with occasionally steep sections of trail.

In 1759, Daniel Boone blazed through the area en route to Kentucky. John D. Imboden, a Confederate general, established Damascus after the Civil War. Imboden intended to capitalize on the iron deposits of the surrounding mountains and develop a steel industry to rival Pittsburgh. Early settlers used the ore to make tools and weapons. As fate would have it, the ore deposits were only on the surface. Instead, profiteers exploited the trees. While Damascus didn't compete with Pittsburgh steel, at the time,

Mile marker on the Iron Mountain Trail

more trees were lumbered in the county than in the entire state of Pennsylvania.

The first obvious water source on the trail is just beyond yellow mile marker 15 at mile 3.2. Walk through a stand of white pine to a gap below a steep section of trail. Next to the trail is a questionable spring—even in the wettest of times. The stand of pine also has a seldom-used campsite. From the spring, climb steeply to a knob. Descend and cross Deer Run Road in a gap. The next road crossing is 8 miles at US 421. Along the ridge are serene views of farms in the valley to the east. To the northeast is Mount Rogers (the highest peak in Virginia) and White Top, and to the west is the Shady Valley.

The geography of the Shady Valley is part of the valley and ridge system of the Appalachian Mountains. The elongated sandstone ridges of Holston Mountain and the Iron Mountains, like folds in a rug, were more resistant to erosion than the softer dolomite rock in Shady Valley.

Continue hiking up and down swells in the ridge until the hiking eases beyond yellow mile marker 10, at mile 8.2. Eventually, leave the ridge and enter a covelike

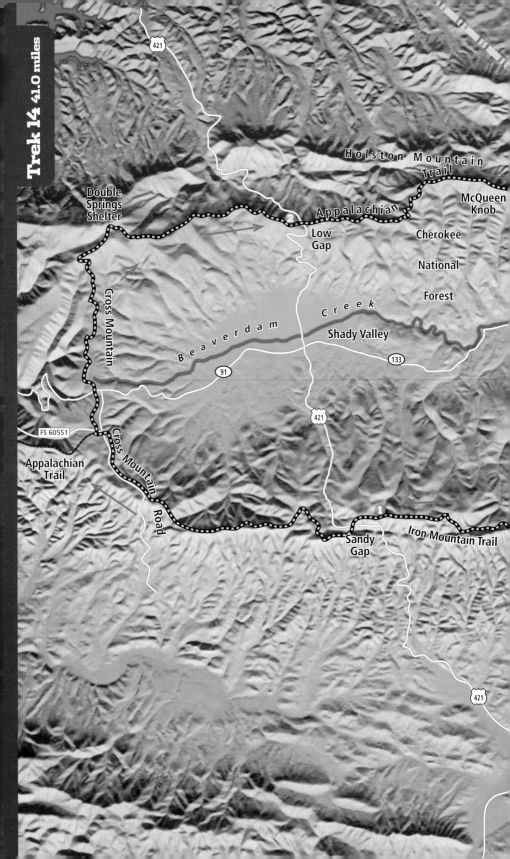

421

Double
Springs
Shelter

Holston Mountain
Trail

McQueen
Knob

2 Appalachian

Low
Gap

Cherokee

National

Forest

Cross Mountain

Beaverdam   C r e e k

Shady Valley

91

133

421

FS 60551

Appalachian
Trail

Cross Mountain Road

Sandy
Gap

Iron Mountain Trail

421

Virginia
Tennessee

ston Mountain

Abingdon
Gap

Jefferson
National
Forest

Laurel Creek

US 58

Mount Rogers
NRA

Damascus

91

Appalachian Trail

T

P

US 58

91

Beaverdam

Creek

Old 91

133

T

Backbone
Rock

Cherokee

National

Forest

Iron   Mountain

Iron Mountain Trail

N
W   E
S

Randy Moore hikes the Shady Valley Loop.

area. Here, cross a creekbed with a spring below Grindstone Ridge. Leave the cove and regain the dominant ridge. At mile 12.5, arrive in a gap with a grassy field on your right. A marshy area fed by a spring is beyond the field. Set camp in the gap or in an established site near the field. During dry conditions, consider stashing water along US 421 less than a mile from the campsite. There are also several campsites just south of the road.

DAY TWO   14+ miles   2900 feet
Past US 421, and beyond mile marker 2 at mile 16 descend steeply to Shady Gap and unmaintained Old Doe Road. Cross the road and climb back to the ridge. Just past mile marker 1 a rock-lined path leads to an excellent overlook to the east. Eventually pass a trashy campsite and reach an old road grade before it dead-ends at paved Cross Mountain Road at the communications towers. From Damascus, Holston Mountain and the Iron Mountains parallel each other for 35 miles. Cross Mountain connects the two ridgelines in the middle.

Turn right and walk the road through a small community. After a grassy field on the right with a small cemetery, turn left onto Forest Road 60551. The Appalachian Trail crosses the road just beyond the gate. Go right onto the Appalachian Trail. For a linear trek, consider turning left on the Appalachian Trail and continue south on the Iron Mountains for another 15 miles to Watauga Dam Road.

Mandatory side trip—Nick Grindstaff Monument: From Forest Road 60551, continue on the Iron Mountains along the Appalachian Trail for approximately 2.5 miles. Fifteen yards north of the shelter is a stone chimney, now a monument to Nick Grindstaff, who according to the monument "lived alone, suffered alone, died alone." According to popular legend, Grindstaff lived as a hermit in the Iron Mountains for dozens of years until his death in 1923. Legend has it that a local found the friendly hermit's four-day-old dead body guarded by his faithful dog.

From Forest Road 60552, cross 91 in less than 1 mile. From here, it is 3.4 miles to Double Springs Shelter (not to be confused with Double Spring Gap at mile 28.6) and 6.9 to US 421 on Holston Mountain. Past 91 are several water sources and campsites. Contour through this pleasant section of forest, eventually merging with an old road grade. Begin a steady climb on the old grade past a muddy campsite with a spring to Double Springs Shelter. The small shelter may be full on weekends and in the spring and summer when northbound thru-hikers are in the area.

From the shelter, turn right descending from the gap on Holston Mountain toward Damascus. Notice an old fence line and rock piles marking the boundary of an old farm on Locust Pole Knob. Cross an obscure road that used to connect Bristol and Shady Valley. Just prior to Low Gap at US 421 are several campsites. There is a reliable spring in the gap on the roadside.

DAY THREE 14+ miles 3100 feet
For much of the way beyond US 421, the Appalachian Trail follows an old road grade. The route skirts high points and the grade is gentler than the Iron Mountain Trail. Generally speaking, water sources are more numerous on the Appalachian Trail and well marked. At mile 30.1 McQueen Knob has one of the oldest shelters on the Appalachian Trail—built in 1934. The shelter has no water and is suitable only as an emergency campsite. At mile 31.5, the Abingdon Gap Shelter has a good water source several hundred feet down the marked spur trail to the right. Other campsites are scattered along the trail.

East Tennessee sunset (© shullphoto)

At mile 36.9, reach a spur trail that descends to the valley and Backbone Rock. If you are up for it, walk 2.3 miles to the rock, or stay on the Appalachian Trail to Damascus and, later, drive south to the tourist attraction on TN 133. Backbone Rock is a 75-foot-tall spine of rock 20 feet thick. In the early 1900s, the Empire Mining Company blasted a short tunnel to accommodate a railroad. These days TN 133 follows the grade and the U.S. Forest Service manages the area as a camping and picnic grounds.

Staying left at the Backbone Rock spur trail, begin a steady descent to Damascus. Cross the state line at mile 38 and switchback directly into Damascus. Stay on the trail through town and return to your vehicle.

Trail Summary and Mileage Estimates

0	Old Virginia 91 (1900 feet), trailhead at gated road on right
5	Deer Run Road (3500 feet), cross road
12.5	Campsite in field (4050 feet), continue straight on trail
13	Sandy Gap/US 421 (3800 feet), cross highway, continue on trail
16.4	Shady Gap/Old Doe Road (3450 feet), cross road, continue on trail
18.2	Cross Mountain Road (3280 feet), turn right onto road through town
19.3	Forest Road 60551 (3600 feet), turn left onto road
19.4	Appalachian Trail (3600 feet), turn right onto trail
19.8	TN 91 (3400 feet), cross road, continue on trail
23.2	Double Springs Shelter (4100 feet), bear right onto Appalachian Trail
26.7	Low Gap/US 421 (3380 feet), cross road, continue on trail
28.6	Double Spring Gap (3530 feet), continue straight on trail
30.1	McQueen Knob, log shelter built in 1934 (3650 feet)
31.5	Abingdon Gap Shelter (3700 feet)
36.9	Backbone Rock Trail (3250 feet), continue on Appalachian Trail
38	Virginia/Tennessee state line (3200 feet)
41	Damascus (1900 feet)

Suggested Camps Based on Different Trekking Itineraries

Night	10 mpd	10–20 mpd	>20 mpd
One	12.5 miles - field campsite	12.5 miles - field campsite	23.2 miles - Double Springs Shelter
Two	20 miles - Tennessee 91	26.7 miles - Low Gap/US 421	
Three	31.5 miles - Abingdon Gap Shelter		

Mountains-to-Sea Trail— Great Balsam Mountains (NC)

Difficulty:	Strenuous
Distance:	35 Miles
Elevation gain:	8000 feet
Best season:	April through November
Recommended itinerary:	3 days, 4 nights (14 miles per day, camping at one end of the trail)
Water availability:	All streams marked on maps carry water year-round under normal conditions. There are quite a few other seeps and streams where it is possible for the creative and dedicated (or thirsty) to fill a water bottle. The only area with large gaps in water is where the trail closely follows the Blue Ridge Parkway from the Rabb Knob Overlook (mile marker 442) to Grassy Ridge Mine Overlook (mile marker 436).
Logistics:	This trek's proximity to the Blue Ridge Parkway is a tremendous asset, as shuttles and restocking supplies are easily facilitated, and the scenic overlooks so prodigious on the Parkway can be used strategically. There is no camping available from US Route 74 to near Old Bald—about a 14-mile section. Also, this section is well marked with the white dot of the Mountains-to-Sea Trail, except the section from Haywood Gap to NC Route 215. These two characteristics serve to heighten the adventure, as well as the need for reading the map a bit more closely. We suggest hiking from US 74 to North Carolina Route 215. While it is a bit more strenuous (the elevation gain is all positive in this direction), you will be rewarded with the best panoramic views near the end of your trip. It is possible to park a shuttle vehicle on North

Carolina 215, north of the Parkway in one of the many pullouts near the Mountains-to-Sea trailhead.

Jurisdictions: Blue Ridge Parkway (828-271-4779); Pisgah Ranger District (828-877-3665), Pisgah National Forest; and Highland Ranger District (828-526-3765), Nantahala National Forest. No camping is permitted on the Park Service corridor along the Parkway, nor on private lands within the National Forest boundary, which the trail winds in and out of from US 74 to Old Bald.

Maps: National Geographic Trails Illustrated 785, *Nantahala & Cullasaja Gorges*. For more detail, refer to USGS Hazelwood and Sams Knob.

Trail location: From Asheville, North Carolina, drive west on Interstate 40. Merge onto US Route 74 at exit 27 toward Clyde/Waynesville/Murphy/Atlanta/Maggie Valley, and follow for approximately 13 miles. Take the Blue Ridge Parkway entrance on the right, just before US 74 passes through Balsam Gap. Head north on the Parkway approximately 0.7 mile and park in the lot at the Park Ranger and Maintenance Station on the right. You can pick up the trail in the southwest corner of the ranger station property, adjacent to US 74.

Long views of the surrounding wild hills and deep valleys are common along the high ridges that define this section of the Mountains-to-Sea Trail (MST). Looking out on what historically has been the heart of Cherokee land gives perspective to their legend of the buzzard that formed the mountains. According to legend, when the earth was still wet and muddy, a great buzzard shaped the land. After a particularly long flight, on return to the land of the Cherokee, the tired buzzard's flapping wings hit the soft earth. Where his wings landed, valleys were created, and where he lifted them, mountains swelled in the space below his feathers. Flying north into the mountains we know as the Great Smokies, his wings first touched down near Brevard, North Carolina, and again at Waynesville, North Carolina. The wilderness his wings conjured in between are the Balsam Mountains. All along this

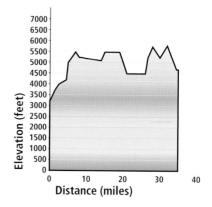

section of the MST are views to the south, where Buzzard still flew high above the land, and also views north to the Plott Balsams and beyond to the Smoky Mountains. In this direction, Buzzard's wings created the wildest wilderness and it is there the Eastern Band of the Cherokee Indians still reside.

DAY ONE   14 Miles   3800 feet

US 74 and the Blue Ridge Parkway intersect in Balsam Gap, dividing the Plott Balsams to the north from the Balsam Mountains in the south. This section of the MST winds its way from Balsam Gap (3250 feet) east to North Carolina Route 215 near Mount Hardy (6110 feet).

The trek begins from the southwest corner of the ranger station property just east of Balsam Gap. The first several miles of trail quickly gain enough elevation to leave behind the two nuisances of day one: poison ivy on the trail and the sound of truck engines on US 74. Keep your eyes out for the one, and seal your ears to the other while ascending through the mixed hardwood southern cove forest and an understory of ferns, holly, and dogwood.

Along mile 2 you'll see the few houses that the MST circumnavigates on its right-of-way through this small strip of private land. You also will see the infrequent mountain maple, with their distinctive green and white striped bark—some quite large. Also, notice the jewelweed mixed in with its constant companion, stinging nettle. In wildflower season, fire pinks and spiderwort are common.

The trail begins to switchback, climbing into the Balsams alongside the Parkway for several miles. After 2.5 miles, encounter a good stream and a trail junction. Fill up here, as water is scarce to absent until the trail passes near the Grassy Ridge Mine Overlook in several miles. The MST is the trail going uphill closest to the stream and is marked with a hiker's blaze within sight of the junction.

The trail continues to switchback over the next few miles, and the forest takes on a slightly more remote feel as the trees are bigger and more gnarled. The next few miles feature nice stonework

Thick sea of fog in the Balsams (© shullphoto)

74
19/23

Balsam
Gap

P T

74
19/23

Blue   Ridge

Grassy
Bald

Parkway

Ridge

Lone
Bald

Bald

Balsam Mountains

Nantahala

National

Forest

Piney Mountain

Piney Mountain Creek

Richland
Balsam

Blue Ridge Parkway

Middle Prong

215

Pisgah

National

Forest

Middle Prong

Wilderness

2

Rough Butt
Bald

Blue Ridge Parkway

T
P

Mount
Hardy

215

along the trail maintained and built by the Carolina Mountain Club. Enjoy views of the Plott Balsams to the north on the distinctive and highly enjoyable ridge walk along the narrow crest leading to Wesner Bald. There are also a few places on the ridge between Wesner Bald and Steestachee Bald where trees have fallen and created wide vistas to frame photos.

About half a mile after passing near Deep Gap and the Grassy Ridge Mine Overlook is Cabin Creek, the next reliable water source. Fill up here or at Dark Ridge Creek just a little farther on. A few miles of easy walking will put you on the ridge below Old Bald. The trail at this point merges with a jeep road and is still well marked. Continue until arriving at the large open field with terrific panoramic views of Judaculla Ridge, Richland Balsam, and everything wonderful that lies to the south and south east. This site makes great camping, and there is a good water source located another 15 minutes along the MST.

DAY TWO   11 Miles   2000 feet

The MST stays along the top of the field that concluded day one. Follow it to the tunnel of rhododendron so characteristic of the region. The trail follows the jeep road for a few hundred yards and then breaks left, contouring as the jeep track turns downhill. Fill up water at the stream about half a mile from the field, or wait another mile or so and use any of the three streams you'll step across in quick succession.

The forest varies between younger, denser stands, and older stands of locust, hickory, oaks, and maples, with soft understories of ferns and long grasses. These larger trees also have interesting insect burls along this section of trail. The balsam woolly adelgid is an extremely small insect that has had a disproportionately devastating effect on the balsams in this area of the Nantahala National Forest. In the south, the trees called balsams are actually Fraser firs nearly everywhere else. The various local names that Appalachia has bestowed on its natural inhabitants are just another layer of getting to know these mountains. Balsams grow alongside red spruce trees,

Basswood (Photo by Ben Walters)

and are ordinarily difficult for the untrained eye to distinguish between. However, the combination of acid rain and the unchecked spread of the adelgid (size of a huckleberry seed) have decimated the balsam trees (which generally grow at elevations above 5000 feet). As the trail approaches Judaculla Ridge, notice all the bone white poles that are spread throughout the forest. These are the remnants of balsam tree trunks, and lend a surreal feel to the landscape.

The route on the east side of Judaculla Ridge follows a pleasant, grassy abandoned roadbed that easily accommodates two hikers walking side by side. The trail enters the valley drained by Beechflat Creek below Richland Balsam. There is an obvious Y intersection—the left fork is marked No Trespassing, and the right fork takes you along the MST toward the Middle Prong Wilderness Area.

Note: Some maps show the trail connecting with the Blue Ridge Parkway at the Cowee Mountain Overlook (mile marker 431). Actually, the trail stays low, and doesn't approach the Parkway until a trail junction several miles farther near Rough Butt Bald at the Bearpen Gap Overlook.

The trail descends approximately 700 feet below Reinhart Knob. Once the trail begins contouring on an old road, arrive at a fork after about half a mile. Veer left here, but as for all intersections and forks in the trail, a little scouting will usually reveal a telltale hiker's blaze to point you in the right direction. You can either fill up your water at Piney Mountain Creek or wait until the east branch of the creek. If one is flowing well, then the other is likely to have water also. A field for camp is about half a mile after Piney Mountain Creek and a tenth of a mile before the east branch.

DAY THREE   10 Miles   2200 feet

This section of trail starts out well marked. After passing into the Middle Prong Wilderness Area on the north side of the Blue Ridge Parkway, however, there are almost no markings. A hundred yards down the trail from the field is the East Branch of Piney Mountain Creek. Fill up here before you begin all the elevation gain that today has in store. After about 0.25 mile, come to a fork in the trail. Go left and up. After about a mile are two other trail intersections. In both cases stay left—also watch for the trail's white blaze to ensure you are on the right track.

After attaining a small level shelf and following that for 0.75 mile, a trail breaks up and right to Bearpen Gap. Stay right on the MST to go through the most beautiful bald area on this side of the Parkway. After passing the gate that prohibits vehicular traffic on the old jeep track, go left and up at the next trail intersection. After 0.75 mile enter a good-size open field, enjoy views of Rough Butt Bald, and mountains to the east. The MST crests a small hill through a thicket of trees and then dives left and down toward Haywood Gap.

Investigating the field here for a small stopover is worth the time. The open grassy area is actually quite large. In the lower part is a lively pond with tadpoles

Bryan Haslam on the Mountains-to-Sea Trail
(© shullphoto)

galore, small birds, and enormous dragonflies. In the southeast corner of the field is a 30-foot side path that leads to a small rock outcrop with must-see views of every mountain nook and cranny from the southeast to the west.

From here, follow the well-marked trail up a few switchbacks and down to the Parkway at Haywood Gap. The trail picks up directly across the Parkway and winds northeasterly 20 or 30 yards to a sign proclaiming the Middle Prong Wilderness Area proper. Be aware that within the wilderness area, new rules apply: no groups larger than ten people and no campfires. The Cherokee began retreating from this area in the 1780s as white settlers arrived in increasing numbers. After more than a century of tension and conflict with settlers, the Cherokee were removed by the U.S. government during the winter of 1838-1839 along what became known as the Trail of Tears. Some Cherokee managed to hide in the mountains (or chose U.S. citizenship) and later formed what is now known as the Eastern Band of the Cherokee Indian. Just north of this area is the Qualla Boundary, which marks the edge of their present reservation, centered around the town of Cherokee just on the southeastern boundary of the Great Smoky Mountains National Park.

The forest in this watershed is second growth. The trail picks up a little here in physical and navigational difficulty, but is a kingdom of solitude in the tradeoff. There is good water in the first drainage east of Buckeye Gap. Follow the trail up a large bald for the best views of the trek. The MST puts on its disguise here as a humble footpath until it reaches NC 215.

Follow the footpath out the north end of the bald as it climbs a little farther and bears east. At the first fork bear right and down toward Mount Hardy Gap. At the next fork (0.1 mile), go east (left) down toward NC 215. The trail winds south through a beautiful and remarkably open rhododendron forest.

Parallel a creek before passing through another open meadow. June is a nice time of year at this elevation with field hawkweed and hawthorn. This field would make a good camp at the end of a long third day (or the beginning if you elect to hike this in reverse). Water and a road are found within one-third of a mile. Shortly after leaving the field there is a Mountains-to-Sea Trail blaze, and then it's 0.2 mile to NC 215.

Alternate finish: At the first fork in the trail after leaving the bald is the choice to bear right and continue on the MST to NC 215, or go left and down a mellow ridge into the Middle Prong Wilderness. Forest Service Trail 113 heads north, paralleling NC 215's progress toward Waynesville. There is not likely to be any water along this section, so be sure to fill up near Buckeye Gap. This side hike adds approximately 2.5 miles to the day, and concludes at a park service campground called Sunburst (877-444-6777). There are tent sites and flush toilets, but no showers. It is open from April to October and is $8 per night per site.

Trail Summary and Mileage Estimates

0	Blue Ridge Parkway Ranger Station (3250 feet)
0.1	Trail crosses small creek (3250 feet)
1.5	Trail crosses gravel road (3750 feet)
2.5	Significant stream and trail intersection (4000 feet)
4.5	Trail loses sight of the Parkway (4200 feet)
5	Trail follows crest of knife-blade ridge (5000 feet)
7	Trail follows ridge between Wesner Bald and Steestachee Bald (5500 feet)
8	Grassy Ridge Mine Overlook (5250 feet)
8.5	Cabin Creek (5250 feet)
10	Dark Ridge Creek (5200 feet)
14	Field for suggested campsite (5100 feet)
15	Cross three creeks within 0.25 mile of each other (5500 feet)
19	Triple uphill switchback (5500 feet)
21	Piney Mountain Creek (4500 feet)
25	Big field, suggested campsite for day two (4500 feet)
25.75	East Branch of Piney Mountain Creek (4500 feet)
26	Trail makes sharp left uphill (4500 feet)
26.75	Trail junction, left to Bearpen Gap, right to stay on MST to Haywood Gap (5250 feet)
28	High bald field with views of Rough Butt Bald (5750 feet)
30	Trail crosses Parkway at Haywood Gap (5250 feet)
32	Trail summits bald with views of Middle Prong Wilderness Area (5800 feet)
34.5	Trail passes through large field (4700 feet)
35	Trail crosses NC 215 (4700 feet)

Suggested Camps Based on Different Trekking Itineraries
Night >10 mpd

One	14 miles - field near Old Bald
Two	25 miles - field past Piney Mountain Creek

Pisgah Loop (NC)

Difficulty:	Easier
Distance:	33.5 miles
Elevation gain:	5700 feet
Recommended itinerary:	3 days (10 miles per day)
Water availability:	Water is abundant throughout most of the hike. Avoid water from the South Mills River and Bradley Creek and use smaller streams instead. Sources are less obvious on the Laurel Mountain section covering roughly 7 miles.
Logistics:	Consider hiking this trek in the off-season (November through April) or on weekdays. The South Mills River is popular with a variety of users—in particular consider avoiding the opening of shotgun deer season on Thanksgiving weekend. Winter is not ideal due to many river crossings on the South Mills River and Bradley Creek that may be dangerous in cold weather or high water.
Jurisdictions:	Blue Ridge Parkway (828-271-4779) and Pisgah Ranger District (828-877-3265), Pisgah National Forest
Maps:	USGS Cruso, Shining Rock, Dunsmore, and Pisgah Forest
Trail location:	The trailhead is located at the end of Turkey Pen Road off of US Route 280 east of Brevard, North Carolina. From Interstate 26, take exit 40 and travel west 10.5 miles on US 280. Keep eyes peeled for Turkey Pen Road on the right. Follow the gravel road 1.3 miles to its end at the parking area.

This route loops through the heart of the Pisgah Ranger District of the Pisgah National Forest, one of the most popular sections of forest in western North Carolina among recreational users. This trek will give you a deep-down immersion in the heart of the Pisgah Forest—from the flanks of Mount Pisgah to the South Mills River—and deep into George Vanderbilt's former holdings and the site of the country's first forestry school. Although big views on the hike are infrequent, gorgeous scenes of dazzling mountain streams through thick forest are plentiful. On this loop, you will encounter people fishing, hunting, running, mountain biking, hiking, and horseback riding. Fishing enthusiasts should take note of this trek as it follows two excellent fishing streams, the South Mills River and Bradley Creek.

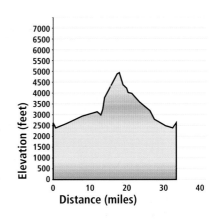

DAY ONE 13 miles 1300 feet

Begin this route at the Turkey Pen Gap parking area. The 12-mile section from Turkey Pen Gap to Forest Road 476 is sandwiched between two busy parking areas. From the kiosk at the trailhead follow the South Mills River Trail less than 1 mile to the river—follow the trail rather than the road grade that is longer and more gradual for horses. Cross the swinging bridge over the river and walk a short distance forward then left on the primary South Mills River Trail, which is a wide footpath and was once a railbed. The trail rises above and out of sight of the river for a short distance. Stay left at the Mullinax trailhead (1.5 miles). Eventually the trail descends through an open forest and campsite as it meets the river again. Most of the trail along the river is an old wide grade. In some spots the trail is typically wet and muddy, especially during wet spells.

Pass the Poundingmill Trail (2.5 miles) on the right and then cross the river on another swinging bridge. Pass another trail on the left, Wagon Gap Road Trail, and

Rhododendron bloom in grass (Photo by Ben Walters)

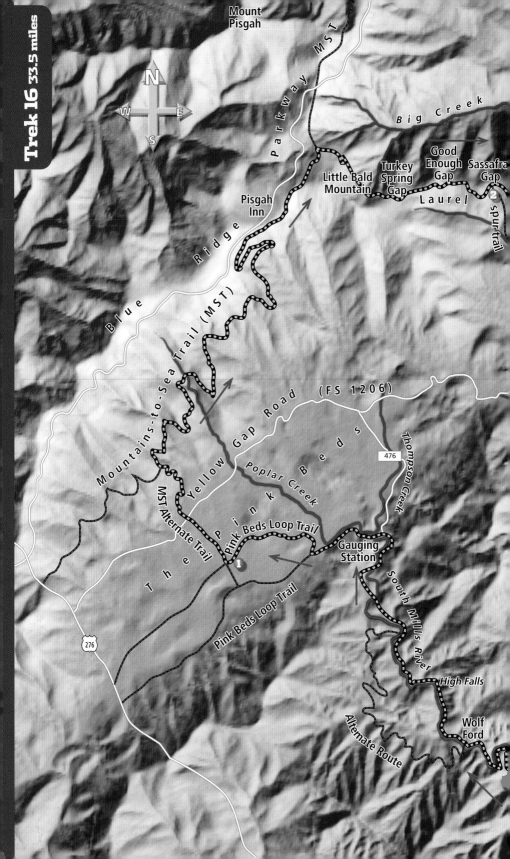

Mount
Pisgah

Parkway MST

Big Creek

Little Bald
Mountain

Turkey
Spring
Gap

Good
Enough
Gap

Sassafras
Gap

Pisgah
Inn

Laurel

spur-trail

Blue

Ridge

Mountains-to-Sea Trail (MST)

Yellow Gap Road (FS 1206)

Poplar Creek

Beds

Thompson Creek

476

MST Alternate Trail

Pink

Pink Beds Loop Trail

The

Gauging
Station

South Mills River

276

Pink Beds Loop Trail

Alternate Route

High Falls

Wolf
Ford

Big Creek

Johnson Gap

Rich Gap

Mountain

Yellow Gap Road (FS 1206)

Slate Rock Creek

Yellow Gap

Yellow Gap Creek

Yellow Gap Road (FS 1206)

Bradley Creek

Bradley Creek

Pea Branch

Pea Gap

Cantrell Creek

Cantrell Creek Lodge

Turkey Pen Gap parking area

South Mills River

Janie Faucette Moore crossing Bradley Creek

then cross the third and final swinging bridge until Wolf Ford at mile 8. Beyond the bridge, wander through a large serene field scattered with trees that looks a bit like a lawn. Cross Cantrell Creek and arrive at a tall stone chimney wrapped with vines (mile 3.6). The old chimney was first stacked a hundred years ago and stands tall and solid like an oak. The chimney is the remains of Cantrell Creek Lodge. The lodge has been reconstructed at the Cradle of Forestry near the Pink Beds. The lodge served as one of several locations for rangers to watch for game poaching and illegal timber harvesting.

From Cantrell Creek to Wolf Ford there are nine crossings. The fords are frequent and can be refreshing or a burden depending on your mood. Along the way are several small waterfalls and deep pools that allow fish ample oxygen during hot summer days. Classified as a wild trout stream and open to fishing year-round, there is a healthy population of native brown and rainbow trout.

Continuing upstream, the trail weaves through a narrow winding corridor bordered by steep slopes and covered with thick forest. Here the sun comes up late and disappears early. Pass an intersection with the Squirrel Gap Trail and cross at Wolf Ford, continuing upstream and departing the primary South Mills River Trail, which actually leaves the river. The South Mills River Trail climbs uphill and over Grassy Ridge before rejoining the river upstream.

At mile 12, arrive at a gate at the end of Forest Road 476. On the left is a campsite and a stone gauging station from bygone days. Find the trailhead for the Pink Beds Connector Trail at the campsite. Follow the connector trail upstream on level terrain. A few hundred yards beyond the trailhead, Thompson Creek and Poplar Creek meet to form the South Mills River. The trail crosses Thompson Creek and follows Poplar Creek. In about 0.25 mile, cross the creek on a log bridge and turn right at the trail junction, then arrive at another well-marked trail junction with the orange-blazed Pink Beds Loop Trail. Turn right here, following the Pink Beds Loop counterclockwise.

Known as the Pink Beds, the flat valley has one of the largest upland bog and marsh systems in the North Carolina mountains. In the Pink Beds are bogs that are often flooded by beavers and occasionally impede hiker traffic. Within a mile, reach another intersection—this time with the Mountains-to-Sea Alternate Trail. At the intersection is an obvious campsite or you can choose to camp at several more secluded campsites between the gauging station and the Mountains-to-Sea Alternate Trail in the Pink Beds.

DAY TWO   7+ miles   2100 feet

Turn right at the Mountains-to-Sea Alternate Trail heading north, leaving the Pink Beds Loop behind. In less than a half-mile the trail intersects Forest Road 1206 (also known as Yellow Gap Road). Cross the road and follow the Barnett Branch Trail. Climb for less than a mile to a junction with the primary Mountains-to-Sea Trail/Buck Springs Trail, and turn right. Water is plentiful, and the trail generally stays near the 4000-foot contour line. There is an established campsite on a ridge past Poplar Creek with water nearby. The trail grade was once a primary route established by George Vanderbilt to reach his Buck Springs Lodge near Mount Pisgah. Vanderbilt once held an enormous amount of land that was sold to the government nearly one hundred years ago. His heirs still own a large chunk of land in Asheville and his home, the 250-room Biltmore Estate.

Soon the casual walking ends as the trail climbs, sometimes switching back, nearly 1000 feet to the Pisgah Inn on the Blue Ridge Parkway and the highpoint of the trek at 5000 feet. The trail temporarily enters a buffer of land around the Blue Ridge Parkway

Dusk in the Pisgah National Forest

managed by the National Park Service. The trail cuts through the inn's parking lot. Follow the white blazes through the lot and regain the trail at a large trail map.

At the inn are all the amenities a hiker could want: bathrooms, a restaurant, a pay phone, and overnight accommodations. Plan ahead to reserve a room and dinner table (828-235-8228) or stay in the campground managed by the Blue Ridge Parkway (sites are $12 and available as first come, first served) located across the Parkway. The campground and the inn are open seasonally from April until October.

From the inn, the trail straddles a relatively flat ridge with good views. In less than 1 mile, pass the Pilot Rock Trail and descend steps. At the base of the steps look right for the Laurel Mountain Trail. The trail descends Laurel Mountain contouring around knobs and into several gaps. Laurel Mountain separates two watersheds: Big Creek on the east and Slate Rock Creek to the west. From the trailhead, the trail is rocky and full of roots and crosses several seeps as it makes its way around Little Bald Mountain to Turkey Spring Gap in 1 mile.

After a brief climb from Turkey Spring Gap, the trail descends steeply to Good Enough Gap. Here, a trail goes left and down to Big Creek. Continue straight on the Laurel Mountain Trail to Sassafras Gap. If you have hiked more than once in the southern Appalachians, it's likely you've been in a Sassafras Gap or on a Sassafras Mountain. Sassafras typically grows below 4000 feet and is a short tree with leaves that vary in shape—some with three lobes others with two or one lobe, like a mitten. Once used to flavor root beer, the leaf stem has a refreshing flavor.

To the right in Sassafras Gap is a steep connector trail to Slate Rock Creek. To reach the campsite, bear right on the connector trail to a level spot in an established campsite below the gap. Water is farther down the connector trail.

DAY THREE 13+ miles 2300 feet

Continue on the Laurel Mountain Trail to Johnson Gap, contouring around Johnson Knob to arrive at Rich Gap. Continue descending Laurel Mountain and arrive at Forest Road 1206 in Yellow Gap, about 3 miles from Rich Gap. Turn right onto the road and head downhill for about 1.3 miles. Take care walking on the well-traveled Yellow Gap Road. Stay close to the road's edge and especially watch for blind curves.

At the end of the downhill, look left for a large campsite and the Bradley Creek trailhead. Cross the creek at the campsite and head downstream on the Bradley Creek Trail. The trail meanders along and often crosses the shin-deep, bubbling creek underneath a canopy of poplars, sycamore, and Carolina hemlock with shady campsites and a dandy swimming hole.

The trail crosses the creek several times, so prepare for wet feet again. If you prefer to tempt fate, some of the crossings are possible by hopping on wet, slimy rocks. However, at a decent flow, put on your water shoes and jump in.

At 1.5 miles from the road the trail crosses the creek in front of Bradley Creek Reservoir—a good place for a swim. At the small reservoir is a large campsite flanked by a moss-covered, overhanging cliff about 20 feet high. Continue on the wide trail staying near the creek. At mile 30.5, pass the Riverside Trail on the left and bear right, staying on the Bradley Creek Trail going uphill, leaving Bradley Creek and following Pea Branch upstream. Soon cross Pea Branch and arrive at Pea Gap after a short climb. Descend and meet up with the South Mills River for the last time. Take care crossing the river, or consider turning right on the trail downstream through campsites, passing another ford then arriving at the swinging bridge crossed at the beginning of the trek.

Fern fields in the Pink Beds

If wading across the river, cross and then turn right going downstream until arriving at the swinging bridge. Turn left and uphill and in less than 1 mile arrive at the Turkey Pen Gap parking area.

Trail Summary and Mileage Estimates

0	Turkey Pen Gap parking area (2640 feet)
0.7	South Mills River Trail (2400 feet), cross swinging bridge, continue straight briefly, then go left on South Mills River Trail
2.5	Poundingmill Trail (2500 feet), continue on South Mills River Trail
3.6	Remains of Cantrell Creek Lodge (2600 feet)
8	Wolf Ford (2950 feet), continue upstream
12	Gate at Forest Road 476 and gauging station (3150 feet), follow Pink Beds Connector Trail
13	Mountains-to-Sea Alternate Trail (3000 feet), turn right
13.5	Barnett Branch Trail (3250 feet), cross Forest Road 1206, also known as Yellow Gap Road, to trailhead
14	Mountains-to-Sea Trail/Buck Springs Trail (3800 feet), turn right onto trail
17.4	Pisgah Inn (5000 feet), pass through parking area, continue on Mountains-to-Sea Trail
18	Laurel Mountain Trail at base of steps (4960 feet), turn right onto trail
19	Turkey Spring Gap (4400 feet)
20	Good Enough Gap (4240 feet)
20.4	Sassafras Gap (4040 feet)
21.4	Johnson Gap (4000 feet)
23.5	Rich Gap (3600 feet)
26.3	Forest Road 1206 (3200 feet), turn right onto road
27.5	Bradley Creek Trail (2800 feet), cross creek and go left
30.5	Pea Branch (2500 feet), bear right upstream
32.5	South Mills River (2400 feet), cross river and turn right
33.5	Turkey Pen Gap parking area (2640 feet)

Suggested Camps Based on Different Trekking Itineraries

Night	<10 mpd	10 mpd	>10 mpd
One	8 miles - Wolf Ford	13 miles - Pink Beds	15 miles - Near Poplar Creek on MST
Two	15 miles - Near Poplar Creek on MST	20 miles - Sassafras Gap	
Three	20 miles - Sassafras Gap		
Four	29 miles - Bradley Creek Reservoir		

Art Loeb Trail (NC)

Difficulty:	Strenuous
Distance:	30 miles
Elevation gain:	9700 feet
Best season:	March through November
Recommended itinerary:	4 days (less than 10 miles per day)
Water availability:	There are few water sources on the ridgelines although springs and creeks are enough to keep your bottles full through dry stretches. Take advantage of water sources and fill bottles.
Logistics:	The trail is officially broken down into four sections as a reference for day hikers. Since the traditional sections are not necessarily convenient to campsites, this itinerary does not stick to the traditional four sections. A four-day thru-hike is recommended; many of the views are the finest in the area and there are several worthy spur trails. The trail is marked by a blue blaze.
Jurisdictions:	Blue Ridge Parkway (828-271-4779) and Pisgah Ranger District (828-877-3265), Pisgah National Forest
Maps:	National Geographic Trails Illustrated 780, *Pisgah Ranger District*; USGS Pisgah Forest and Cruso, and a small portion of Sams Knob and Waynesville.
Trail location:	The southern terminus of the trail begins near the Davidson River Campground on US Route 276, 1.3 miles from the junction with US 276/64 and North Carolina Route 280 in Brevard, and 0.2 mile south of the Pisgah District Ranger Station. Turn left toward the campground and park in the lot to the left before the bridge. The northern terminus is at the Daniel Boone Boy Scout Camp off US Route 215, 4 miles south of Bethel. Notify camp staff that you are leaving a car.

The plaque mounted on the broad summit of Black Balsam Knob in the Pisgah National Forest is easy to miss. At 6214 feet, the small monument is located at the highest point on the Art Loeb Trail. The plaque has an uncomplicated map of the trail and a few words about the man whose name the trail bears. While many hikers and visitors to the forest are familiar with the trail and the grand views of the Blue Ridge Mountains along its path, few are aware of the memory and legacy of the

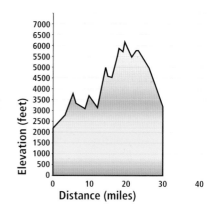

man it honors. Unbeknownst to most hikers, Art Loeb (1914–1968) played a major role in exploring new areas, maintaining trails, and reverently promoting his favorite pastime. A premiere thru-hike in North Carolina, this national recreation trail is a fitting tribute to Loeb. The trail traverses from south to north nearly the entire length of the Pisgah Ranger District.

DAY ONE 7.8 + miles 2600 feet

From the parking lot on the Davidson River, hike downstream and cross the river on the suspended bridge. The trail climbs to High Knob, sticking to ridgelines for most of the rest of the trek. The trail leads over several knobs of the Shut-In Ridge toward the crest of the Pisgah range.

Near the trail's southern terminus at the Davidson River, the sounds of the town of Brevard are audible: car horns, truck gears grinding, and once the whistle at the now-closed Ecusta paper plant. Until his untimely death of a brain tumor at the age of 54, Loeb was general manager of the plant. An unlikely occupation for a conservationist, Loeb didn't begin hiking until he suffered a serious heart attack in his midforties. As part of his recovery, Loeb began walking. His walks took him to the woods, where he discovered his delight in being outdoors.

He joined the Carolina Mountain Club (CMC) and every weekend explored new trails or hiked his favorites. One of Loeb's favorite ongoing projects was linking scattered sections of hiking trails from the Davidson River to Cold Mountain. Loeb never finished the project. In 1968 he was diagnosed with brain cancer and died shortly after. The CMC and the U.S. Forest Service decided to finish the trail in 1969 and name it in his honor.

Once on the ridge, cross a gravel road at Joel Branch, there is water to the right of the trail down the gravel road. Continue past the North Slope Ridge Trail just north of Stony Knob and summit the first of two mountains named Chestnut on the hike (there are also two Deep Gaps). Mountain laurel, rhododendron, poplars, and oaks shade the trail. Also be aware of the occasional American chestnut sprout.

Trio of hikers on Black Balsam

The sides of the long (5 to 10 inches) narrow leaf have a jagged pattern, like shark teeth. Disease wiped out the once mighty giants of the southern Appalachians by the 1940s, although roots still sprout before they too perish.

Drop into Catpen Gap, then arrive in Cat Gap at mile 6.3 and the intersection of several trails. The Cat Gap Loop Trail meets at Cat Gap with both trails on the right leading to the Davidson River fish hatchery. A third trail on the left descends to King Creek. Follow the blazes and the uphill ridge trail over a small knob then descend to Sandy Gap. Here a steep spur trail leads to the summit of Cedar Rock, a 4000-foot knob flanked by several giant faces of granite. The Cedar Rock Summit Trail leads to fabulous views of Pilot Mountain and the Pisgah Crest and rejoins the Art Loeb in Butter Gap.

The Art Loeb Trail goes left from Sandy Gap, skirting the granite east face of Cedar Rock to a shelter just south of Butter Gap. (Butter Gap is marked incorrectly on USGS quads—it is the next gap to the west of its label.) If you choose to summit, there are two scrambles down granite slabs on the opposite side of the mountain. The second, Coffee Break Ledge, is sketchy with a large pack, especially when wet. Both routes arrive at Butter Gap at mile 8.8 (the summit trail roughly cuts the distance in half).

Camping in the shelter below Butter Gap is not recommended. The area is heavily impacted and favored by local summer camps and wilderness programs. Instead, sleep in an unnamed gap less than half a mile past Sandy Gap at the base of Cedar Rock's east face. Water is farther down the trail and the traffic is minimal.

DAY TWO   7+ miles   2900 feet
Butter Gap is the meeting place of several trail junctions. To the north, the Grogan Creek trail leads down to the fish hatchery via Picklesimer Fields. To the east is the

W
N
S
E

Black
Balsam
Knob

Farlow
Gap

Pilot
Mountain **2**

Sassafras
Knob

Shuck Ridge

FS 816

Tennent
Mountain

Deep
Gap

FS 229

Gloucester
Gap

Rich
Mountain

FS 475

Blue Ridge Parkway

Pisgah Parkway

Pisgah

National

Forest

Davidson River

Chestnut
Mountain

FS 471

Butter
Gap

Cedar Rock
Mountain

1

Looking
Glass
Rock

Cat Gap

FS 475

276

Chestnut
Knob

Davidson
River
Campground

Pisgah
District
Ranger
Station

T P

64 280

276

Brevard

280

64

Daniel Boone
Boy Scout Camp

P T

Cold Mountain

Shining
Rock

Shining

Rock

Wilderness

estor
Gap

spur trail
to Cold Mountain

Ridge

Blue

276

Ridge

276

Parkway

Pink Beds

Mount
Pisgah

Pisgah

National

Forest

Autumn colors on Cedar Rock Mountain

Cedar Rock Summit Trail and a road grade that contours to a rock climbing area. To the left, the Art Loeb Trail splits between two road grades. The road on the right contours and meets up again at Low Gap (also known as Margerine Gap). Follow the Art Loeb Trail as it goes east on the ridge.

At Low Gap, ignore the road grades again—choose the single track up the ridge. Eventually arrive at several steep switchbacks to the forested top of Chestnut Mountain. The descent from Chestnut is more gradual, eventually passing a logged area on the right then immediately climbing to Forest Road 471. Cross the road to a set of steps, and quickly rise and fall over Rich Mountain to Gloucester Gap at mile 12.2 and the intersection of Forest Road 471 and Forest Road 475. Beyond Gloucester Gap, FS 471 becomes FS 229. The gap is considered the end of section one. There are no campsites at the intersection for thru-hikers, however.

From here, begin a heart-pounding 2-mile climb up switchbacks to the narrow summit of Pilot Mountain (5020 ft) at mile 14.4. The trail gets steeper and the switchbacks more frequent near the top. It's worth it—there are brilliant 360-degree views from the top.

Descend to Deep Gap at mile 15 and the site of a shelter with a spring nearby. Follow the road grade from the gap to the shelter or choose among several established camp areas in Deep Gap. Forest Road 229, the old Gloucester Lumber Company railroad terminates just shy of Deep Gap, so visitors are common.

DAY THREE   6+ miles   2500 feet
From Deep Gap, climb over Sassafras Knob to Farlow Gap and the junction of the Farlow Gap Trail. Continue up Shuck Ridge and notice the transition from hardwood to the spruce and fir forests common at higher elevations. Intersect with the Blue Ridge Parkway at mile 17.6 and look left across the road for the trail's continuation.

Climb steadily from the Parkway to the Pisgah Ledges, a relatively flat ridgeline at 6000 feet. Merge with the Mountains-to-Sea Trail on Silvermine Bald at mile 18. The two trails overlap until deviating at paved Forest Road 816 at mile 19.1. The area around Black Balsam Road (FR 816) is one of the most popular in the Pisgah Ranger District, and the most heavily traveled section of the Art Loeb Trail—visitors are not obligated to hike up 4000 feet, the Blue Ridge Parkway brings them right there. It's obvious why Mr. Loeb's favorite section of trail is hard to resist. It's among the most striking areas in the region with unmatched scenery from its 6000-foot peaks.

Spending the night somewhere in the area is a must. Of course, inclement weather days are an exception. There are dozens of camping options beginning around Silvermine Bald and into the Shining Rock Wilderness. Again, depending on the season and the weather, other campers are typical, especially near the road.

Cross Forest Road 816 and bear left onto the Art Loeb. The Mountains-to-Sea Trail heads down to the right toward Graveyard Fields. After a small stand of trees, the Art Loeb gently climbs through treeless, grassy terrain to the broad top of Black Balsam. A maze of trails crisscrosses the top—take care to stay on the main trail and visit the Art Loeb Plaque on top, where there are exceptional views of the Pisgah National Forest in every direction.

In fact, there is nary a place for the next several miles where there are not drop-dead views. This wasn't always the case. In the 1920s, thousands of acres were burned in a massive wildfire ignited by railroad sparks. The intense fire destroyed the forest and consumed layers of organic soil, leaving the grassy balds behind.

All trails on Black Balsam lead toward Tennent Mountain, the next obvious peak to the north. Once on Tennent, drop to a gap then over a small knob to Ivestor Gap at mile 21.5. A small knob has several nice camp spots shielded by trees. Ivestor Gap is the boundary of the Shining Rock Wilderness. The gap is the intersection of several old road and rail grades. East of the gap, a rail grade, the Graveyard Ridge Trail, switchbacks down to a stream. On the west, a grade runs from Shining Rock to the north and south to a parking area at the end of the pavement on Forest Road 816.

DAY FOUR 8+ miles 1700 feet

At Ivestor Gap, the trail holds steady above 5000 feet contouring to the right around Grassy Cove Top. The 18,000-acre Shining Rock Wilderness is the largest wilderness in North Carolina. Named for the strip of white quartz beyond Shining Rock Gap at mile 23.3, easy access leaves solitude sometimes elusive, but it's still quite beautiful. Pass a water source right of the trail beyond Flower Gap. Shining Rock Gap would be a stellar place to camp if not for the impact from frequent campers. A short spur trail from the gap leads to the chunk of shiny quartz that gives the area its name and is a worthy side trip of less than half a mile.

The Art Loeb Trail heads north from Shining Rock Gap. Pass a trail on the right that leads to Dog Loser Knob and continue to Crawford Creek Gap, over Stairs Mountain and then through the Narrows to Deep Gap. From Deep Gap, a spur heads north less than 2 miles to Cold Mountain. The original Art Loeb Trail plans involved the summit of Cold Mountain. In the spirit of Art, summit the 6030-foot peak. The Art Loeb Trail makes a sharp left-hand turn and descends nearly 3000 feet to the trail's terminus at the Daniel Boone Boy Scout Camp.

A band of rock on Black Balsam

Trail Summary and Mileage Estimates

0	Davidson River (2200 feet), hike downstream and cross the swinging bridge
3.3	Neil Gap (2800 feet), continue on Art Loeb
5.5	Chestnut Knob (3800 feet), continue on Art Loeb
6.3	Cat Gap (3350 feet), continue on Art Loeb
8.8	Butter Gap (3100 feet), turn left up ridge on Art Loeb
9.9	Chestnut Mountain (3700 feet)
12.2	Gloucester Gap (3150 feet), cross Forest Road 475, continue up ridge
14.4	Pilot Mountain (5020 feet), continue on Art Loeb
15.2	Deep Gap (4600 feet), continue on Art Loeb
16.1	Farlow Gap (4550 feet), continue on Art Loeb
17.6	Blue Ridge Parkway (5550 feet), cross Parkway to continue on Art Loeb
18	Merge with Mountains-to-Sea Trail on Silvermine Bald (5900 feet)
19.1	Forest Road 816 (5750 feet), cross road and bear left
19.6	Black Balsam Knob (6200 feet), stay on Art Loeb
21.5	Ivestor Gap (5500 feet), continue on Art Loeb
22.7	Flower Gap (5800 feet), continue on Art Loeb
23.3	Shining Rock Gap (5800 feet), continue on Art Loeb
23.9	Crawford Creek Gap (5800 feet), continue on Art Loeb
26.2	Deep Gap (5000 feet), go left still on Art Loeb
30	Trail turns to left to descend to Daniel Boone Boy Scout Camp (3200 feet)

Suggested Camps Based on Different Trekking Itineraries

Night	<10 mpd	10 mpd	>10 mpd
One	7.8 miles - East face of Cedar Rock	8.8 miles - Butter Gap	15.2 miles - Deep Gap
Two	15.2 miles - Deep Gap	21.5 miles - Ivestor Gap	
Three	21.5 miles - Ivestor Gap		

Mountains-to-Sea Trail— Pisgah Crest (NC)

Difficulty:	Strenuous (very strenuous if done in reverse)
Distance:	40 miles
Elevation gain:	8200 feet
Best season:	April through November
Recommended itinerary:	3 days (10–20 miles per day)
Water availability:	Long sections of abundant water mixed with long dry sections. Water is scarce along sections of trail on the ridge. Take advantage of water sources to keep a full tank. All creeks south of the Blue Ridge Parkway drain into the French Broad River—the terminus of this trek.
Logistics:	This section of the Mountains-to-Sea Trail (MST) is extremely well marked by signposts and white dots. The trail generally parallels the Blue Ridge Parkway and crosses the road often. Several trail sections stray from sight and sound of the Parkway, however. The road gives hikers many options for shuttles and shorter versions of the trek. Campsites along the trail are extremely scarce due to camping restrictions. We suggest going from North Carolina Route 215 to the French Broad River. The opposite direction is also recommended, although it's more strenuous. Foot Travel in Black Mountain offers a shuttle service (*www.bighike.com* or 866-BIGHIKE).
Jurisdictions:	Blue Ridge Parkway (828-271-4779) and Pisgah Ranger District (828-877-3665), Pisgah National Forest. No permits required, but camping is prohibited on park service property, and much of the trail is within the boundary. The restriction significantly limits camping options, so plan accordingly.
Maps:	National Geographic Trails Illustrated 780, *Pisgah Ranger District*; USGS Shining Rock, Cruso, Dunsmore, and Skylands

Trail location: Drive Interstate 26 to Asheville and take exit 33 (old exit 2). Turn south onto North Carolina Route 191 and follow signs to the Blue Ridge Parkway. The trail terminus is along the entrance ramp. Park at your own risk along the French Broad River on NC 191 in a gravel parking area just north of the Parkway. To start the hike, drive south on the Parkway for approximately 30 miles and go north toward Canton on North Carolina 215. Soon, look for a gravel parking area on the left side of the road. The well-marked intersection of the Mountains-to-Sea Trail is just beyond the parking area on the right.

At the crest of the Pisgah mountain range is Asheville's most recognizable peak, Mount Pisgah. The communications tower perched on its summit knob at 5712 feet is an unmistakable landmark and near the midpoint of this trek. The mountain was once part of George Vanderbilt's sprawling Victorian-era estate. The crest of the Pisgah range is not difficult to access, since the Blue Ridge Parkway straddles

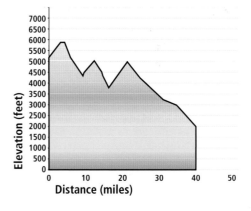

its skyline. Although close to the asphalt, this 40-mile section of the Mountains-to-Sea Trail gives a much more intimate look at this strikingly beautiful section of mountains than is possible from behind a windshield.

DAY ONE   9+ miles   1200 feet

Beech Gap, at the intersection of North Carolina 215 and the Blue Ridge Parkway, roughly separates two ranges of the Blue Ridge Mountains: the Balsam Mountains and the Pisgah Range. From the Gap, the Balsam Ridge winds to the northwest. To the northeast is the Pisgah Range.

The trailhead on North Carolina 215, marked by a wood post with a hiker blaze and the Mountains-to-Sea emblem, is just north of the Parkway. From the trailhead ascend several hundred feet to the Pisgah Ledges leveling out at 6000 feet. Just past Chestnut Bald, on Silvermine Bald are spectacular views of the mammoth granite domes of the Pisgah National Forest with the giant Looking Glass on the left and the more humble John Rock and the multiple faces of Cedar Rock to the right.

110

276

215

Pigeon River

276

N

W   E

S

Pisgah

National

Forest

Moun
Pisga

Little Pisga
Mounta

Buck
Springs
Gap

Pisgah
Inn

Shining

Rock

Wilderness

Yellowstone Prong

Pisgah Crest

Pink
Beds

Green
Knob

276

215

Tennent
Mountain

Black
Balsam
Knob

Graveyard
Fields

P

FS 816

B l u e   R i d g e   P a r k w a y

Looking Glass
Rock

To
Brevard

T P

151

191

To Asheville

T

MST

P

Bent Creek

Experimental

Forest

Ferrin
Knob

3

Bent
Creek
Gap

Parkway

151

Blue   Ridge

Pisgah Crest

Pisgah

National

Forest

191

280

280

Looking Glass Rock

At mile 3.2, the Art Loeb Trail and the MST form the same path on Silvermine Bald. The alternate MST descends Shuck Ridge leaving the Pisgah Crest for many miles. Stay left on what is considered the primary MST to its intersection with Black Balsam Road (Forest Road 816) at mile 4.3. Here, the MST and Art Loeb Trail diverge. The area to the north is among the most spectacular in North Carolina with several 6000-foot mountain balds. The treeless, craggy mountains look more like a scene in Scotland than the southern Appalachians. Make a short diversion to the top of Black Balsam via the Art Loeb Trail for superb views and drop-dead sunsets—the broad summit marked with a plaque is less than a mile.

Cross the road and stay right on the MST descending through an open forest. At mile 5.9 reach Graveyard Gap at 5200 feet between Black Balsam and Graveyard Ridge and the intersection of several trails, including an old railroad grade. The railroad had several semipermanent cars fashioned to house families that logged and mined the area a century ago. Bear left at the trail sign and walk on the north side of Graveyard Ridge above a remote drainage flanked by Black Balsam and Tennent Mountain. For the next few miles, the trail strays from the Parkway, although motorcycles, recreational vehicles, and cars are never far.

Soon the dominant sound is rushing water. Pass several trail intersections and contour around a small knob winding down a splendid section of trail through deciduous trees to the Yellowstone Prong of the East Fork of the Pigeon. The trail crosses the Prong on a bridge at mile 9.3 below Skinny Dip Falls and a premiere swimming hole. There are several well-established campsites along the north side of the creek among boulders and shady trees.

DAY TWO 9+ miles 2100 feet

For the next 5 miles the MST stays near the Parkway on the crest of the ridge. From the Yellowstone Prong, hike uphill a short distance to the road. Arrive at a short spur to the right leading to a Parkway clearing with views of Looking Glass Rock. The giant chunk of granite is a favorite among climbers. In view is the Nose area of the rock, the site of the first technical ascent of Looking Glass in the 1960s.

Stay on the MST and climb the ridge to the top of Chestnut Knob (4720 feet) at mile 10.5, drop again and begin a more demanding climb to the grassy top of Green Knob (5050 feet) at mile 13.5. The narrow summit has a craggy fin and is covered in grass. There are good views along this section of the trail toward the fire tower on Frying Pan Knob and the communications tower on Mount Pisgah.

Switchback down Green Knob and cross the Parkway at Pigeon Gap then descend and cross US Route 276. The trail leaves the spine of the Pisgah Range for several miles until its return at the Pisgah Inn. Instead of following the crest, the Buck Springs section of trail wraps around short, fingerlike ridges, each separated by small creeks. At mile 16.3, pass the Buck Springs Trail at 3800 feet elevation. Water is plentiful and the trail generally stays close to the 4000-foot contour line. There is one established campsite on a ridge past Poplar Creek. Use this campsite or consider the Mount Pisgah camping area across the Blue Ridge Parkway from the Pisgah Inn.

Harrision Shull on the Mountains-to-Sea Trail

DAY THREE   21+ miles   4900 feet

It is possible to make this a shorter day. Consider camping at the Mount Pisgah campground to knock a couple of miles off the day. The next available campsite is just beyond Bent Creek Gap at mile 31.1.

The stiff task of hiking back to the Parkway becomes apparent with occasional views of the Pisgah Inn above. The trail climbs, sometimes switching back, nearly 1000 feet over 2 miles to the Mount Pisgah complex. At the inn are all the amenities a hiker could want: bathrooms, a restaurant, a pay phone, and overnight accommodations. Plan ahead to reserve a room and dinner table (828-235-8228) or stay in the campground managed by the Blue Ridge Parkway (sites are $12 and available on a first come, first served basis). The campsite and the inn are open seasonally from April until October.

The development of the area is a legacy of the former landowner, George Vanderbilt. Heir to a fortune, Vanderbilt graded a path at the turn of the twentieth century to shuttle guests from his Asheville estate to his Buck Springs hunting lodge located in Buck Springs Gap just beyond the inn along the MST. The lodge was dismantled by the park service several decades ago. Vanderbilt's estate has the largest private residence in the United States and is Asheville's marquee tourist attraction. Completed in 1895, the house was the centerpiece of an estate that once included Mount Pisgah and more than 100,000 acres. Thanks to the Vanderbilts, a large chunk of the terrain surrounding Asheville is in the public domain. In 1914, the family sold 87,000 acres of their estate to become part of the Pisgah National Forest, established in 1916.

The MST cuts through the Pisgah Inn parking lot and reenters the forest on

Shed on top of Mount Pisgah

The MST on Green Knob

the other side of the lot at a trail sign. Continue on the relatively flat ridge past two trailheads to the right. After the second trailhead arrive in Buck Springs Gap—the site of the lodge. Climb over a small knob then into a paved parking area at an overlook and sign marking the terminus of the Shut-In Trail—a trail carved by Vanderbilt from his estate to the lodge. The original grade is mostly gone and it's now a portion of the MST. The 17.8-mile Shut-In section follows the Pisgah Ridge over several knobs, occasionally contouring on century-old stone embankments draped by dense undergrowth. From the Mount Pisgah parking area to the French Broad River, the trail loses more than 5000 cumulative feet in elevation, although expect some climbing.

Mandatory side trail: From the Shut-In Trail sign, cut through the parking lot to the Mount Pisgah trailhead. The 1.5-mile, must-do side trip climbs to the communications tower on Mount Pisgah with excellent views of the forest.

Stay on the MST, following the ridge. Trail signs and mile markers are abundant on this section as the trail crosses the Parkway and cuts through several parking areas with lookouts. Be aware that water is relatively scarce until you reach Bent Creek Gap, so keep bottles full. As usual, navigation along the well-marked trail is straightforward, so enjoy the views and the forest. Typically the best views (and the least solitude) are found at overlooks on the Parkway.

From the Shut-In Trail sign, climb over Little Pisgah Mountain and begin a steep hike down to Elk Pasture Gap and the meeting of North Carolina Route 151 with the Parkway at mile 24.8. Cross the Parkway and contour on an old road grade. For the next several miles the hiking is casual until Beaver Dam Gap. From the Beaver Dam parking area, climb 450 feet up the ridge to the top of Ferrin Knob (4000 feet), once the site of an old fire tower. The Parkway passes through a series of three tunnels before meeting the MST again in Bent Creek Gap. Cross the gravel road linking the Bent Creek Experimental Forest with the Mills River Recreation Area. Not long past the gravel road on the MST look left for a small campsite on a ridge near the trail. Water is 200 feet past the campsite. This is the final resting place until the Holiday Inn in Asheville.

Continue through unremarkable, but pretty forest on the way to the French Broad River valley. The trail contours through the Bent Creek Experimental Forest. Climb Grassy Knob, then go through Sleepy Gap and pass the Sleepy Gap Trail that descends to the experimental forest. Eventually, the French Broad River comes into view and the end is near. Cross through a fenced area that is the North Carolina Arboretum and arrive at the entrance ramp to the Parkway and the terminus of the Shut-In Trail. If you choose to continue on the MST, the trail crosses the river on the roadway bridge and regains the forest on the other side.

Trail Summary and Mileage Estimates

0	Mountains-to-Sea trailhead at NC 215 (5200 feet)
3.2	MST merges with Art Loeb Trail (5900 feet), stay left on primary MST
4.3	Intersect Forest Road 816 (5900 feet), stay right on MST
5.9	Graveyard Ridge Trail (5200 feet), stay left on MST
9.3	Yellowstone Prong of the East Fork of the Pigeon (4350 feet), cross creek on bridge
9.6	200-yard spur trail to Looking Glass Rock Overlook (4500 feet)
12.4	Green Knob (5050 feet)
14.4	Pigeon Gap (4530 feet), cross Blue Ridge Parkway
14.7	NC 276 (4350 feet), cross highway
16.3	Buck Springs junction (3800 feet), go straight
21.3	Mount Pisgah/Shut-In Trail terminus (5000 feet), straight on MST
24.8	NC 151 at Elk Pasture Gap (4250 feet), cross Blue Ridge Parkway and contour on old road
29.2	Beaver Dam Gap (3550 feet)
31.1	Bent Creek Gap (3250 feet), cross gravel road
34.7	Sleepy Gap (3000 feet)
40	NC 191 and French Broad River (2000 feet)

Suggested Camps Based on Different Trekking Itineraries

Night	>10 mpd	10 mpd
One	9.3 miles - Yellowstone Prong	9.3 miles - Yellowstone Prong
Two	21.3 miles - Mount Pisgah Campground	21.3 miles - Mount Pisgah Campground
Three		31.1 miles - Just past Bent Creek Gap

Mountains-to-Sea Trail— Asheville to Mount Mitchell (NC)

Difficulty:	Very strenuous
Distance:	34 miles
Elevation gain:	12,200 feet
Best season:	April through November. Perfect summer hike to escape summer dog days. The Blue Ridge Parkway, which provides the primary shuttle access to Mount Mitchell from Asheville, is subject to closures due to ice and snow in the winter. Call the Blue Ridge Parkway info line for updated status (828-298-0398). The Mount Mitchell State Park is open year-round.
Recommended itinerary:	3 days (10–20 miles per day)
Water availability:	Carry plenty of water; sources are infrequent on the high ridgelines.
Logistics:	It is necessary to run a shuttle from Mount Mitchell. Since this section of the Mountains-to-Sea Trail parallels the Blue Ridge Parkway (BRP), it is possible to vary the length of this hike. Exit and entry to the Mount Mitchell parking area is restricted when the park is closed—hours vary depending on the season. Register your car at the park office. Overnight parking is permitted in the lower parking area and at the Folk Art Center. If parking elsewhere on the Parkway, notify them that you plan to leave a vehicle. The MST is blazed throughout with a white dot. Foot Travel in Black Mountain offers a shuttle service (*www.bighike.com* or 866-BIGHIKE).
Jurisdictions:	Blue Ridge Parkway (828-271-4779); Mount Mitchell State Park (828-675-4611); and Appalachian Ranger District (828-622-3202), Pisgah National Forest. No permits are required, but camping is prohibited on

Park Service property and in the state park, barring a small car camping area that is typically full. Much of the trail is within the Park Service boundary. The restrictions limit camping options, so plan accordingly.

Maps: USGS Mount Mitchell, Montreat, Craggy Pinnacle, Oteen, and Asheville; USFS South Toe River, Mount Mitchell, and Big Ivy Trails

Trail location: Begin the hike at the Folk Art Center on the Blue Ridge Parkway in Asheville. The Folk Art Center is at mile marker 382 on the Blue Ridge Parkway. Access the Parkway from US Route 70, then go north to the center parking area. The entrance to Mount Mitchell State Park, the trek's end, is 0.6 mile past mile marker 356. Turn left from the Parkway onto North Carolina Route 128 and drive to the parking lot, just shy of the summit.

From the Asheville city limits, the Blue Ridge Mountains surge impressively to the northeast, eventually cresting at the Black Mountains and their apex, Mount Mitchell—the highest point east of the Rockies. Connecting the Black Mountains and the city of Asheville are the Great Craggy Mountains. The Craggy spine rises from 3000 feet to more than 6000, spanning a wide range of microclimates and forests that include several infrequently traveled sections of trail. Along the way

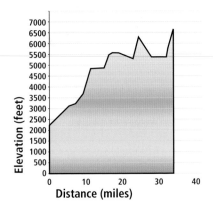

are savory views of the Swannanoa Valley and the Burnett Reservoir with some of the finest photo opportunities in the area. While the drive from Asheville to Mount Mitchell via the Parkway is less than an hour drive, the hike up will challenge even the fittest backpackers.

DAY ONE 17+ miles 7000 feet

Before starting your trek, visit the Folk Art Center featuring traditional and contemporary crafts of the Appalachians. Because of the Parkway's access to the Mountains-to-Sea Trail (MST), hikers can begin this trek in several locations for a shorter or longer first day. At the center parking lot, look for a monument honoring Arch Nichols, one of the area's trail visionaries. An employee of the Forest Service, Nichols was a lively participant in creating new trails in the area, including the Art Loeb Trail and the MST. One of his accomplishments was linking trails from Mount Pisgah to Mount Mitchell.

View from Potato Knob (Photo by Ben Walters)

Alternative start: Consider beginning this trek closer to the first campsite. Start at Craven Gap where Town Mountain Road reaches the Parkway. There is a small parking area at the trailhead. The Parkway authority suggest notifying them if you plan to leave a vehicle overnight. Starting at Craven Gap will shorten the first day by 5.4 miles, taking some of the edge off of the otherwise 7000-foot-gain day.

A buffer of forest insulates the Blue Ridge Parkway and the MST from development within the city limits. The Folk Art Center is on the east side of town, although it is possible to include a longer section of trail through Asheville. From the Folk Art Center, the MST rolls up and down, sometimes contouring, eventually gaining a ridge. Not long after leaving the Folk Art Center, cross to the east side of the Parkway and begin a pleasant walk along a ridge system. From this vantage, it is obvious that Asheville's suburban growth is not deterred by its rugged geography, as houses have crept up the coves and over the ridgelines surrounding the town proper. On the left, get a bird's eye view of old and new development in Haw

Pisgah

National

Forest

FS 63

Craggy
Pinnacl

1

Potato
Gap

Bee
Tree
Gap

Lane
Pinnacle

Parkway

Great Craggy Mountains

Craggy
Garden
Visitor
Center

Bull
Mountain

Rattlesnake
Lodge

Ox Creek
Road

Ridge

Parking

Craven
Gap

Blue

Town Mountain Road

Haw
Creek
Valley

Swannanoa

River

Asheville

Folk Art
Center

T
P

70

40

Mount Mitchell
State Park

Mount Mitchell

Black Mountains

Camp Alice

Pisgah

Balsam Gap

Great Craggy Mountains

Blackstock Knob

Clingmans Peak

128

National

Forest

Blue Ridge

Pisgah

National

Forest

Parkway

Graybeard Mountain

Burnett Reservoir

Montreat

Black Mountain

70

70

40

40

40

70

Creek Valley and trophy homes along Town Mountain Road. Thankfully, the establishment of the Parkway restricted development on the ridge you are walking.

Climb a small knob with several switchbacks, descending slightly to a portion of trail that contours below the Parkway. The next couple of miles of trail are a pleasant surprise, due in part to a few mammoth poplars and oaks towering above the trail. It's surprising to find such a mature forest so close to the city limits. Look for water in this section of trail to fill your bottle from small seeps.

At mile 5.4, cross the Parkway at Craven Gap. There is a small gravel parking lot and a good alternative to beginning the hike here, closer to the first campsite. In the winter, the Parkway is often closed beyond Craven Gap. From the Gap, begin the steady ascent up the Great Craggy Mountains. Soon cross Ox Creek Road and regain the MST. Stay right in Bull Gap and switchback up Bull Mountain. Portions of the trail follow an old wagon road—the legacy of Dr. Chase Ambler. The wealthy doctor carved the road to reach his summer home, Rattlesnake Lodge, 2.1 miles farther up the trail. Ambler was also a forerunner of trail development in the area, helping establish the southern chapter of the Appalachian Mountain Club, Mount Mitchell State Park, and dozens of miles of trail.

At mile 9.3 arrive at the former site of Rattlesnake Lodge. Ambler sold the property in 1920, and the lodge burned to the ground in 1926. A trailside sign displays the resort's layout and several of the remnants are obvious, such as an old pool. It takes some imagination to grasp the ambiance of the old estate—less than a hundred years is plenty of time for the voracious Appalachian vegetation

Weathered tree near Craggy Pinnacle

to swallow even the grandest castle. There are several good spots here for water. Although others have obviously camped on level spots in this area, overnight stays are prohibited.

Just beyond the Ambler estate, the trail crosses a creek and then switchbacks and gradually ascends to a gap. Beyond the gap is a section of trail that is seldom used by day hikers. Nevertheless, the Carolina Mountain Club takes care to keep the trail tidy. At Rich Knob stay right at the fork on the ridge and parallel the rusty, barbed wire fence. To the left is the city of Woodfin's watershed. Reach the first of many superb views on Lane Pinnacle. From here, look down at the Burnett Reservoir (which supplies water to Asheville) and toward Graybeard Mountain—on the ridge crest beyond the reservoir.

Make no mistake where the name Craggy comes from: Between Rich Knob and Lane Pinnacle, are several interesting formations of exposed rock to explore, with perches from which to take photos. Descend Lane Pinnacle and merge with the Parkway in Potato Gap, then reenter the forest, contouring and then climbing above the Parkway. The trail turns right at the Snowball Trail above Bee Tree Gap.

Cross the access road to the Craggy Gardens Picnic Area in Bee Tree Gap at mile 15.1. Pass the picnic area on your left (with eighty-six tables and comfort stations), and walk through a stand of birch.

Easy access to Craggy Gardens and its heath balds attract hoards of visitors to this gorgeous area. Arrive at a pavilion (5630 feet) built by the Civilian Conservation Corps and surrounded by mountain shrubs. There are good views of the valleys and mountains to the north and south. June and July are an ideal time to visit this area when wildflowers such as flame azalea, violets, and may apples are in bloom long after they have disappeared at lower elevations.

In 0.25 mile the MST makes a sharp left turn onto the Douglass Falls Trail at mile 16.4. No worries if you miss the trail—the Craggy Gardens Visitor Center is just a few steps beyond the turn. Stop here for water and a pit stop. From here, the MST contours around Craggy Pinnacle, temporarily leaving the Parkway boundary. Near a rock outcrop on the north side of Craggy Pinnacle, look for a grassy area in national forest territory with a few flat spots to stay for the night. Carry your water in from the visitor center, or look for several small streams about a mile beyond the campsite before the Parkway.

DAY TWO   10+ miles   3500 feet

Wrap around Craggy Pinnacle to climb back to the Parkway, eventually crossing the road. After crossing the Parkway, the walking traffic on the MST is denser, although there are still several sections beyond the reach of many walkers. From Bullhead Gap to the end of the Great Craggies are dozens of views and some of the finest hiking on the trek, although not entirely casual. From here, the remainder of the hike rises and falls but never dips below 5000 feet.

In this section, the MST crosses through several parking areas with remarkable overlooks and settings for reliable photo compositions in every season. Here, the forests vary from low bushes to birch stands, hawthorns, and conifers.

Consider short stops at the Glassmine Falls and Graybeard Overlooks. From the Graybeard Overlook, climb over Bullhead Mountain and then to the Glassmine Falls Overlook. Climb again, this time over Walker Knob and cross the Parkway in Balsam Gap. Before Balsam Gap, look for seeps of water but expect a dry section until approaching the road to Mount Mitchell.

From the parking area in Balsam Gap, Big Butt Trail is on the left, an old road heads up the middle, and the MST climbs right to Blackstock Knob (6320 feet). The climb up the knob is the biggest of the day. Switchback through a forest of shady conifers. The dark green forest is a surprising contrast to the grasses and bushes of Craggy Gardens.

Eventually reach a long narrow ridge near the top looking for views of Mount Mitchell—Mitchell's summit has an observation tower, not to be confused with the communications towers on Clingmans Peak. From the top of Blackstock at mile 24.5, walk along the forested section of trail with downed trees covered in green moss like shag carpet, eventually descending on rock steps alongside short, overhanging cliffs. Below the dripping boulders are several small streams. Just beyond the water source, the views open on the flanks of Potato Knob. Below Potato Knob take notice of the fine trail work.

Cross a grassy ridge and descend through trees to NC 128—the Mount Mitchell access road at mile 28. Cross and descend stone steps to the trail—which is an old road grade known as the Buncomb Horse Range Trail. The trail to Mount Mitchell goes left, but walk a short distance to the right to a clearing and a suitable spot to camp. Or consider hiking the final 5 miles to the top of Mount Mitchell. Water is in the direction of Mount Mitchell about 200 yards from camp.

DAY THREE   6 miles   1700 feet
The final day is relatively casual compared to the first two days. Follow the MST as it contours along the east side of the Black Mountains ridgeline. The trail follows the original railroad grade built in the early 1900s by logging barons. The trail is easy going to Camp Alice, leveling out at 5700 feet at the base of the spruce and fir forest. Along this section are streams, meadows, and great views of the surrounding mountains.

In the early 1900s, Governor Craig of North Carolina supported a movement to preserve the Black Mountains from further logging. In 1915, an act set in motion the creation of the first state park in North Carolina. For his efforts, Mount Craig (6647 feet) in the Black Mountains is named for the governor. Although

Opposite: Morning on Bull Mountain

much of the forest had been logged or razed by fire by 1915, the act eventually added 1700 acres to the public domain.

Below Mount Mitchell, the trail switchbacks left. To the right, the trail heads toward Commissary Ridge. Bear left and follow the MST to the site of Camp Alice, once a logging outpost and later a tourist resort. Cross Lower Creek, then turn right at the boulder and reenter the forest on a single-track trail through a forest of spruce and fir. The trail climbs steeply toward the summit of Mount Mitchell.

Run into the Mount Mitchell Trail and turn right, eventually merging onto the wide tourist trail to the observation tower on Mount Mitchell and the resting place of Elisha Mitchell, the mountain's namesake who perished not far from the summit more than a century ago. In the summer there is hardly a busier spot in the mountains than the top of Mount Mitchell, in the winter there is not a more remote and desolate place in all of North Carolina than the highest point east of the Rockies.

Trail Summary and Mileage Estimates

0	Folk Art Center (2240 feet), turn right onto MST
5.4	Craven Gap (3130 feet), cross Parkway, turn right onto MST
7.2	Ox Creek Road (3240 feet), cross road and regain MST
9.3	Site of Rattlesnake Lodge (3700 feet)
11.4	Rich Knob (4860 feet), bear right at fork
15.1	Bee Tree Gap (4890 feet), cross paved road and pass picnic area
16.4	Douglass Falls Trail (5500 feet), turn left onto trail
17.4	Campsite at Craggy Pinnacle (5600 feet)
19.1	Graybeard Overlook (5590 feet)
23	Balsam Gap (5320 feet), cross Blue Ridge Parkway, turn right onto MST
24.5	Blackstock Knob (6320 feet)
28	NC 128 (5400 feet), cross road, descend steps, and turn left onto Buncomb Horse Range Trail/MST
32.1	Camp Alice (5400 feet), turn left at switchback
32.5	Cross Lower Creek (5800 feet), turn right onto MST
34	Mount Mitchell (6684 feet)

Suggested Camps Based on Different Trekking Itineraries

Night	10 mpd (begin at Craven Gap)	>10 mpd
One	12 miles - Craggy Pinnacle	17.4 miles - Craggy Pinnacle
Two	22.6 miles - Buncomb Horse Range Trail and NC 128	28 miles - Buncomb Horse Range Trail and NC 128

Mountains-to-Sea Trail— Linville Gorge to Mount Mitchell (NC)

Difficulty:	Very strenuous
Distance:	51.6 miles
Elevation gain:	15,700 feet
Best season:	Year-round; late April is best for wildflowers and early October is best for fall colors. At any time of year, Mount Mitchell is rugged and hosts some of the region's most extreme weather, including powerful thunderstorms, high winds, and cold temperatures.
Recommended itinerary:	5 days (10 miles per day, with time to play and relax)
Water availability:	Springs are few and far between. Plan to carry lots of water and make long side trips (at least 15 minutes each way). It is not advised to drink the water from the Linville or Catawba Rivers as both receive heavy runoff from agriculture, light industry, and busy roads. Use feeder creeks and springs instead.
Logistics:	It is a long but beautiful 1.5-hour drive between the Linville Gorge and Mount Mitchell along back roads and the Blue Ridge Parkway, so plan on leaving a vehicle at Mount Mitchell for getting back to the trailhead. The Mountains-to-Sea Trail (MST) is usu-ally well marked by a white dot about 3 inches in diameter. Two dots stacked atop one another but slightly offset indicates that the trail turns to the left or right. The Catawba and Linville Rivers are usually benign river crossings, but during periods of rain each can swell and become dangerous or impassable. A good portion of this trek follows high ridges exposed to lightning.
Jurisdictions:	Grandfather Ranger District (828-652-2144), Pisgah National Forest; Blue Ridge Parkway (828-271-4779);

and Mount Mitchell State Park (828-675-4611). Camping in the state park is permitted in designated areas only and a fee is required. There is no fee for leaving a shuttle vehicle for an extended period of time, but you must register your vehicle with the park. Camping is not permitted on National Park Service property along the Blue Ridge Parkway.

Maps: USGS Linville Falls, Ashford, Little Switzerland, Marion, Celo, Old Fort, and Mount Mitchell

Trail location: The trailhead at the Table Rock picnic area is located about 1 hour north of Morganton, North Carolina. From exit 105 on Interstate 40 in Morganton, follow North Carolina Route 18 north through town. At the north end of downtown, NC 18 becomes NC 181. Follow NC 181 into the mountains for approximately 24 miles. Turn left at the sign for the Table Rock picnic area onto Gingercake Road, at the bottom of a small hill, and enter the Gingercake Acres community. Follow Gingercake Road for about 0.25 mile and bear left at the Y intersection onto Table Rock Road. In less than a mile, the road turns to gravel and becomes Forest Road 210. Follow Forest Road 210 for approximately 4.5 miles to another sign for the picnic area, and turn right onto Forest Road 210B. In a little more than 0.5 mile, pass the driveway and sign for the North Carolina Outward Bound School. Continue straight for approximately 2 miles to the Table Rock picnic area and trailhead parking. The last stretch of road to the picnic area is closed during the winter, so be ready to park further away and add a couple of extra miles to the beginning of the trek.

To get to Mount Mitchell State Park, continue north on NC 181 past the Table Rock turn to the Blue Ridge Parkway. Head south on the Parkway to milepost 355 and turn right onto North Carolina Route 128. The park entrance is a few miles ahead.

In 1857, Professor Elisha Mitchell perished on the slopes after measuring what is now considered the highest peak east of the Rocky Mountains. Nicknamed Black Dome for the thick crown of Fraser fir that once covered its summit, its claim as the

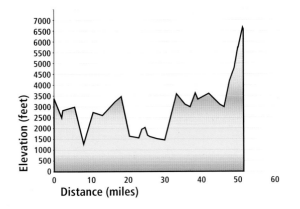

Distance (miles)

highest peak was challenged by a former student of Mitchell's. Renamed Mount Mitchell in the professor's honor, today there is no question of the 6684-foot peak's stature as the tallest. The mountain is among several 6000-foot peaks in the Black Mountains. Due to logging, air pollution, and a non-native pest, the woolly adelgid, the spruce and fir forest is in peril—only skeletons of the ecosystem that Mitchell once knew exist today. This trek links two of North Carolina's most extreme features: Mount Mitchell and the Linville Gorge, a 16-mile-long wilderness gorge shrouded by steep rocky faces.

DAY ONE   9+ miles   2200 feet

Most of the campers near Table Rock are either climbers or hikers exploring the Linville Gorge Wilderness. A rare soul will be following your footsteps to Mount Mitchell.

Find the MST trailhead at the south end of the parking area, just past the pit toilets, and wind your way through the picnic area. For the next 0.5 mile, the trail follows a deeply rutted path along the exposed southeastern rim of the Linville Gorge Wilderness. Stop at any of a number of rocky outcrops for a breathtaking view of the gorge, often called the "Grand Canyon of the East." Look for peregrine falcons, which regularly nest on cliffs in the gorge, broad-winged hawks, and two species of vulture soaring on updrafts created by the high ridges. Scramble up and around the rocky ridgeline and begin a hairy descent through a torrent of fallen trees and loose rocks to Chimney Gap (2509 feet). Along the way, glimpse a rare view of Table Rock's southeastern face. Once in Chimney Gap, consider making the half-hour round trip to Chimney Branch, a reliable water source except during drought.

Leaving Chimney Gap, climb steadily up switches to an unmarked junction with the Cambric Branch Trail (Trail 234), and bear left. As you reach the main ridge of Shortoff Mountain (3161 feet), the MST bends to the southwest and winds its way along smooth trail through mixed hardwood, pines, and mountain laurel. Near the southern end of the ridge, the trail approaches high cliffs with sweeping views of the abrupt end of the Linville Gorge with Lake James in the

Spruce
Pine

19E

N
W E
S

80

South Toe River

Armstrong Creek

Black Mountains

Mount
Mitchell
State
Park

Mount
Mitchell T

Woods Mountain 3

Betsy Ridge

Big Laurel
Mountain

Singecat Ridge

Rattlesnake Branch

128

80

Sams
Knob

Blue Ridge Parkway

P i s g a h   N a t i o n a l   F o r e s t

70

Catawba River

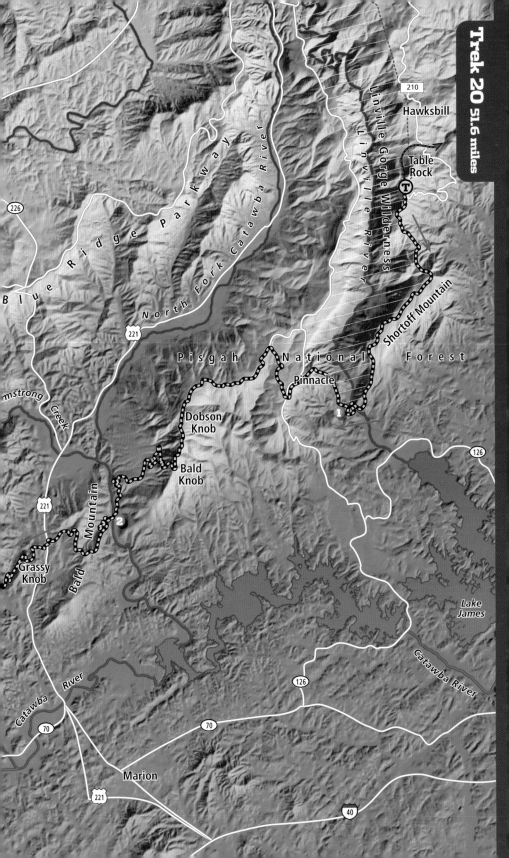

210

Hawksbill

Table
Rock

T

226

B l u e   R i d g e   P a r k w a y

North Fork Catawba River

Linville Gorge Wilderness

Linville River

221

Shortoff Mountain

mstrong

Creek

P i s g a h   N a t i o n a l   F o r e s t

Pinnacle

1

Dobson
Knob

Bald
Knob

126

221

Bald   Mountain

2

Grassy
Knob

Lake
James

Catawba River

River

126

Catawba

221

70

70

Marion

40

Linville Gorge (Photo by Corey Hadden)

distance. Respect seasonal closures of the high cliffs to protect critical nesting habitat for the peregrine falcon by staying on trail.

Drop steadily to the Linville River via a chaotic network of crisscrossing trails further confused by fallen trees. Follow the white dots and you won't go wrong. At the river's edge (1250 feet), head left for camping or, if you plan to cross, turn right and head upriver for a few hundred feet until you come to a fan of large rocks, tumbled into place by thousands of years of floods. The MST crosses the Linville River here, sandwiched between steep terrain to the left and private property to the right. Carefully cross the swift water and stay on the trail, turning left onto a gravel road. Climb the tree-covered bluff overlooking the river and listen for birds not loud enough to overcome the rushing water: belted kingfisher, Louisiana waterthrush, and northern parula. Turn right onto the MST, climb up and over a steep knob, and camp near Sandy Branch.

DAY TWO   12+ miles   3000 feet
Ahead is one of the steepest ascents of the trek: 1200 feet in a mile with only two short switchbacks. Take care climbing to the Pinnacle (2800 feet), and use the

Opposite: Shortoff Mountain and the Linville River (Photo by Corey Hadden)

mountaineering rest step (take a step, then straighten your leg out, locking your knee, for a brief rest) to save your calves for the rest of the day. A small observation platform beneath the Pinnacle has stunning views of Shortoff Mountain and the foothills to the southeast.

Bear right and head down the gravel road to the Pinnacle trailhead, turn left onto the Kistler Memorial Highway, and look for the MST on the right in 0.8 mile. Follow a gently descending path often filled with water toward Yellow Fork and then slightly uphill to Forest Road 106. Turn left on the gravel road and follow it 3.4 miles to its end near Dobson Knob. The MST gradually climbs an old logging road up Dobson Knob, and makes its way up and over a wooded peak on its way to Bald Knob (3495 feet). A spring near Dobson Knob appears in wet years. Just past Bald Knob, a short spur trail doubles back through a boulder field to a perch that closes the chapter on the Linville Gorge to the east, and opens a new one through the North Fork of the Catawba River to the west.

The trail from Bald Knob to the North Fork of the Catawba River has recently been rerouted to avoid private property. Mapping its new path over and through countless microridges and drainages as it descends to the river is still a work in progress. As the trail leaves Bald Knob, it descends a narrow ridge to the south before beginning a long series of switchbacks that will leave even the best map and compass users dizzy from micronavigation. As the trail begins to level out, the forest opens up to reveal its gentle topography and your whereabouts. A beautiful campsite by the North Fork of the Catawba River is close to railroad tracks. For some, this could be a sleepless night. If the thought of sleeping so close to a train is a bit unsettling, make camp before the junction of the MST at the old logging road. Otherwise, hike along the old logging road, cross the tracks, and make camp near the river.

DAY THREE   12+ miles   4100 feet

Cross the North Fork of the Catawba River and pick up the MST on the other side. Have plenty of water since the next reliable source isn't for several miles. Hike through the lush floodplain forest and follow an unimproved road as it ascends a small ridge; the MST breaks off to the right. Climb steadily up the trail choked with mountain laurel toward the top of Bald Mountain, savoring views over your shoulder of Dobson and Bald Knobs. At the top, the MST follows a few gravel roads down and up before turning left into the woods. Be on the lookout for white dots and you will stay on track. Back in the woods, the MST switches its way downhill just south of Graveyard Mountain only to meet up with Forest Road 150. Stay on Forest Road 150 this time, pass a helipad, and come to US Route 221, a busy four-lane road with limited visibility to the north. Cross carefully and regain the MST at the north end of the rest area.

Leaving the rest area, turn left onto the MST and follow a network of trails and old logging roads leading to Grassy Knob and Toms Creek. Two miles later, the MST makes a sharp right turn and descends to Toms Creek, a tranquil stream beneath a gallery of hemlocks and tulip poplars. Across the creek, bear left onto a grassy road and cruise up a gentle grade, contouring around a small ridge that affords you a pleasant view inside the forest canopy. Stop briefly at the South Fork of Toms Creek, the last water source crossed by the trail for the next 15 miles. Just past the creek, the MST turns once again into the woods and climbs steeply toward Betsy Ridge through an open oak forest. Shift into low gear and listen for scarlet tanager, black-throated green warbler, and red-eyed vireo singing high in the trees. Near the top of the ridge, the trail rejoins the grassy grade and passes through a small gap. Bending sharply north onto Betsy Ridge, the trail is suddenly covered with flakes of shiny mica the size of quarters. To the west, the main ridge of Mount Mitchell looms blue on the horizon.

Climb in fits and spurts up Betsy Ridge through thin stands of pine, oak, and mountain laurel until you gain the main ridge of Woods Mountain (3600 feet), planted firmly east to west in defiance of other mountains in the area. Camp is west on the MST in a small saddle, about 1.5 miles away. Water can be found in Rattlesnake Branch, Little Buck Creek, or Bad Fork, all some distance from camp.

DAY FOUR   10+ miles   2500 feet

For several miles, Woods Mountain undulates like the back of a dinosaur. Just as you catch your breath on the way down from one little peak, the MST clambers up another one. Head west along the spine of Woods Mountain toward the Blue Ridge Parkway. Top off water bottles in Armstrong Creek, a quarter mile away and 200 feet down from a small saddle west of Timber Ridge. Begin the steady 2-mile climb toward Hazelnut Gap, searching for a break in the trees and a closer view of Mount Mitchell and Commissary Ridge, the route to the top. At Hazelnut Gap, turn left onto an old logging road leading to the Blue Ridge Parkway, North Carolina Route 80, and Buck Creek Gap (3350 feet).

Cross the bridge, turn right onto the MST, and switchback up a small ridge. The trail parallels the Parkway for several miles and crosses it three more times. Curiously, the second crossing is in the same direction as the first. In between the first and second crossing, the Parkway passes through two tunnels, the second secretly passing beneath the trail. After the third crossing, the MST continues to parallel the Parkway for another three-quarters of a mile before bending westward and contouring around Big Laurel Mountain (4105 feet), and descending to Neals Creek, Forest Road 2074, and the base of Mount Mitchell. Camp by the creek in designated roadside camping spots or back up the trail, away from the road. Either way, get a good night's sleep and plan for an early start to avoid mountain weather that may roll in as the day progresses.

Skeletal Fraser firs on the approach to the summit of Mount Mitchell (Photo by Corey Hadden)

DAY FIVE 6+ miles 3900 feet

From Black Mountain Campground via Forest Road 2074 and Forest Road 472, cross the bridge over the South Toe River and turn left through the campground. The MST follows the Mount Mitchell Trail approximately 5.6 miles to the summit of Mount Mitchell. Begin by climbing long switchbacks up Long Ridge through forests of tulip poplars and hemlocks. Rhododendrons gradually give way to mountain laurel on drier slopes. Bear left on the trail toward Higgins Bald, jump over Setrock Creek, and regain the Mount Mitchell Trail. Pause amid a grand stand of giant hemlocks, several of which are two to three arm widths around, and listen to the eerie silence, interrupted only by the chatty voice of the red-breasted nuthatch and the soft whistle of the brown creeper. As you approach Commissary Ridge, find your way through two trail junctions and gain the main summit ridge. The rutted trail twists through thick forests of spruce and fir and passes boulders dripping with moss, as slippery as the day Elisha Mitchell fell to his death while resurveying the mountain. As it levels out, the spruce and fir trees give way to heath and blackberries. Grey skeletons are all that remain of the Fraser fir. Ahead is the summit tower.

Trail Summary and Mileage Estimates

0	Mountains-to-Sea Trail at Table Rock picnic area (3400 feet)
2.1	Chimney Gap (2509 feet)
2.4	Cambric Branch Trail (2840 feet), bear left onto MST
5.6	South end of Shortoff Mountain (3000 feet)
8	Gravel road (1280 feet), turn left onto road, then right onto MST
10.6	Kistler Memorial Highway (2750 feet), turn left onto road, right onto MST
13.1	Forest Road 106 (2610 feet), turn left onto Forest Road 106
16.5	End of Forest Road 106 (3235 feet), bear right onto MST
18.2	Spur trail to Bald Knob Overlook (3480 feet), bear right on MST
20.4	Old logging road (1640 feet), turn left onto road
22.9	MST (1560 feet), turn right onto MST
23.7	Unimproved road (1960 feet), bear right onto road
24.6	MST (2050 feet), turn left onto MST
25.3	Forest Road 150 (1680 feet), turn right onto Forest Road 150
25.9	US 221 (1620 feet), cross highway and regain MST at north end of rest area
27.9	MST (1520 feet), bear right onto MST
30	MST mile marker 440 (1460 feet), sharp right onto MST
33.3	Woods Mountain (3600 feet), turn left onto MST
35.6	Spur trail to Rattlesnake Branch (3120 feet), continue straight on MST
37	Spur trail to Armstrong Creek (3000 feet), continue straight on MST
38.4	Hazelnut Gap (3640 feet), turn left onto old logging road
39.1	Blue Ridge Parkway and NC 80 (3350 feet), cross bridge and turn right onto MST
42.1	Blue Ridge Parkway (3620 feet), cross Parkway and regain MST
45.2	Forest Road 2074 (3100 feet), turn right onto Forest Road 2074
46.3	Black Mountain Campground (3000 feet), cross bridge and bear left
51.4	Mount Mitchell (6684 feet)
51.6	Summit parking lot (6600 feet)

Suggested Camps Based on Different Trekking Itineraries

Night	<10 mpd	10 mpd	10–15 mpd
One	7.9 miles - Linville River	9.1 miles - Sandy Branch	12.8 miles - Yellow Fork
Two	16.5 miles - Dobson Knob	22 miles - N. Fork Catawba River	28 miles - Toms Creek
Three	25.3 miles - northeast of helipad	34.8 miles - Woods Mountain	45 miles - Neals Creek
Four	34.8 miles - Woods Mountain	45 miles - Neals Creek	
Five	45 miles - Neals Creek		

Peaks of the Black Mountains (NC)

Difficulty:	Very strenuous
Distance:	31.3 miles
Elevation gain:	6900 feet
Best season:	Consider this trek during any season. The area around Mount Mitchell tends to be crowded when the weather is mild from April through November. Beware of afternoon thunderstorms on the high ridge in the heat of the summer, and haze typically obscures midyear views. The harsh conditions in the winter may be a challenge to consider when visitors are few, but only if you like cold and wind.
Recommended itinerary:	2 days (10–20 miles per day)
Water availability:	Much of the hike is on high and steep ridgelines, so water sources are relatively scarce but located in convenient places.
Logistics:	We suggest traveling north to south. There is a small spot to park a car at the northern terminus of the trail on Watershed Road (Forest Road 5578) at the Forest Service boundary, although a vehicle with good clearance is necessary to drive to the trailhead.
	At the southern terminus, parking is available at the campus of SUWS of the Carolinas, a youth wilderness program, beyond the southern trailhead on Graphite Road. Foot Travel in Black Mountain offers a shuttle service (*www.bighike.com* or 866-BIGHIKE).
Jurisdictions:	Appalachian/Toecane Ranger District (828-652-6146), Pisgah National Forest; Mount Mitchell State Park (828-675-4611); and Blue Ridge Parkway (828-271-4779)
Maps:	USGS South Toe River, Mount Mitchell, and Big Ivy Trail
Trail location:	To reach the southern terminus trailhead from Interstate 40, follow exit 72/US Route 70 east toward Old

Fort, and turn left onto Mill Creek Road toward Andrews Geyser. Turn right onto Graphite Road at the first road junction and continue to the trailhead just past the Brookside Church. The trailhead is not marked and begins on a gravel road beyond the church near a fenced tennis court used as a parking area. Park about 100 yards beyond the trailhead in a grassy area on the left used by SUWS staff.

To reach the northern terminus trailhead from Interstate 40, follow exit 72/US 70 east through Old Fort and in approximately 10 miles turn left onto NC Route 80 on the outskirts of Marion, North Carolina. Follow NC 80 over the mountains and turn left onto US Route 19E. In Burnsville turn left onto NC Route 197, then turn left again onto Low Gap Road (SR 1109), also known as Bowlens Creek Road. Before the gap and at a cluster of homes on the hairpin turn, go left up Forest Road 5578 to the Forest Service property line.

Don't be snookered by the relatively short distance spanning the mountains between the western North Carolina hamlets of Burnsville and Old Fort. To link the two areas by foot requires a strong back and sturdy foot. The route in question walks the breathtaking and storied crest of the Black Mountains. The crest is only 15 miles long, but includes six of the ten highest peaks in the eastern United States, old-growth timber, and an abundance of plant and wildlife habitat. The exposed crest of

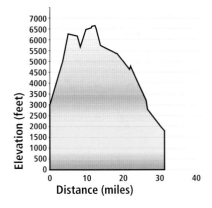

the high ridge is an enticing winter challenge too as it holds the mark for the lowest recorded temperature in North Carolina—minus 34 degrees.

DAY ONE   12+ miles   5800 feet

The first section of trail ascends the Bowlens Creek watershed on the western slope of the Black Mountains toward Celo Knob. From a cluster of homes on the hairpin turn on Bowlens Creek Road, begin up Watershed Road (Forest Road 5578). Walk a short distance uphill past houses to the national forest boundary and cross an old bridge to the north side of the creek following the Black Mountain Crest Trail (#179).

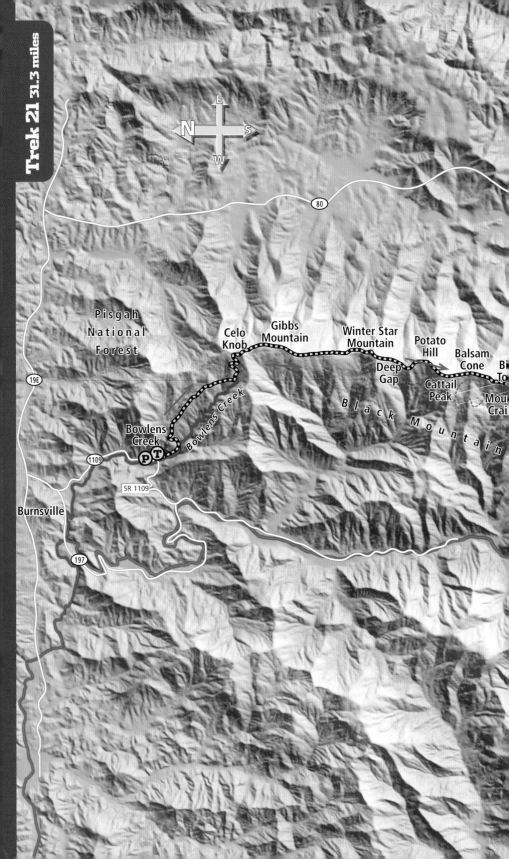

N
E
W
S

80

Pisgah
National
Forest

19E

Celo
Knob

Gibbs
Mountain

Winter Star
Mountain

Potato
Hill

Balsam
Cone

Bi
To

Deep
Gap

Cattail
Peak

Mou
Crai

Bowlens Creek

Bowlens
Creek

P T

1109

SR 1109

Burnsville

197

B l a c k   M o u n t a i n

Old Fort

Graphite Road

Pisgah
National
Forest

Blue Ridge Parkway

Mount
Mitchell
Wildlife
Mangement
Area

Mount
Mitchell
State
Park

Camp
Alice

alternate

Mount
Mitchell

Licklog
Knob

Heartbreak Ridge

Glass
Rock
Knob

Pritchard Creek

P   T

alternate

128

Clingmans
Peak

Graybeard
Mountain

Blue Ridge Parkway

Barnett
Reservoir

80

Mount Mitchell lookout tower

Hike up a road grade, staying left at two forks. Eventually leave the creek, winding up the side of the mountain to a gap on the ridge marked by a U.S. Forest Service property boundary sign. Switchback to the right and walk the ridge. Where a road grade enters from the left, stay right. Then pass a spring on the right below a boulder at 4700 feet. Shortly after the spring there is a clearing with a campsite at 4800 on the ridgeline.

At 5000 feet, begin the transition to the spruce and fir forest. The northern species of plants and trees at high elevations are remnants of the last ice age. While there were no glaciers here, when the climate warmed, northern species that moved south during the cold became restricted to higher elevations.

The Blacks are an appropriate place to ponder the flora of the range. One of the area's well-known visitors was Andre Michaux, a botanist sent by the French government in the 1790s to bring back trees suitable to grow in France for ship masts—though it's likely that he was more interested in the high mountains' extraordinary biodiversity than shipbuilding.

Cross a stream around 5000 feet and begin broad switchbacks on the road grade toward Celo Knob. After several switchbacks, turn a corner at 6100 feet for a good vantage of the Blacks to the south. Ahead is Mount Mitchell, distinguished by its square summit tower, and beyond is Clingmans Peak topped with radio transmitters. Skirt around the south side of Celo Knob (6317 feet) and gain the crest of the Black Mountains, turning due south on a foot trail.

Pass the weathered Whiteoak Trail sign steadied by a pile of rocks in a meadow on the ridge with exceptional views in every direction. Take time to orient yourself to the North Carolina mountains and the boundaries of the Pisgah National Forest. The forest stretches from the Pisgah Crest to the southwest and beyond Grandfather Mountain and the Linville Gorge to the northeast.

To the east, the obvious landmark is the rectangular Table Rock Mountain—

the beacon of the Linville Gorge several ridgelines east. Linville Gorge parallels the Blacks, and several of its landmarks are obvious. Table Rock is separated by a wide convex-shaped gap from Hawksbill Mountain. Farther south of Table Rock is the long cliff lining Shortoff Mountain before the gorge opens up and the Linville River empties into Lake James. To the north are the Roan Highlands, the Yellow Mountains, and Grandfather Mountain. To the west, beyond Asheville and the French Broad River Valley, are the Great Smoky Mountains and the Pisgah Crest.

The Black Mountain Crest Trail from Bowlens Creek to Cattail Peak is within the Pisgah National Forest. From Cattail to Camp Alice on the southeast side of Mount Mitchell, the route is within Mount Mitchell State Park—North Carolina's first park, established in 1915.

The route from Celo Knob is relatively gentle walking until climbing Winter Star Mountain (6200 feet) and a steep descent to Deep Gap (5700 feet). There are several campsites at Deep Gap and a spring nearby. The Colberts Ridge Trail arrives in the gap from the east. Consider stopping for the night—it's a shame to rush through such a gorgeous area without proper breaks. A small spring is located on the east side of Deep Gap straight down from the campsite. A larger water source

Ian Randall hikes the crest of the Black Mountains near Celo Knob.

is .75 mile down the Colberts Ridge Trail. From Deep Gap, begin the first of several humps—a 750-foot climb over Potato Hill (6475 feet). The trail stays near the spine of the ridge over rock steps suited for giants. Hiking this section of trail on summer afternoons brings a sense of commitment when lightning storms are common.

The hike from Deep Gap to Mitchell is one of the premier sections of trail in this book. The high altitude, the grand views, and challenging footwork add up to a remarkable stretch of trail to the top of Mount Mitchell. The rocky narrow ridge with stunted conifers and meadows is a scene from the West. Typically, the trail follows the crest over each of the six knobs along the way—sometimes the trail skirts the side with occasional rock scrambles.

At one time, the Blacks were considered one mountain. In fact Mount Mitchell has gone through names like a fugitive—finally settling on Mitchell in lieu of Clingmans Peak (for Elisha Mitchell's rival) or the more colorful Black Dome. Any hiker who has walked from Deep Gap to Mitchell will tell you that the Blacks are hardly one mountain and the short but stout climbs up each of the six knobs justify the additional names.

The final hump before Mount Mitchell is Big Tom Mountain (6581 feet) and its close neighbor, Mount Craig (6648 feet). Big Tom Wilson was a local mountain guide who found Elisha Mitchell's dead body in a pool at the base of a waterfall in 1857. A small gap separates Big Tom from Mount Craig, named for the former governor who advocated creating the state park.

Savor fantastic views from Mount Craig at a clearing. For some, the tower and development on Mount Mitchell spoil the view—for others, the development is a necessary price to pay to preserve the magnificent ridge. Thanks to the efforts of early twentieth-century conservationists, the Blacks have been largely untouched in the last seventy-five years and portions are among the wildest areas in the southeast.

Descend to a gap, and then climb toward Mitchell, eventually passing through a picnic area and arriving at the paved road. Cross the road and climb steps to the parking area and follow the tourist trail to the summit tower. Plan to spend time at the tower visiting Elisha Mitchell's tomb and taking in the 360-degree views—solidify your geography of the area by studying pictures in the tower that identify surrounding peaks and ridges. Time your arrival to coincide with the sunset (or sunrise) from the high point of Appalachia.

Be mindful that no camping is permitted in the park with the exception of an established campground south of the summit. The campground has only nine established sites, which are first come, first served, and is typically full. The sites are slightly out of the way, but worth considering in the off-season. To access the campground from the Mount Mitchell lookout tower, descend the tourist trail and turn left onto the Mountains-to-Sea Trail (MST). Descend 0.5 mile through trees. Stay straight at the Camp Alice Trail junction to reach the Mount Mitchell State Park campground on the Campground Spur Trail. If bypassing the campground, the route turns left at this junction.

A second camping option is also slightly out of the way on Commissary Ridge. At the Camp Alice junction, turn left onto the Camp Alice Trail (also the MST) for 0.75 mile through a spruce and fir forest. Arrive at a gravel road and the former site of Camp Alice—once a logging camp and then a resort. Despite it's name, overnight visits are no longer permitted at Camp Alice. Turn left and cross Lower Creek. Follow the road, and arrive at the switchback. To reach Commissary Ridge, bear left. To continue on route, follow the switchback to the right.

A third camping option is in another 4.5 miles from the switchback to the trail junction with the park road, NC Route 128.

DAY TWO   19 miles   1100 feet

From the switchback near Camp Alice, an old rail grade contours the east slope of the Black Mountains. The grade descends very gradually and is a pleasant stroll shaded by silver birch interspersed with meadows and big views. At mile 18.1, pass the Buncomb Horse Range Trail on your left. The horse trail descends to the South Toe River. Cross the Right Prong of the South Toe and reach NC 128. The camping spot in question is through the trees on the east side of the highway.

Turn left onto NC 128 and walk less than a mile on the road to the Mount Mitchell park gate on the Blue Ridge Parkway. The Asheville watershed is to the southwest and due south is the Seven Sisters ridgeline capped by Graybeard Mountain descending to the village of Montreat. The ridge divides the Montreat property line and the watershed.

At the park gate, turn left onto the Parkway and leave the Black Mountains behind—the Black Mountains meet the Craggy Mountains around Potato Knob and Clingmans Peak. Soon pass a gate on the right. The Heartbreak Ridge Trail once began here, but has been rerouted. Continue along the Parkway for approximately 2 miles. Keep your eyes peeled for the elusive trailhead marker for Heartbreak Ridge, Trail 208, shrouded in trees on the right side of the road. The trailhead is just before a sharp left-hand bend in the road. Turn right onto the trail with a short climb over Glass Rock Knob. Bear left onto the ridge at the field below the No Galaxing signs on the ridge. The National Park Service and Forest Service have placed restrictions on harvesting the dark green, heart-shaped plant commonly plucked for use in floral arrangements.

Turn right at the "Camp Woodson Adopt a Trail" sign. Here begin descending Heartbreak Ridge, also a popular mountain bike descent. Take care to stay on the trail at two minor junctions. Climb over a twin knob—between the knobs is a clearing with nice views to the west. Descend again and eventually contour around

MST junction with the Buncomb Horse Range Trail

Licklog Knob (3225 feet) and meet a trail junction in the gap. Turn right and switchback many times down the mountain through a serene forest. At the base of the descent arrive in a heavily impacted campsite at Pritchard Creek. The area to the right is popular among wilderness programs because of its relative seclusion and easy access from the road.

If you have time, follow Pritchard Creek upstream and look for rock walls and foundations—remnants of a community wiped out by the flood of 1916. A culmination of heavy rains and two hurricanes within a week of each other, one hitting the Gulf Coast and the other swamping the Carolina coast, wiped out all previous 24-hour records of rainfall in the United States. According to an account by the Southern Railway Company, the worst flooding was here, between Old Fort and Ridgecrest, causing mudslides that filled deep cuts like Pritchard Creek with "mud, stones, logs, trees, and stumps."

To reach the trailhead, turn left downstream. Soon cross the railroad tracks and arrive at the southern terminus of the route on Graphite Road.

Trail Summary and Mileage Estimates

0	Bowlens Creek Road (3000 feet), follow Watershed Road (Forest Road 5578)
3.5	Cross spring (5000 feet)
5	Celo Knob (6317 feet), bear right
7.5	Winter Star Mountain (6200 feet), continue straight ahead
8.3	Deep Gap (5700 feet), continue straight ahead
9.8	Cattail Peak (6500 feet), continue straight ahead
11.3	Big Tom Mountain (6581 feet)
11.4	Mount Craig (6648 feet)
12.3	Mount Mitchell (6684 feet)
12.6	Turn left onto MST (6560 feet)
13.8	Camp Alice (5780 feet), turn left onto MST
14	MST (5750 feet), go right at switchback
18.1	Buncomb Horse Range Trail (5400 feet), stay straight ahead on MST
18.3	NC 128 (5400 feet), go left onto NC 128
19.3	Mount Mitchell gate, junction with Blue Ridge Parkway, go left onto Parkway
21.8	Heartbreak Ridge trailhead (4650 feet), go right onto Heartbreak Ridge Trail
22.1	Glass Rock Knob (4800 feet), go left
22.2	Camp Woodson Adopt a Trail Sign (4750 feet), turn right
26.3	Licklog Knob (3225 feet), continue straight
26.7	Trail junction (2800 feet), turn right
30.3	Pritchard Creek (2000 feet), turn left
31.3	Brookside Church on Graphite Road (1800 feet)

Suggested Camps Based on Different Trekking Itineraries

Night	<10 mpd	>10 mpd
One	8.3 miles - Deep Gap	13 miles - Mount Mitchell Campground or 14.5 miles - Commissary Ridge
Two	18.3 miles - NC 128	

The Mountains-to-Sea Trail—Table Rock to Grandfather Mountain (NC)

Difficulty: Strenuous

Distance: 46.8 miles

Elevation gain: 11,600 feet

Best season: Year-round. Late April is best for wildflowers and early October is best for fall colors. Summer is best to take advantage of the numerous swimming holes, and winter can be especially breathtaking, offering unobstructed views of forest interiors and distant mountains. Grandfather Mountain is rugged and home to some of the region's most extreme weather: powerful thunderstorms, high winds, deep snow, and freezing temperatures.

Recommended itinerary: 6 days (less than 10 miles per day, with time to play and explore)

Water availability: Water is abundant throughout the trek, except at the Table Rock picnic area.

Logistics: The Table Rock picnic area and Profile trailheads are approximately 22 miles apart, so plan on using two vehicles for a shuttle. The trailheads are about a 2-hour drive from Charlotte and slightly less from Asheville. Camping is not permitted in the Table Rock picnic area, but is allowed a few yards farther down the trail. The Mountains-to-Sea Trail (MST) is usually well-marked by a white dot about 3 inches in diameter. Two dots stacked atop one another but slightly offset indicates that the trail turns to the left or right. It is a fairly simple task to follow the white dots one after the other connecting campsite to campsite.

Thankfully, other trails and junctions are left unmarked, leaving you the challenge of finding your own way. Extended periods of rain may complicate the numerous creek crossings en route to Grandfather Mountain. Don your sandals, wait for the water to come down, or consider an alternate route rather than create a new path to a dry crossing.

Jurisdictions: Grandfather Ranger District (828-652-2144), Pisgah National Forest, and Blue Ridge Parkway (828-271-4779). Grandfather Mountain, locally owned and managed in part by the Nature Conservancy, is a designated International Biosphere Reserve (800-468-7325). A backcountry permit is required for Grandfather Mountain and camping is not permitted on Park Service property along the Blue Ridge Parkway.

Maps: USGS Linville Falls, Chestnut Mountain, and Grandfather Mountain; Grandfather Mountain Trail Map and Backcountry Guide

Trail location: From exit 105 on Interstate 40 in Morganton, North Carolina, follow NC Route 18 north through town. At the north end of downtown, NC 18 becomes NC Route 181. Follow NC 181 into the mountains for approximately 24 miles. Turn left at the sign for the Table Rock picnic area onto Gingercake Road, at the bottom of a small hill, and enter the Gingercake Acres community. Follow Gingercake Road for about 0.25 mile and bear left at the Y intersection on Table Rock Road. In less than a mile, the road turns to gravel and becomes Forest Road 210. Follow Forest Road 210 for approximately 4.5 miles to another sign for the picnic area, and turn right onto Forest Road 210B. In a little more than 0.5 mile, pass the driveway and sign for the North Carolina Outward Bound School. Continue straight for approximately 2 miles to the Table Rock picnic area and trailhead parking. The last stretch of road to the picnic area is closed during the winter, so be ready to park further away and add a couple of extra miles to the beginning of the trek.

To get to the Profile trailhead at the end of the trek, at the junction of Gingercake Road and NC 181, follow NC 181 north for approximately 6 miles, passing NC Route 183 along the way, until it merges with NC Route 221. Bear right and follow NC 181 for 3 miles to Linville. Turn right onto NC Route 105 and proceed for 0.5 mile to the traffic light. Turn left, staying on NC 105 and head toward Boone. In approximately 4 miles, pass through a traffic light and NC Route 184, on the left. The Profile trailhead is approximately 0.7 mile ahead on the right.

As if the mountains in western North Carolina weren't steep enough, Table Rock and Grandfather Mountain thrust skyward with such ferocity you'd think the craggy peaks were in Wyoming. From any angle, Table Rock looks formidable. Its rectangular summit peers 2000 feet down to the bottom of the Linville Gorge Wilderness, while its steep east face reflects the morning sun through

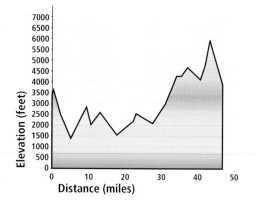

the foothills and piedmont. To the northeast, Grandfather Mountain rises above the folding hills, tearing at the sky with its jagged granite ridgeline. The Mountains-to-Sea Trail (MST) and connecting paths weave together the story of these two peaks with swimming holes, cascading falls, and sweeping views of southern Appalachian highlands.

DAY ONE   7 miles   1300 feet

The first few hundred yards of this trek are steep and probably the most treacherous: tall uneven steps, loose rocks, and roots. You may wonder what you've gotten yourself into, but the grade evens out just as you reach the first great spot to look out into the vast Linville Gorge Wilderness and forget that time matters. In October 2000, a campfire grew out of control and seared through the gorge, burning more than 10,000 acres. Black swaths of charred trees and earth, scars from the fire, stretch from the river to the rim of the gorge. Along the trail, leafless skeletons of mountain laurel, rhododendron, and the blackened trunks of fire-resistant pines stand in contrast to healthy spring wildflowers and lush summer growth. From here, the MST turns right and climbs gently on steady footing for a couple of hundred yards to its junction (unmarked) with the Table Rock summit trail, a worthwhile side trip totaling 0.5 mile with broad views of

Grandfather Mountain in early October

the Linville Gorge Wilderness, Grandfather Mountain, and Mount Mitchell (see Trek 20, MST—Linville Gorge to Mount Mitchell [NC]). The MST drops left and begins its steady and, at times, confusing descent away from the Linville Gorge. Jog along and cross two gravel roads before darting back into the woods just before a large turnaround. There are no water sources for a while, so top off in nearby Buck Creek.

The trail undulates for the next couple of miles through tunnels of rhododendron and mixed forests of pine, hemlock, and tulip poplar before plunging 1000 feet to Steels Creek in about a mile with few switchbacks. The MST turns left at Steels Creek, skips across Buck Creek, and begins to climb up and away from the water, periodically returning to the water's edge. Large sunny rocks in the middle of the creek provide a peaceful place to rest and have lunch. Soak your feet in the creek and breathe deep the moist earthy scent of the southern Appalachians. Around the bend, picturesque cascades form kettles of cold mountain water that make for a refreshing swim. Begin the last mile to camp with a ridiculous crawl up 50 feet of unswitched trail that levels out through open woods and fields of fern. Cross Steels Creek four times in the last 0.5 mile before making camp at 2000 feet on the edge of a meadow near Steels Creek and a small tributary.

Pisgah

National

Forest

221

N E S W

Boy Scout Trail

Watauga River

Grandfather

Daniel Boone

Rough Ridge

Yancey Ridge

Hughes Ridge

Timber Ridge

S

Profile Trail

Mountain

4

Beacon
Heights

Grandmother
Mountain

Lost Cove Creek

T

184

105

Linville

Blue Ridge Parkway

181
221

181

Linville River

221

194

Newland

Wilson Creek

Brown
Mountain

Upper Creek

Harper Creek

Chestnut
Mountain

2

North Harper Creek

181

P i s g a h

N a t i o n a l

F o r e s t

1

210

181

Hawksbill

Table
Rock

T

Linville Gorge Wilderness

Linville River

Linville River

221

221

Late winter storm over Table Rock and Hawksbill (Photo by Corey Hadden)

DAY TWO   10+ miles   2200 feet

Leave camp and immediately begin the steady climb up an old logging road for the next 1.3 miles. As you ascend, moist coves thick with rhododendron give way to dry slopes covered by mountain laurel, which are more tolerant of the sunnier and drier conditions found on higher and more exposed slopes. As the trail levels, bear right onto the MST, contour around, and step carefully across a simple, yet daunting creek crossing just a few feet above a 50-foot cascade. Safely across, follow the MST along trail and gravel road to its junction with NC 181. Quickly cross four lanes of intermittent mountain traffic and regain the MST on the other side at 2850 feet.

In the woods again, the MST drops through thick rhododendron forests over the next mile to Upper Creek (2040 feet). Cross the fast-moving water and regain the MST on the other side and climb an old logging road gently through open forests of tulip poplar toward Burnthouse Branch (2600 feet). Along the way, rickety timbers from old logging operations barely hold the trail together as it passes over small yet steep drainages. As you near Burnthouse Branch, views of the valley below emerge through the trees and a rare sidelong glimpse of Table Rock's north ridge can be seen.

At the top of the creek, Burnthouse Branch meets Forest Road 198. Bear left and continue along the old logging road, steadily ascending the northwest flank of Chestnut Mountain (3330 feet). Pass through the saddle (2850 feet), and begin the graduated descent down a broad ridge with views of Chestnut Mountain's forested northern slope before dropping quickly to Raider Camp Creek (1600 feet). Parallel the creek a short distance before crossing Harper Creek. Camp is just on the other side of the crossing, but don't rush it—the river is fast moving and the footing unstable. Once across, camp under large hemlocks and explore the creek upstream or down, or break out your fly rod and see what luck has for you today.

DAY THREE 6+ miles 1600 feet gain

Day three traces the path of Harper and North Harper Creeks for several miles before climbing up and over Long Ridge to Lost Cove Creek. After you sweep camp, head east and pick up the MST. Turn left at the first junction, just a few feet from camp, and make a short climb up and away from the river. The trail winds slightly, high above Harper Creek, passing short cliff bands with young hemlocks sprouting from vertical cracks.

If you have not already discovered what's down the path at the next junction, drop your pack and grab your camera. Hint: It is loud, thundering, and at the bottom is the area's greatest swimming hole. Otherwise, let out a loud sigh and bear right onto the MST, gaining a few feet in elevation before the river rises to meet the trail again.

Follow Harper Creek for another mile and begin the first of eight creek crossings, separated by a few yards to as much as a mile. All are benign with loose and slippery rocks being the most common hazard. During dry spells, usually in late summer, several of the crossings are low enough to keep the water from coming in over the tops of your boots. Stay alert for wildlife sightings along the creek: spotted sandpiper, kingfisher, and the occasional great blue heron can be seen.

Shortly after the last crossing, the MST heads away from the river and wanders to the top of Long Ridge (2550 feet), turns right onto Forest Road 464 and in 10 minutes dives back down the trail toward Huntfish Falls (1800 feet). Camp next to the creek in an open wood about 0.5 mile east of the falls. Tomorrow is a short day; hike back to the falls in the morning and spend a few hours on the sunny slabs of rock pondering your navel or taking some photos.

If you want to get away from the water and back into the high country, consider this alternative: Hike to Little Lost Cove Cliffs, which offer panoramic views of Grandfather Mountain, via North Harper Creek. Reconnect with the MST east of Roseborough via well-defined but unmarked trails over Bee Mountain and Timber Ridge.

DAY FOUR 6+ miles 1600 feet gain

From camp, the MST crosses Lost Cove Creek and sticks to the creek bottom despite the trail on the map which heads up the ridge. As you near the confluence of Lost Cove Creek and Gragg Prong, the MST enters private property that is not thoroughly signed. Bear left on the MST, up the Gragg Prong, and out of the private property. The trail crosses the Gragg Prong and periodically climbs above the river on steep slopes, returning before its junction with the Timber Ridge Trail and Forest Road 981.

Follow the MST across the bridge over Gragg Prong and immediately turn left onto Forest Road 192. Climb steadily toward Old House Gap up this winding dirt road for approximately 3 miles. As you near Old House Gap, an old logging road on the left leads to camping near Major Branch, or continue ahead to the old gated road that leads to Gragg Cemetery. Find a level area to camp past the cemetery among the rhododendrons. Visit the cemetery and mull over the dates and names on some of the older gravestones and notice the same names on your map, immortalized in the features of your journey. Members of the Gragg family still live in the area.

DAY FIVE   11.4 miles   3500 feet

On day 5, contour around the base of Grandfather Mountain and climb to a camp within easy reach of its summit. At Old House Gap (3000 feet), turn left and head uphill on the MST along an old overgrown logging road. Switchback up through moist forests carpeted with galax, a small, but pungent evergreen plant collected by locals for flower displays. High above, at 4200 feet, side trails to Beacon Heights and the Blue Ridge Parkway offer stunning views of your route so far.

Once past the trail junction for Beacon Heights, the MST contours along the Blue Ridge Parkway, dipping in and out of boulder-strewn drainages on its way to Shiprock. Stop by the Linn Cove Visitor Center and see the display about the innovative architecture of the viaduct, which is 5 minutes down a short paved section of the MST leading away from the visitor center. From here, the MST follows the Tanawha Trail above the Blue Ridge Parkway, rising and falling with the ridges shooting off from Grandfather Mountain. Break for lunch atop Shiprock (4700 feet), and carefully investigate the endangered plant communities composed of heath and lichens that favor exposed rocky outcrops.

Continue ducking in and out of small coves for 3.6 miles until you reach the turnoff for the Daniel Boone Boy Scout Camp and Trail. Leave the MST for good, and gradually switchback up a broad ridge to a junction with the Cragway Trail. The Daniel Boone Campsite is just a few minutes farther along the main trail. Pitch your tent on the platform, recently built to help reduce the amount of erosion in the campsite. A small spring near the camp is slow but reliable. The highest peak on the mountain, Calloway Peak, is a 1-hour hike up steep, rough trail flanked by fragrant firs. Carefully ascend craggy terrain with the help of fixed cables and ladders. Consider climbing Calloway Peak twice, tonight after dinner when the stars are bright and tomorrow fully loaded on your way over the mountain.

DAY SIX   4.7 miles   1400 feet

Make sure to get an early start to beat any mountain weather that tends to build up during the day. Leave camp and negotiate several rocky slabs and ladders before reaching the rocky summit of Calloway Peak (5948 feet). Take a deep breath of mountain air and look down on the valleys and ridges you've come to know over the last few days and find Table Rock above them, sticking out like a

Opposite: Lush spring greens along the Tanawha Trail (Photo by Corey Hadden)

thumb on the horizon. When you're ready, continue along the ridge to Calloway Gap and the Profile Trail. Turn right and swiftly descend a few hundred feet to the reliably wet Shanty Spring. From here, the uneven trail winds its way down the mountain for 2.7 miles to the trailhead.

Trail Summary and Mileage Estimates

0	Mountains-to-Sea Trail at Table Rock picnic area (3400 feet)
0.4	Spur trail to Table Rock summit (3640 feet), bear left on MST
2.3	Forest Road 210B (2500 feet), sharp left onto MST
5.1	Steels Creek (1400 feet), bear left on MST
8.3	Spur trail to Forest Road 496 (2500 feet), bear right on MST
9.4	NC 181 (2850 feet), cross highway and regain MST on opposite side
10.6	Upper Creek (2040 feet), ford Upper Creek and regain MST
13.1	Forest Road 198 at Burnthouse Branch (2600 feet), turn left onto MST/Forest Road 198
17.7	Spur trail to State Road 1328 (1560 feet), sharp left on MST
22.2	North Harper Creek Trail 266 (2200 feet), turn right onto MST
23	Forest Road 464 (2550 feet), turn right onto Forest Road 464 for 0.5 mile, then left onto MST
27.5	Timber Ridge Trail and Forest Road 981 (2100 feet), cross bridge and turn left onto Forest Road 192
31	Old House Gap (3000 feet), turn left onto MST
34.1	Spur trail to Beacon Heights trailhead (4300 feet), turn right, then left onto MST
35.4	Linn Cove Visitor Center (4300 feet), MST follows viaduct trail
37.1	Shiprock (4700 feet)
40.7	Daniel Boone Boy Scout Trail (4270 feet), turn left onto Daniel Boone Boy Scout Trail
42	Cragway Trail (4800 feet), stay straight on Daniel Boone Boy Scout Trail
43.3	Calloway Peak (5948 feet)
43.8	Profile Trail (5642 feet), turn right onto Profile Trail
46.8	Profile trailhead at NC 105 (3900 feet)

Suggested Camps Based on Different Trekking Itineraries

Night	<10 mpd	10 mpd	>10 mpd
One	7 miles - Gingercake/Steels Creek	10.6 miles - Upper Creek	13.1 miles - Burnthouse Branch
Two	17.7 miles - Raider Camp Creek/ Harper Creek	20.7 miles - North Harper Creek	30.7 miles - Major Branch of Gragg Prong
Three	24.3 miles - Lost Cove Creek	30.7 miles - Major Branch of Gragg Prong	42.1 miles - Daniel Boone Boy Scout Campsite
Four	30.7 miles - Major Branch of Gragg Prong	42.1 miles - Daniel Boone Boy Scout Campsite	
Five	42.1 miles - Daniel Boone Boy Scout Campsite		

TREK 23

Mountains-to-Sea Trail— Bluegrass Highway (NC)

Difficulty:	Strenuous
Distance:	40.5 miles
Elevation gain:	7200 feet
Best season:	Year-round, though mid- to late-winter conditions can be quite severe on Grandfather Mountain.
Recommended itinerary:	2 days (15–20 miles per day)
Water availability:	Reliable sources are often several miles apart along much of the Blue Ridge Parkway. Be sure to top off at every opportunity.
Logistics:	The Mountains-to-Sea Trail (MST) from Deep Gap to Blue Ridge Parkway milepost 291.5, approximately 16 miles, remains unfinished at this writing. Thru-hikers and other users have permission from the Park Service to hike along the grassy shoulder, though camping is not permitted along the Parkway except at designated campgrounds. If lugging your pack for 16 miles beside a road followed by 10 miles of moderate trail is not your idea of an adventure, consider setting up camp at Price Memorial Park ahead of time, and take only what you need for a day's exploration.

Until the official opening of this section of the MST, and for those not wanting to hike along the Parkway, a trailhead may be found 0.2 mile south of the Parkway just off US Route 321 on Old Camp Catawba Road. Look for the 3-inch white dots blazing the way. Or, like many other "hikers," bring a bike and ride along the Parkway, a leisurely trip of about 2 hours. Trekking should be an adventure and fun, whatever style you choose.

Jurisdictions:	Blue Ridge Parkway (828-271-4779) and Grandfather Ranger District (828-652-2144), Pisgah National Forest. A camping fee is required for sites at Price

Memorial Park Campground and for hiking the trails at Grandfather Mountain, the world's only privately owned International Biosphere Reserve. The reserve is managed in partnership with the Nature Conservancy to protect endangered species and fragile southern Appalachian subalpine ecosystems.

Maps: USGS Deep Gap, Boone, Valle Crucis, and Grandfather Mountain

Trail location: The beginning of the trek along Blue Ridge Parkway at Deep Gap is approximately 12 miles east of Boone and 25 miles west of Wilkesboro, North Carolina, on US Route 421. The entrance to Grandfather Mountain Preserve, the end of the trek, may be found on US Route 221, 2 miles east of Linville and 1 mile west of the junction of US 221 and the Blue Ridge Parkway. A bike shuttle is highly recommended for this trek due to the scenic nature of the 30-mile ride from Grandfather Mountain to Deep Gap, 28 miles of which is along the nation's most scenic road.

Rising from the rolling hills of the piedmont like a tidal wave of rock and forest, the Blue Ridge Mountains are the epitome of everything southern and Appalachian: lush forests, craggy peaks, and bluegrass music. The Mountains-to-Sea Trail from Deep Gap to Grandfather Mountain begins just a fiddle's neck away from the front porch of legendary bluegrass picker Doc Watson.

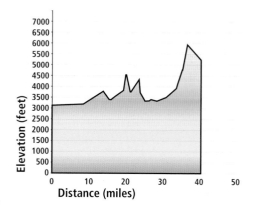

Like his fingers across the strings of a guitar, this trek rolls along through high mountain meadows and lush creek bottoms en route to the highest and craggiest peak in the Blue Ridge, Grandfather Mountain. Along the way, explore carriage roads and trails that wander through the once private estates of Moses Cone and Julian Price, now maintained by the National Park Service to preserve the natural beauty and character of the eastern Blue Ridge.

DAY ONE   26+ miles   3600 feet

The goal of day one is to reach Price Memorial Park, a park service campground nestled among flowering rhododendrons and tulip poplars in the shadow of

Grandfather Mountain nearly 27 miles away! The first 16 miles are a gentle walk beside the Blue Ridge Parkway, which parallels much of the MST's course through western North Carolina on its way from the Atlantic Ocean to the Great Smoky Mountains. The trail here does not yet exist, necessitating a road walk or bike ride to the first section of trail in Moses H. Cone Memorial Park.

With your lightweight hikers on and plenty of water, turn right (south) onto the Parkway and begin a gradual climb passing several scenic overlooks, any of which makes for the perfect place to rest and greet the sunrise. At mile 8.5, the Parkway begins to parallel Goshen Creek, the day's first reliable source of water. A small picnic table can be found near here at Boones Trace, a pull-off surrounded by farmland rumored to have been used by Daniel Boone on his way to Kentucky.

Here beside Goshen Creek, according to the North Carolina Geological Survey, evidence can be found of the ancient continental collision when layer upon layer of rock was thrust over one another, stacking up to form the Appalachian Mountains. As time passed, rivers and uplift exposed deep layers of rock underneath, opening a geologic window through time, which can be seen here and there along the Parkway and MST.

In a gap void of trees at Thunder Hill Overlook, mile 13.9, one can straddle the eastern Continental Divide, which has been making a series of S turns with you since Deep Gap. Here at 3795 feet, sweat dripping off your shirt is just as likely to

Hemlocks (Photo by Corey Hadden)

421

321

Rich Mountain

N
W   E
S

Boone

421 321

321

105

22

Pisgah

National

Forest

Moses H. Cone
Memorial
Park

Rich
Mountain

Flat Top
Mountain

Martin
Knob

Hanging
Rock

Julian
Memorial

Price
Park

Trout
Lake

Green
Knob

Bass
Lake

Blowin
Roc

105

1

Price
Lake

184

Mountain

Blue Ridge Parkway

221

Calloway
Peak

2

Grandfather

Backbone Ridge

Rock
Kno

T

221

Grandmother
Mountain

Pisgah

National

Forest

Yancey Ridge

221

South Fork New River

Deep Gap

421 221

T

Osborne Mountain

421

Blue Ridge Parkway

Elk Creek

Grassy Knob

Chestnut Knob

Buffalo Creek

Yadkin River

321

Licklog Mountain

Fork Mountain

Yadkin River

end up in the Gulf of Mexico as the Atlantic Ocean. To the north, the South Fork of the New River, believed to be the oldest river in North America, will eventually take that water away to West Virginia, where it will add to the flows of the Kanawha and Ohio Rivers, and later, the mighty Mississippi. To the south, more than 1600 feet down the dramatic Blue Ridge escarpment, which separates all that is Appalachian from the piedmont, the Yadkin River first fakes left, then right, before finally setting a southeasterly course for the Pee Dee River, South Carolina, and the Atlantic Ocean.

Across the road from the parking area, a footpath leads through the fence line and tall grass to the top of a knoll with an even more spectacular view. The footpath may one day be included in the official Mountains-to-Sea Trail, but for now it simply breaks the monotony of walking beside the road. Continue along the path down the west side of the knoll to a clearing flanked by flame azaleas and regain the Parkway for the remaining mile or so to the turnoff for US 321 and the first trail section of the MST.

At US 321, cross the busy road and bear left for 0.3 mile to Old Camp Catawba Road, and turn right. Look for a trailhead and old carriage road on the left in 0.2 mile. Step over a cable gate and then Penley Branch, the first water source in many miles, and breathe deep as you walk quietly through a dark cathedral of giant hemlocks. A sign pointing to Cone Manor indicates that you have entered the 3517-acre estate formerly owned by textile magnate Moses H. Cone, now managed by the Park Service. The MST lazily follows old carriage roads that traverse the estate through a variety of interesting landscapes and plant communities including northern hardwoods, nearly pure stands of hemlock, and high open meadows above 4000 feet.

At 17.1 miles, pass a spur trail that leads left to the old apple barn, and begin a series of gradual switchbacks stacked one on top of the other until you reach a three-way junction at a hairpin turn. Stay right, and proceed 0.6 mile to Cone Manor, which now houses the Parkway Craft Center. Take a few minutes and peruse the shop and its displays of Appalachian folk art: quilts, baskets, and the like. Out the door and down the steps, jog back a few yards along the carriage road and bear left toward the Parkway, passing underneath via a short stone tunnel.

The MST leads left toward Trout Lake, but a carriage road leads straight for a couple of miles through high meadows and beautiful woods to Cone Cemetery and an observation tower atop Flat Top Mountain (4558 feet). You've already hiked 20+ miles, with 6 to go. Your call. But if nothing else, trot down the road a few yards for an impressive view of Grandfather Mountain looming on the horizon.

Back on the MST, cross gravel Flannery Fork Road in about a mile and then come to Trout Lake. Despite their beauty, lakes in the unglaciated southern Appalachians are not naturally occurring, and this one is no exception. Turn left over the

Sunset over Grandfather Mountain from Moses Cone Memorial Park (Photo by Corey Hadden)

dam and begin the gradual ascent toward Rich Mountain, staying right on the MST at all trail junctions. Once atop a semibald ridge just south of Rich Mountain, make a sharp right then left on the MST, contouring around a small open valley before re-entering the woods on a wide two-track. In 0.5 mile, on a narrow ridge shooting off the west side of Rich Mountain, the MST turns sharply left. Step cautiously on rotten steps over an old barbed wire fence and zigzag down a series of broad switchbacks through open woods before coming to Shulls Mill Road. Descend wooden steps cut from a single log, and jog right on the road for a hundred yards to an old gate in the fence on the left.

The MST climbs out of the pasture and into the woods for several miles passing through thick tunnels of rhododendron and stands of dying white pine, their lifeless forms stricken by the southern pine bark beetle. Cross from one small creek bottom to another and finally descend stone steps to the rippling waters of the Boone Fork, sandwiched here between giant boulders and cool hemlocks. Camp is 1.5 miles to the left at the Price Memorial Park Campground, which is down the Boone Fork Trail to the Price Memorial Park Picnic Area and right on an unmarked footpath through a grassy field and rhododendron tunnel, an easy walk after a long day of trekking.

DAY TWO   13+ miles   3600 feet

Day two's total mileage is half that of yesterday's, but get an early start nonetheless, especially if you're traveling in the summer when afternoon thunderstorms can catch you on top of Grandfather Mountain. Retrace your steps back to the MST where it crossed the Boone Fork, and head north. The trail winds along beside the river as it tumbles through a series of congested waterfalls and boulder fields, occasionally coming to a slow pause before beginning another tumultuous descent. At the confluence of the Boone Fork and Bee Tree Creek, bear left and begin an often mucky climb up the creek bottom past Buck Knob to drier pastures and Holloway Mountain Road. Pass through a stile in the fence and follow a dry footpath through tall grass, snaking in and out of small islands of oak, maple, and peculiar rocks leaning over like old grave markers. If it is late May or June, flame azaleas compete with the sun with their bright orange flowers.

In 2.8 miles, bear right onto the MST and cross a stout bridge over the upper Boone Fork, here a raging mountain stream 30 feet below. In 0.5 mile, turn right onto the Daniel Boone Boy Scout Trail and begin the final climb up and over Grandfather Mountain's craggy summits. The first high, exposed rock is Grandfather's highest point, Calloway Peak (5948 feet), but to get there requires a scramble over boulders and steep slabs of rock. Fixed ladders and hand lines may seem unsightly amid the deep green of the spruce trees, but are a godsend when the rock is slick after an afternoon shower or late-winter snowmelt.

From here, the Grandfather Trail tumbles across rocky summits, subalpine meadows, and chutes of boulders for 3.5 miles to trek's end at the Grandfather Mountain Visitor Center, with panoramic views nearly the entire way.

Cross-country travel through Price Memorial Park (Photo by Corey Hadden)

Trail Summary and Mileage Estimates

0	Blue Ridge Parkway at US 421 (3140 feet), head south on the Parkway
8.5	Boone's Trace Overlook (3200 feet)
13.9	Thunder Hill Overlook (3795 feet), side trail to knoll
15.4	US 221/321 access ramp (3440 feet), turn right onto access ramp
15.5	US 221/321 (3420 feet), cross and turn left onto US 221/321
15.8	Old Camp Catawba Road (3410 feet), turn right onto Old Camp Catawba Road
16	Mountains-to-Sea Trail and Moses H. Cone Memorial Park (3410 feet), turn left onto unmarked carriage road
17.1	Side trail to Apple Barn (3560 feet), stay right on MST
19.4	Carriage road (3840 feet), stay right on MST
20	Cone Manor and Parkway Craft Center (3980 feet), turn right on unmarked carriage road
20.2	Carriage road to Cone Cemetery and Flat Top Observation Tower (4558 feet), turn left for MST and Grandfather Mountain
21.2	Flannery Fork Road (3780 feet), cross gravel road and regain MST
21.4	Trout Lake (3770 feet), turn left over dam and stay on MST
23.6	Trail to Rich Mountain (4340 feet), turn left onto MST
23.9	Shulls Mill Road (3740 feet), turn right onto paved road
24	MST (3710 feet), turn left onto MST
25.2	Boone Fork Trail (3350 feet), turn left onto Boone Fork Trail for campground
26.3	Price Memorial Park Picnic Area, (3360 feet), turn right onto footpath to campground
26.8	Price Memorial Park Campground (3420 feet)
28.4	MST junction (3350 feet), stay left on MST/Boone Fork Trail
30.9	Holloway Mountain Road (3520 feet), cross gravel road and regain MST
33.7	Side trail to Boone Fork Parking Area (3940 feet), stay right on MST
34.1	Daniel Boone Boy Scout Trail (4270 feet), bear right onto Daniel Boone Boy Scout Trail
35.3	Cragway Trail (4800 feet), stay straight on Daniel Boone Boy Scout Camp and Trail
35.4	Daniel Boone Boy Scout Campsite (4800 feet)
36.7	Calloway Peak (5948 feet)
40.5	Grandfather Mountain Visitor Center (5260 feet)

Suggested Camps Based on Different Trekking Itineraries

Night

One	26 miles - Price Memorial Park, NPS Campground (fee collected)

Note: Daniel Boone Boy Scout Camp on Grandfather Mountain offers a chance for a second night out.

Mountains-to-Sea Trail— A Thru-hiker's Guide to Western North Carolina's Mountains (TN/NC)

Difficulty: Strenuous

Distance: 305.8 miles from Clingmans Dome to Deep Gap. The recommended itinerary includes an additional 21.6 miles of day hikes and travel to resupply locations for a total of 327.4 miles.

Elevation gain: 67,700 feet

Best season: Year-round. For winter months, consider bringing gaiters and in-step crampons for snowy and icy sections of trail, and be sure your cold weather and winter camping skills are solid. It's not uncommon for higher elevations to experience major snowstorms. Intense summer afternoon thunderstorms are a daily occurrence in the southern mountains. Plan on getting wet. Spring and fall have excellent weather and displays of color in the form of wildflowers or changing leaves.

Recommended itinerary: 28 days (averaging 12 miles per day, with rest days)

Water availability: Water sources occur irregularly along the trek. Some days you will pass numerous sources, while other days may involve long waterless stretches. Where water does not cross the trail for many miles, springs often may be found down drainages to either side of the trail, especially during wet years. Consult your map and check out recent weather patterns.

Logistics: The trek ends approximately a 4-hour drive by paved roads from its beginning. Arrange to be dropped off and picked up, or use one of the local shuttle services to pick you up at trek's end and shuttle you back to your car at one of the national park visitor centers.

It's nearly impossible to carry all of your provisions for three and a half weeks. Don't even try. Instead, purchase your food en route at local groceries within a few miles of the trail. Or plan out your meals and have a package shipped to a local post office along the route in a timely manner so that it arrives before you do. Address your packages to: Your name, General Delivery, the town, state, and zip code. Add "Attn: Long-distance hiker resupply. Please hold until date." And don't forget to bring your ID. Only two post offices are within reasonable walking distance of the trail: Jonas Ridge, zip code 28641, and Linville, zip code 28657. If you can get a ride, other trail towns to consider are Cherokee, Asheville, and Marion.

For much of the trek, camping is available along the trail at obvious locations within the Nantahala and Pisgah National Forests at designated campgrounds and at one site on Grandfather Mountain. However, several long sections of trail are bound on either side by private land, tribal land, park service, or preserve property where it is illegal to camp. This may be frustrating to some, but instead of breaking the law, please help bring backcountry campsites to these areas by appealing to the local hiking clubs to lobby for permission. Contact the Carolina Mountain Club (*www.carolinamtnclub.org*) and the Friends of the Mountains-to-Sea Trail (*www.ncmst.org*).

For now, the easiest solution is to find a friendly landowner who will allow you to pitch a tent, or spend a total of seven nights in motels along the way, based on the recommended itinerary. One night, near Balsam Gap, requires the willing landowner approach—see day four for details. Call the recommended motels and make your reservations in advance before tourists fill them up. Two park service campgrounds, Mount Pisgah and Price Memorial Park, require a fee and are closed in winter. These also fill up on weekends and even weekdays during the summer, so a reservation is recommended. Details are provided in the daily logs.

Jurisdictions: Great Smoky Mountains National Park (423-436-1231). A free permit is required for all backcountry campsites, but only some require an advance reservation. Blue Ridge Parkway (828-271-4779); Highlands Ranger District (828-526-3765), Nantahala National Forest; Pisgah Ranger District (828-877-3265) and Grandfather Ranger District (828-652-2144), Pisgah National Forest; Mount Mitchell State Park (828-675-4611); Grandfather Mountain (800-468-7325); Price Memorial Park (828-295-7938); and Cone Memorial Park (828-963-5911).

Maps: National Geographic Trails Illustrated 229, *Great Smoky Mountains National Park*, is recommended through Balsam Gap on the Blue Ridge Parkway. This map indicates the future route of the Mountains-to-Sea Trail (MST) from Soco Gap to Balsam Gap, but at this writing only a short section from the Orchards Overlook to Balsam Gap is open for use. Check with the Carolina Mountain Club to see if sections of trail farther west are open. National Geographic Trails Illustrated 785, *Nantahala & Cullasaja Gorges*, covers Balsam Gap to NC Route 215. Be aware that the current edition of this map does not show the MST as a trail until Old Bald, but it's there. National Geographic Trails Illustrated 780, *Pisgah Ranger District*, covers the route from NC 215 to the French Broad River with reasonable accuracy.

At the French Broad River begin using USGS Skyland, Asheville, Oteen, Craggy Pinnacle, Montreat, Mount Mitchell, Celo, Old Fort, Little Switzerland, Ashford, Linville Falls, Chestnut Mountain, Grandfather Mountain, Valle Crucis, Boone, and Deep Gap. Keep in mind that the trail has been rerouted and constructed in locations that these out-of-date maps do not indicate.

If you'd like more information about the MST's history or eastern reach, Allen de Hart's book, *Hiking North Carolina's Mountains-to-Sea Trail* (University of North Carolina Press, 2000) is the undisputed champ. De Hart was one of the first to thru-hike the trail from end to end.

Trail location: The starting point on Clingmans Dome at the top of the Smokies is 7 miles up Clingmans Dome Road from Newfound Gap. Be aware that this road is closed in the winter. Call the National Park for details (865-436-1231). From Cherokee, North Carolina, Newfound Gap is 18 miles north on US Route 441, on the left, and from Gatlinburg, Tennessee, it is 16 miles south on US 441. Deep Gap is conveniently located in North Carolina at the crossroads of US Route 421 and the Blue Ridge Parkway, 12 miles east of Boone and 25 miles west of Wilkesboro. There is no parking in the vicinity.

One day, the Mountains-to-Sea Trail will stretch uninterrupted for nearly 1000 miles from the spruce-covered summit of Clingmans Dome to North Carolina's Outer Banks and the Atlantic Ocean. Why thru-hike the MST through western North Carolina's mountains? It's a true adventure. Compared to the well-loved and overrun Appalachian Trail, you are unlikely to meet another thru-hiker on the MST, and if by chance you do, you'll have something extraordinary in common to sit down and talk about. At 327 miles, the western reach of the MST is also a long, rugged trek through western North Carolina's profound landscape. You'll discover lush cove forests, craggy mountains, rich cultures, great waterfalls, and perfect swimming holes. And best of all, when you reach trek's end, you can decide for yourself how badly you want to jump in the ocean, and keep hiking.

The MST is a work in progress aided by several regional groups that help organize and construct the trail. Among these, Friends of the Mountains-to-Sea Trail and the Carolina Mountain Club are most pertinent to the trail's development in western North Carolina.

Like the trail itself, the process of planning and building the trail has undulated

Turkey beard (Photo by Corey Hadden)

over the years between great peaks of accomplishment and pitfalls as low as the deepest gap. According to Allen de Hart's *Hiking North Carolina's Mountains-to-Sea Trail*, the trail was first proposed in the late 1970s as the "flagship" trail of North Carolina's burgeoning trail system. Connecting the Appalachian Trail with the Atlantic Ocean in order to reveal to all passersby the great natural and cultural history of North Carolina became paramount. Its initial momentum was somehow lost with the changing of the

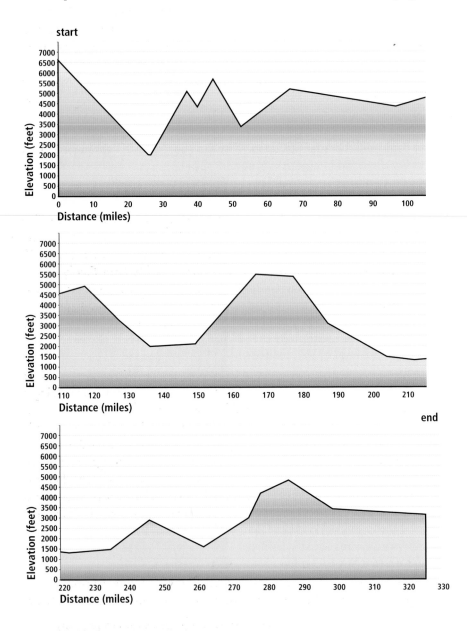

guard in the 1980s, and the trail almost lost entirely, only to be revitalized by dedicated volunteer planners and trail builders. To learn more about the dreamers, politics, ego, and most importantly, the hard-working volunteers that truly are the keepers of the trail, read deHart's book, or call any member of the Friends of the MST or Carolina Mountain Club. They'll set you straight.

For now, the mountains of western North Carolina are home to the two longest continuous segments of trail, split by a 25-mile road walk along the grassy shoulder of the Blue Ridge Parkway as it leaves the Smokies. Admittedly, walking the road can be a drag after a while, and downright dangerous when caravans of summer tourists race their motorcycles, recreational vehicles, sports cars, and SUVs along the winding and scenic highway. But truth be told, this road walk is one of the most spectacular sections of any trek in this guide, and well worth the occasional near miss.

The following itinerary includes a brief description of the terrain, logistics, and other notes of interest. Also refer to other treks in this guide that address sections of the MST in more detail.

DAY ONE   12+ miles   1400 feet

Clingmans Dome to Camp 56, Burnt Spruce, or Camp 57, Bryson Place. Plan for a late-morning start and head first for the top of Clingmans Dome, the second highest mountain along the route at 6643 feet. For its first 3.5 miles, the MST shares its path with the Appalachian Trail along the crest of the Great Smoky Mountains. Camp along picturesque Deep Creek with its perfect moss-covered boulders—just be sure to have your backcountry permit on hand (available at any visitor center or by calling the backcountry reservations office at 865-436-1231).

DAY TWO   14+ miles   4500 feet

Deep Creek to Cherokee. Leave Deep Creek with plenty of water and climb over Thomas Ridge toward Newton Bald, now reclaimed by the forest and Mingus Creek. At US Route 441, turn right and walk along the shoulder toward the national park visitor center and hop onto the Oconaluftee River Trail. At the trail's end, step back onto busy US 441, and head for Cherokee, grab a cheap motel room—there is an Econo Lodge 0.7 mile south of the Blue Ridge Parkway entrance (828-497-2226)—and plan for an early start for tomorrow's hike along the Parkway. In town, visit the Museum of the Cherokee Indian, or catch the drama *Unto These Hills*, which depicts Cherokee life and their removal known as the Trail of Tears.

DAY THREE   14+ miles   3800 feet

Cherokee to Soco Gap. Enter the Blue Ridge Parkway and immediately cross a bridge over the Oconaluftee River to begin the gradual climb toward Wolf Laurel

Tennessee

French Broad River

441

40

North Carolina

Great
Smoky
Mountains
National
Park

Asheville

T

1

2

19

Balsams

3 Waterrock Knob

11 12

10

Plott

4

74

Pisgah

National

9

Forest

Cherokee
Indian
Reservation

Richland
Balsam

5

8

6   7

Nantahala

National

Forest

441

North Carolina

South Carolina

Georgia

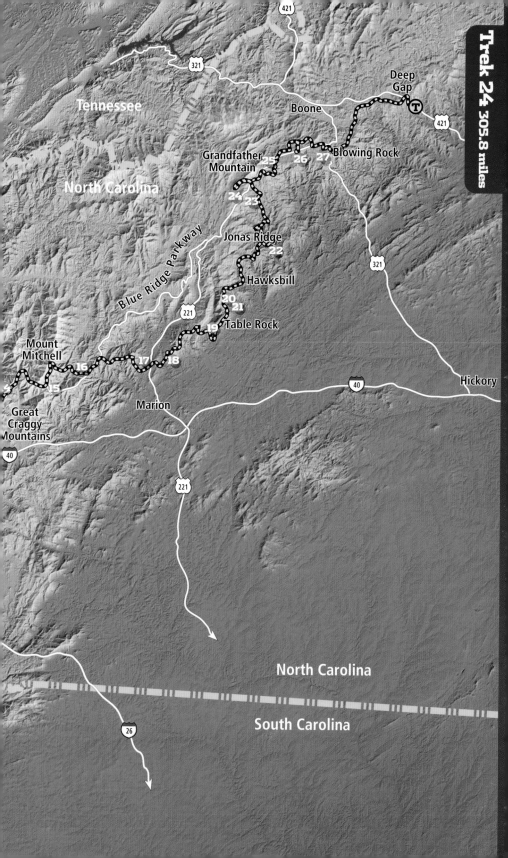

Thick sea of early morning fog near the Blue Ridge Parkway (© shullphoto)

Gap, and water, at 5100 feet. Pass by numerous overlooks and through several tunnels before turning south onto US 19 for another lavish motel room—the Blue Ridge Motel is 0.25 south of Soco Gap (828-926-1879).

DAY FOUR   13+ miles   1600 feet
Soco Gap to Balsam Gap. At mile 4.5, turn up the access road for Waterrock Knob and climb the 0.5-mile trail to its rocky summit with otherworldly views. True to its name, Waterrock Knob's numerous springs gush reliably in all but the driest years. Camp in a church yard 1 mile south of Balsam Gap on NC Route 1701. Or strike up a conversation with a local and a campsite might be offered or suggested.

DAY FIVE   15 miles   4100 feet
Balsam Gap to south of Old Bald. Pick up the trail near the ranger station and gain significant elevation. Water is frequent in the first few miles, but scarce until Cabin Creek. Camp in a big field south of Old Bald with breathtaking views of Richland Balsam.

DAY SIX   10 miles   1900 feet
Old Bald to Piney Creek. Continue the now gradual climb through the skeletons of Fraser fir, rendered lifeless from the miniscule balsam woolly adelgid. Water is abundant later in the day, found between tributaries on either side of camp in a field past Piney Creek.

DAY SEVEN   9+ miles   2200 feet
Piney Creek to NC 215. Cross over the Blue Ridge Parkway at Haywood Gap to enter the Middle Prong Wilderness and climb an unnamed bald for glorious views of Mount Hardy and the Middle Prong. Camp close to water in a field near NC 215.

DAY EIGHT   9+ miles   1300 feet

NC 215 to Yellowstone Prong. Pass through one of the southeast's most extraordinary landscapes: the treeless balds surrounding Graveyard Fields. From Silvermine Bald, take in the granite domes of Looking Glass, John Rock, and Cedar Rock, seemingly out of place in the great forests of the south. Make a side trip up to the broad summit of Black Balsam before descending down to Yellowstone Prong and several great swimming holes.

DAY NINE   12 miles   3100 feet

Yellowstone Prong to Mount Pisgah. Parallel and cross the Blue Ridge Parkway several times before settling in and contouring along its south side toward Mount Pisgah, the highest peak on Asheville's skyline. Numerous water sources line the way to the Mount Pisgah Campground, where a fee is required to pitch your tent.

DAY TEN   10 miles   2600 feet

Mount Pisgah to Bent Creek Gap. Hike down Vanderbilt's famous Shut-In Trail, once evenly graded for easy travel to and from his estate beside the French Broad River. The route now hosts the famous Shut-In Ridge Trail Run, a grueling 17-mile uphill run. Count your blessings as you head *down* the trail. Water sources are few and far between today, so carry several liters when leaving camp, and fill up at every opportunity.

DAY ELEVEN   10+ miles   1400 feet

Bent Creek Gap to US 191. Continue the descent to the French Broad River and head for a hot shower in a motel—there's a Comfort Inn on US Route 191 (800-622-4005)—a bite to eat, and maybe a movie.

DAY TWELVE   0 miles   0 feet

Resupply, visit Asheville, catch a movie, but most importantly, lay low and rest as the next two days are back-to-back killers.

DAY THIRTEEN   16+ miles   1500 feet

US 191 to US 70. Expect easy walking around Asheville through pretty hardwoods, but it's also noisy where the trail passes over Asheville's major arteries. Head up to the Folk Art Center to check out the small museum and local crafts before hitting a motel—there's a Motel 6 (828-299-3040) 1 mile east on US Route 70.

DAY FOURTEEN   18+ miles   7100 feet

US 70 to Craggy Pinnacle. Burly is the only word to describe this day. Start early and carry plenty of water, as there are few on-trail sources until you reach the visitor center at Craggy Gardens. Camp on the north side of Craggy Pinnacle.

DAY FIFTEEN 10+ miles 2900 feet

Big Fork Ridge to Buncomb Horse Range Trail. Ease up a bit now on the mileage as you approach the southern reach of Mount Mitchell and the east's highest ridgeline. Water is scarce once again, but can be found near camp by the junction of NC 128 and the Buncomb Horse Range Trail.

DAY SIXTEEN 9+ miles 1600 feet

Buncomb Horse Range Trail to Neals Creek. Crest the east's highest peak and celebrate with candy from the snack bar near the parking area. Then tumble down through boulders and spruce and pure stands of hemlock en route to Neals Creek, a frisky river at 3000 feet. Water can be found halfway down the mountain in Setrock Creek.

DAY SEVENTEEN 17 miles 3500 feet

Neals Creek to Toms Creek. Another big day—hope for clear weather as you traverse the exposed narrow ridge of Woods Mountain before descending to gentle Toms Creek, perfect for soaking tired feet. There is virtually no water between camps today, unless you make a quick trip down to Rattlesnake Branch from Woods Mountain.

DAY EIGHTEEN 8 miles 1000 feet

Toms Creek to the North Fork of the Catawba River. Head north 1 mile to stock up on supplies at a small gas station and grocery near a motel, or go south 5.5 miles to a supermarket, chain stores, and chain motel. Find a campsite 3.3 miles down the MST on the other side of the North Fork of the Catawba River. Alternatively, if you end up squandering your day in town, or simply want to have more down time, find a campsite 0.6 miles down the MST from US Route 221, in the woods where the trail leaves the Forest Service road. A nearby water source is unreliable.

DAY NINETEEN 11+ miles 3200 feet

North Fork of the Catawba River to Sandy Branch. Climb the recently constructed trail up dozens of switchbacks past sheer rock faces to Bald and Dobson Knobs. Walk the gated gravel road and cross over to the gravel Kistler Highway and the Pinnacle, where an observation platform reveals the gaping mouth of the Linville Gorge Wilderness. Descend straight down fire lines dug in November 2000 when more than 10,000 acres of the Linville Gorge burned. Water is available on Dobson Knob and at Yellow Fork.

DAY TWENTY 11+ miles 4400 feet

Sandy Branch to Five Points. Five Points is named for the junction of five trails that meet here. Water is nearby, down a drainage to the west. Look for peregrine falcons from Shortoff to Table Rock, and be sure to explore the craggy ridge in between.

Fire scars and lush renewal after the November 2000 forest fire in the Linville Gorge (Photo by Corey Hadden)

DAY TWENTY-ONE 0 miles 0 feet

Take another day to rest and explore the magnificent Linville Gorge Wilderness. The nearby Spence Ridge Trail leads down into the heart of the wilderness, or you can test your off-trail skills by heading for Hawksbill (a trail from its summit leads to the gravel road near your camp for the return trip).

DAY TWENTY-TWO 15+ miles 3200 feet

Five Points to Raider Camp Creek. Another burly day through beautiful southern Appalachian coves. Steels Creek has several premier swimming holes, and distant Upper Creek is a stream-crossing challenge. In between, paved North Carolina Route 181 leads 4 miles north to Jonas Ridge if you need to schedule another supply stop. Camp under towering hemlocks and Poplars beside Raider Camp Creek, or walk another 0.5 mile and make a late-afternoon crossing of Harper Creek and camp on the other side.

DAY TWENTY-THREE 13 miles 2900 feet

Raider Camp Creek to Major Branch of Gragg Prong. Cross Harper and North Harper Creeks several times today, often over your boots. Consider hiking in your

Pastureland on the Blue Ridge Parkway near Blowing Rock (Photo by Corey Hadden)

sandals to expedite the process. Camp down an old forest road from spooky Gragg Cemetery.

DAY TWENTY-FOUR   6+ miles   1700 feet
Gragg Prong to Linville, North Carolina. Resupply 3 miles west of Beacon Heights on US 221 in Linville at a gas station/convenience store, or pick up your General Delivery package at the Linville post office. Stay at the Pixie Inn (828-733-2597) and grab a meal at the Scottish Tartan Restaurant.

DAY TWENTY-FIVE   11 miles   3000 feet
Linville to Daniel Boone Boy Scout Camp. Retrace your last steps of yesterday and follow the MST to the Linn Cove Visitor Center, which details the construction of the Linn Cove Viaduct, the elevated road engineered to meet the needs of the Blue Ridge Parkway without causing too much disturbance of the forest and rocks beneath. Leave the MST for a high camp up the Daniel Boone Boy Scout Trail and an evening summit of Grandfather Mountain. Water is unusually abundant along this stretch and available at camp.

DAY TWENTY-SIX   12+ miles   600 feet
Daniel Boone Boy Scout Camp to Price Memorial Park Campground. Traverse some of the high country's lushest landscapes where the MST shares the treadway with the Boone Fork Trail. A camping fee is required at the Price Memorial Park Campground.

DAY TWENTY-SEVEN   17 miles   1200 feet
Price Memorial Park Campground to Blowing Rock, North Carolina. After about 7 miles, drop your pack and head 2.5 miles up the carriage road to the Flat Top Mountain observation tower on the old Moses Cone estate to celebrate all that you've done in the past three and a half weeks. Head into Blowing Rock, grab some pizza or Mexican food, and call it a trek, or find a motel and gear up for one last day along the Blue Ridge Parkway.

DAY TWENTY-EIGHT   17 miles   2000 feet
Blowing Rock to Deep Gap, North Carolina. Follow the Blue Ridge Parkway. Beyond Blowing Rock, through-hiking the MST is a logistical challenge as there are no Park Service campgrounds and no adjacent Forest Service land within easy reach for someone on foot. One day, hopefully, campsites for hikers will be established to enable a true Appalachian Trail–style through-hike without the need for motels or lengthy road walks. For now, if you feel led to see where the Blue Ridge and the southern Appalachians drop away to the piedmont, drop your pack and head for Deep Gap, the easternmost trailhead in our guide and 15.4

miles down the Blue Ridge Parkway. It's a long stretch of road walking, to be sure, but one filled with sublime overlooks and the last of the lush southern Appalachian landscape.

Trail Summary and Mileage Estimates

Note: The cumulative mileages listed here represent points along the MST only, and do not include side hikes or travel to and from resupply locations. That mileage is included in the recommended daily itineraries, however.

0	Clingmans Dome (6643 feet)
25.8	Oconaluftee Visitor Center (2030 feet), bear right onto Oconaluftee River Trail
26.5	Blue Ridge Parkway (2015 feet), turn left onto BRP
37	Wolf Laurel Gap (5100 feet)
40	Soco Gap (4345 feet)
44.5	Waterrock Knob access road (5700 feet), trail from parking area leads 0.5 mile to summit (6296 feet)
52.5	Balsam Gap (3380 feet)
66.5	Camp south of Old Bald (5200 feet)
77.5	Camp in field past Piney Creek
87	Field near NC 215
96.8	Yellowstone Prong (4350 feet)
108.8	Mount Pisgah Campground (4940 feet)
118.6	Bent Creek Gap (3280 feet)
127.5	US 191/French Broad River (2000 feet)
140.6	US 70 (2120 feet)
141.1	Folk Art Center (2240 feet)
158	Craggy Gardens Visitor Center (5500 feet)
168.6	NC 128 and Buncomb Horse Range Trail (5390 feet)
178.4	Neals Creek (3100 feet)
195.4	Toms Creek (1480 feet)
203.4	North Fork of the Catawba River (1320 feet)
215.3	Sandy Branch (1480 feet)
226.5	Near Forest Road 210 (2900 feet)
242.1	Raider Camp Creek (1600 feet)
255.1	Major Branch of Gragg Prong (3000 feet)
258.5	Beacon Heights (4200 feet)
266.5	Daniel Boone Boy Scout Camp (4830 feet)
279	Price Memorial Park Campground (3420 feet)
289.8	Old Camp Catawba Road/US 321
305.8	US 421 at Deep Gap (3140 feet)

The Appalachian Trail (GA/NC/TN/VA)

Difficulty:	Strenuous
Distance:	462 miles
Elevation gain:	120,000 feet
Recommended itinerary:	6-8 weeks (10 miles per day)

Imagine for a moment: It's midmorning and you're at work. Behind the spreadsheet of the meaningless data you're sorting is a discount airfare website. Your bid for a one-way ticket to Atlanta has been accepted, and you'll be flying out tonight. The next morning, at the visitor center at Amicalola Falls State Park, at the base of Springer Mountain, you ask sheepishly if anyone can point you toward the Appalachian Trail. "Just walk through the double doors," they'll say, "pass under the stone arch, and follow the blue-blazed Approach Trail. It's about 9 miles."

Contrary to what many people believe, walking the Appalachian Trail is not only for the veteran wilderness explorer; it is for anyone and everyone with a desire to get away from their routine and be alone. Walking the Appalachian Trail, however far you go, is less about your ability to light a stove with wet matches than it is about less tangible skills like determination and patience. The campcraft skills will be second nature after a few days on trail. Perhaps what matters most of all is taming your imagination over such a long and physical trip.

This chapter is intended to give you an introduction to planning a through-hike along the southern Appalachian portion of the AT. Hiking the AT is a topic for a book all its own, and one that has already been written by more experienced veterans of the trail. Our aim is to whet your appetite for a long-distance hike by demystifying some of the logistics and providing a brief overview.

"Thru-hiker" is the term associated with the determined individuals that elect to hike from one end of the AT to the other, usually from Georgia to Maine, though a handful go against the grain and begin up north. Section hikers are folks hiking the AT in chunks because of time constraints, finances, or simply the wish to time a hike with a particular season's natural wonders. While the AT through the southern Appalachians is less than a quarter of the entire route to Maine, we suggest it as an alternative for those that shudder at the thought of being gone for six months and walking more than 2000 miles.

start

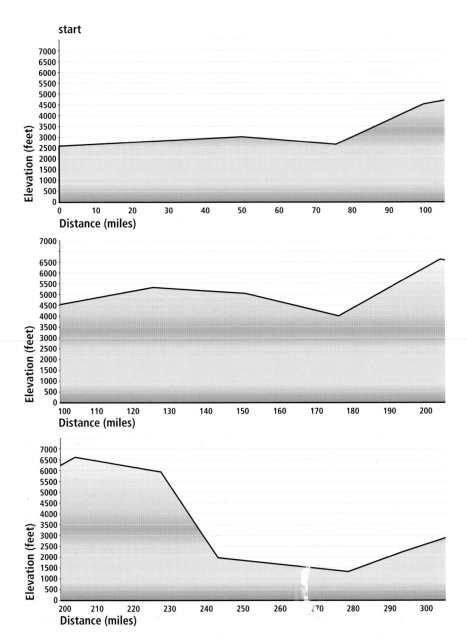

The AT snakes its way through the southern Appalachians for about 455 miles (nearly a quarter of the entire Appalachian Trail) from its southern terminus on the craggy summit of Springer Mountain in Georgia to the small mountain town of Damascus, Virginia, just beyond the Tennessee state line. From the first steps on the Approach Trail in Amicalola Falls State Park to Holston Mountain just south of

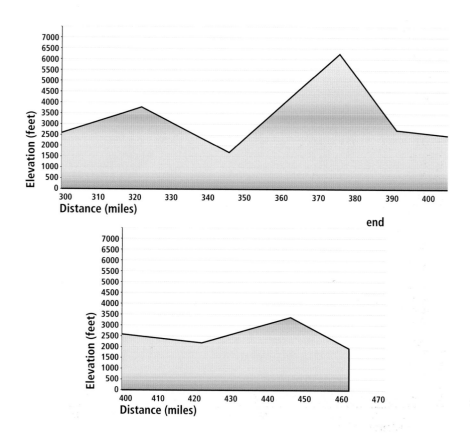

Distance (miles)

end

Distance (miles)

Damascus, the trail climbs hundreds of knobs, crosses even more streams, and cuts through dozens of towns. Along the way the AT traverses five national forests: Chattahoochee, Nantahala, Cherokee, Pisgah, and Jefferson; one national park: Great Smoky Mountains; several wilderness areas, including Blood Mountain, Southern Nantahala, Samson Mountain, Pond Mountain, and Big Laurel Branch; and passes countless fire towers, scenic vistas, coves, and mountain balds.

In 1921, the *Journal of the American Institute of Architects* published an article titled "An Appalachian Trail A Project in Regional Planning." The article marked the first publicly detailed proposal for a foot trail connecting the northern and southern Appalachians. The author was Benton MacKaye, a spirited regional planner from New England. Today, MacKaye (rhymes with "sky") is mostly known as the father of the AT, though he stands with the giants of the modern conservation movement. An Appalachian trail was central to MacKaye's ultimate goal—to control the loss of open space resulting from unplanned growth and development of eastern cities.

According to MacKaye, from his forward in *The Appalachian Trail* by Ronald M. Fisher (National Geographic Society, 1972), two events were pivotal in securing the future of the trail: the creation of the Appalachian Trail Conference to manage

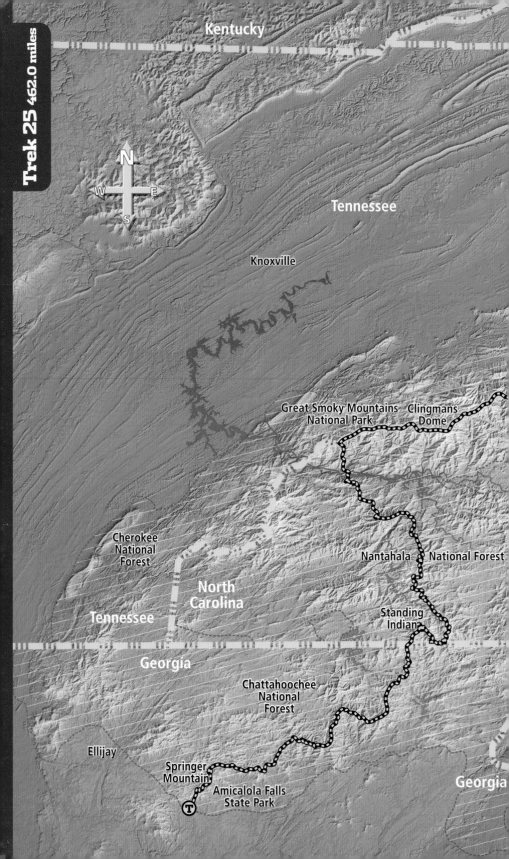

Kentucky

Tennessee

Knoxville

Great Smoky Mountains
National Park   Clingmans
Dome

Cherokee
National
Forest

Nantahala   National Forest

North
Carolina

Standing
Indian

Tennessee

Georgia

Chattahoochee
National
Forest

Ellijay

Springer
Mountain

Amicalola Falls
State Park

Georgia

N
W   E
S

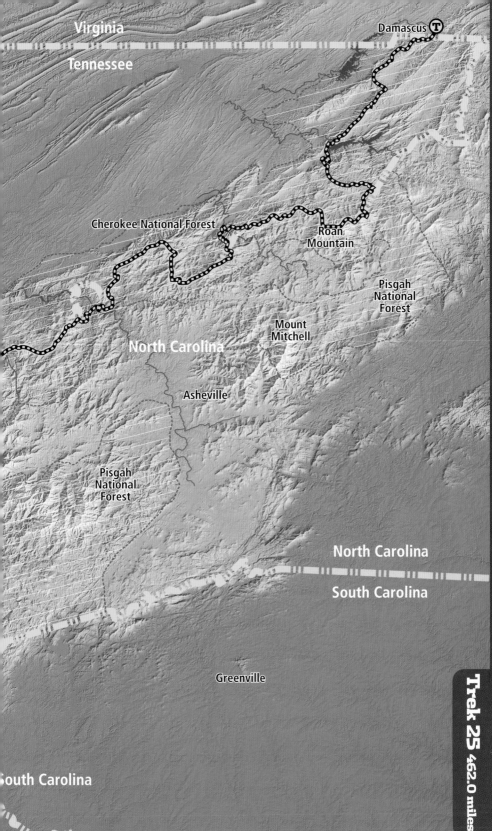

Virginia

Damascus Ⓣ

Tennessee

Cherokee National Forest

Roan
Mountain

Pisgah
National
Forest

North Carolina

Mount
Mitchell

Asheville

Pisgah
National
Forest

North Carolina

South Carolina

Greenville

South Carolina

Trek 25 462.0 miles

Flame Azalea (Photo by Corey Hadden)

regional clubs and actively maintain the trail, and the National Trails System Act of 1968, signed into law by President Lyndon Johnson, which gave the trail federal protection. Suffice it to say, MacKaye's proposal for an Appalachian trail ignited a fire among conservationists, wilderness users, citizens, and elected officials. In the ensuing years, clubs were formed and money was allocated, volunteers were coordinated and regional sections were constructed. Thanks to MacKaye and scores of dedicated volunteers, the AT is the crown jewel of American hiking.

Logistics of a thru-hike: A detailed description of thru-hiking the AT is beyond the scope of this book. We recommend further research to prepare. There's plenty to consider, whether you plan to stop in Damascus or Maine. Here, we highlight a few points to consider, including how to manage food and gear, when to go, and a timeframe.

There are two primary methods for handling food rations and other supplies: outfitting everything from your home base or relying on a credit card and resupplying regularly at small trail towns along the way. The advantages of the latter are that you can hike where and when you want, so if you find yourself passing the turnoff for the Mountains-to-Sea Trail, for example, and suddenly feel pulled to see the ocean, you can follow your inclination. Just about every town that the Appalachian Trail passes through or near has services geared specifically for thru-hikers and other trail users: shuttles, trail food, gear stores, and fuel, handily sold in the quantity you want. The method is convenient, but considerably more expensive than stocking up at home, since the food you buy won't be in bulk. You can buy or have plastic bags on hand for repackaging store-bought food supplies.

Using the home-planning method, many hikers plan elaborate food and gear drops, often mailed by someone at home to a convenient post office along the way. This option, though logistically challenging in the beginning, has several merits:

1. Most food can be bought ahead of time in bulk (i.e., on the cheap) and

repackaged in the quantity and variety desired, reducing cost and difficult-to-carry packaging (e.g., a plastic bag of pasta vs. a cardboard box).

2. Planned drops enable you to phone ahead to your logistics guru and request a specific food item or piece of gear (e.g., it's unseasonably colder than expected, and you want that fleece sooner rather than later).

3. A connection is maintained with those at home. Of course, you can always call home, but there's something refreshingly sweet about receiving a package full of goodies every now and then.

Many hikers use a combination of the two methods, augmenting food shipped or brought from home with fresh fruits and vegetables purchased along the way and whole meals at local restaurants. As you plan your hike consider your reasons for going. This will help you determine the level of support you wish to have from folks at home. Alternatively, it's possible to hire a service to manage the logistics for you.

How much time to set aside for such a long trek really depends on how fast you walk with a backpack, and how you tend to spend your time on trail. We average about 2 miles per hour with a pack, but often take leisurely stops to check out wildflowers or neat rock formations. A day of 10 miles is pretty easy. Conversely, a 15-mile day requires a greater commitment. Twenty-mile days are hard, though not unreasonable with a light pack. Be sure to plan some periods of rest or "zero" days, as thru-hikers refer to days off.

For a month-long trek (or longer) consider at least one rest day per week. This

Blood Mountain shelter (Photo by Corey Hadden)

Winter in the Southern Appalachians

allows time to rest, recover from injury or illness, and stay in camp if the weather is absolutely lousy. A trek of 462 miles averaging 10 miles per day requires six and a half weeks, or about forty-six days of travel. Adding one rest day per week adds another six or seven days, bringing the total to fifty-three days—almost eight weeks.

Consider other time off for each day you plan to spend in town handling your resupply needs and other logistics.

Best season: There is no "best" season for through-hiking the southern Appalachian portion of the Appalachian Trail. Spring is when most thru-hikers are on the trail, for the simple reason that getting to Maine before colder weather takes hold is a priority. Expect trail shelters to be crowded, and to encounter the occasional herd of thru-hikers migrating down the trail. Late-season snow is not uncommon in mid-April at middle and upper elevations, though most days are relatively mild with cool nights.

Summer brings warm, wet weather. Afternoon thunderstorms are a daily occurrence in the mountainous south. The lushness of the southern Appalachian forests is unparalleled in the contiguous United States, in part due to its abundant rainfall. By mid-June and July, the southern mountains are bursting at the seams with luscious greenery. Summer also brings throngs of day hikers, campers, and section-hikers, though most of these folks will be found near popular destinations, such as the Smokies, Springer Mountain, and Roan Mountain. The advantage of summer is that you can travel light, as you won't need thick insulating layers or a warm sleeping bag. Summer is also often the most convenient time for folks to take a month off from work to undertake a section hike.

Fall brings drier weather and stunning colors to the mountains—these features also bring many people to the trail, although they're mostly weekend warriors. You're likely to have much of it to yourself, however. Colder weather sets in early at higher elevations, so plan ahead and bring gear appropriate for cold-weather camping.

As for winter, there is nothing like the peaceful stillness of a snowy landscape, punctuated by the call of a nuthatch or the sudden clump of snow falling from the crown of a pine. Winter is the best season for solitude, but before you go be sure you know how to handle cold and snowy weather. Though southern winters in general are short and mild by northern standards, winter at higher elevations can be fierce and requires solid winter camping skills.

Should you go alone or with someone? The question of whether to embark on a long-distance trek alone or with someone is something only you can answer, but here are some things to consider. Most thru-hikers embark on their journey alone, and friendships made along the trail can be long-lasting. Few hikers headed to Maine who begin with a specific partner finish with that person, citing different goals and different hiking paces among the chief reasons. A shorter, regional thru-hike is a great way to hike with a partner, but be mindful of changing attitudes and expectations along the way and ask yourself before you go if you'd be willing to split up if the need should arise. Hiking for weeks on end is emotionally committing. Choosing the right partner is critical and is a task that is perhaps more monumental than the trek itself. So, the big question now is what are you waiting for?

Appendix

Agency Contacts

National Forests in North Carolina
Supervisor's Office
160A Zillicoa Street
Asheville, NC 28801
828-257-4200
(Take UNCA exit off US 19/23, go
 toward UNCA to first right)

PISGAH NATIONAL FOREST

www.cs.unca.edu/nfsnc

Appalachian Ranger District
French Broad Station
P.O. Box 128
Hot Springs, NC 28743
828-622-3202
(On US 25/70 in Hot Springs)

Grandfather Ranger District
Route 1, Box 110-A
Nebo, NC 28761
828-652-2144
(At exit 90, Nebo/Lake James, off I-40, 9
 miles east of Marion)

Appalachian Ranger District
Toecane Ranger Station
P.O. Box 128
Burnsville, NC 28714
828-682-6146
(On US 19E bypass in Burnsville)

Pisgah Ranger District
1001 Pisgah Highway
Pisgah Forest, NC 28768
828-877-3265
(On US 276 northeast of Brevard)

NANTAHALA NATIONAL FOREST

www.cs.unca.edu/nfsnc

Cheoah Ranger District
Route 1, Box 16A
Robbinsville, NC 28771
828-479-6431
(On US 129 north of Robbinsville)

Highlands Ranger District
2010 Flat Mountain Road
Highlands, NC 28741
828-526-3765
(Follow the signs from US 64 east of
 Highlands)

Tusquitee Ranger District
123 Woodland Drive
Murphy, NC 28906
828-837-5152

Wayah Ranger District
90 Sloan Road
Franklin, NC 28734
828-524-6441
(Turn at sign on US 614, west of Franklin)

CHATTAHOOCHEE NATIONAL FOREST

www.fs.fed.us/conf

Chattahoochee and Oconee National
  Forests
Supervisor's Office
1755 Cleveland Highway
Gainesville, GA 30501
770-297-3000

Armuchee-Cohutta Ranger District
3941 Highway 76
Chatsworth, GA 30705
706-695-6736

Brasstown Ranger District
1881 Highway 515
P.O. Box 9
Blairsville, GA 30514
706-745-6928

Chattooga Ranger District
200 Highway 197 N
P.O. Box 1960
Clarkesville, GA 30523
706-754-6221

Tallulah Ranger District
809 Highway 441 S
Clayton, GA 30525
706-782-3320

Toccoa Ranger District
6050 Appalachian Highway
Blue Ridge, GA 30513
706-632-3031

SUMTER NATIONAL FOREST

www.fs.fed.us/r8/fms

Andrew Pickens Ranger District
112 Andrew Pickens Circle
Mountain Rest, SC 29664
864-638-9568

CHEROKEE NATIONAL FOREST

www.southernregion.fs.fed.us/Cherokee

Cherokee National Forest
Supervisor's Office
P.O. Box 2010
Cleveland, TN 37320
423-476-9700

Ocoee/Hiawassee Ranger District
3171 Highway 64 E
Benton, TN 37307
423-338-5201

Nolichucky/Unaka Ranger District
4900 Asheville Highway 70
Greenville, TN 37743
423-638-4109

Watauga Ranger District
P.O. Box 400
Unicoi, TN 37692
423-735-1500

Tellico/Hiwassee Ranger District
250 Ranger Station Road
Tellico Plains, TN 37385
423-253-2520

JEFFERSON NATIONAL FOREST

www.southernregion.fs.fed.us/gwj/mr

Mount Rogers National Recreation Area
3714 Highway 16
Marion, VA 24354-4097
800-628-7202

NATIONAL PARKS

Great Smoky Mountains National Park
107 Park Headquarters Road
Gatlinburg, TN 37738
865-436-1200
www.nps.gov/grsm
Backcountry reservations: 865-436-1231
Campground reservations:
  800-365-CAMP

Blue Ridge Parkway
199 Hemphill Knob Road
Asheville, NC 28803-8686
www.nps.gov/blri
Information: 828-271-4779
Emergencies: 828-350-3826

STATE PARKS

Amicalola Falls State Park
240 Amicalola Falls State Park Road
Dawsonville, GA 305354
706-265-4703
www.gastateparks.org

Mount Mitchell State Park
Route 5, Box 700
Burnsville, NC 28714
828-675-4611
www.ils.unc.edu/parkprojects/ncparks.html

Gorges State Park
P.O. Box 100
Sapphire, NC 28774-0100
828-966-9099
www.ils.unc.edu/parkprojects/ncparks.html

Jones Gap State Park
303 Jones Gap Road
Marietta, SC 29661
864-836-3647
www.southcarolinaparks.com

Caesars Head State Park
8155 Geer Highway 276
Cleveland, SC 29635
864-836-6115
www.southcarolinaparks.com

Table Rock State Park
158 E. Ellison Lane
Pickens, SC 29671
864-878-9813
www.southcarolinaparks.com

OTHER

South Carolina Department of Natural
  Resources
1000 Assembly Street
Columbia, SC 29201
803-734-3918
www.dnr.state.sc.us

Grandfather Mountain
P.O. Box 129
Linville, NC 28646
800-468-7325
www.grandfathermountain.com

Bad Creek Hydrostation
Duke Energy
SC 130
Salem, SC 29676
864-944-4000

Bibliography

Appalachian Trail Conference. *Appalachian Trail Guide to Tennessee–North Carolina.* 11th ed. National Geographic Trails Illustrated. 1995.

Appalachian Trail Conference. *Appalachian Trail Guide to North Carolina–Georgia.* 11th ed. National Geographic Trails Illustrated. 1998.

Bartram, William. *The Travels of William Bartram.* Naturalist's ed. Edited with commentary and annotated index by Francis Harper. Athens, Ga.: University of Georgia Press. 1998.

Carter, Mark, Carl Merschat, and William Wilson. *A Geologic Adventure Along the Blue Ridge Parkway in North Carolina.* Bulletin 98. Raleigh: North Carolina Geological Survey Section, Department of Environment and Natural Resources, Division of Land Resources. Reprint 2001.

De Hart, Allen. *Hiking North Carolina's Mountains-to-Sea Trail.* Chapel Hill: University of North Carolina Press. 2000.

De Hart, Allen. *North Carolina Hiking Trails.* 3d ed. Boston: Appalachian Mountain Club Books. 1996. Distributed by the Globe Pequot Press.

Duncan, Barbara, Brett Riggs, Blue Ridge Heritage Intiative, and Museum of the Cherokee Indian. *Cherokee Heritage Trails Guidebook.* Chapel Hill: University of North Carolina Press. 2003.

Fisher, Ronald M. *The Appalachian Trail.* Washington: National Geographic Society. 1972.

Garton, John. *Guide to the Foothills Trail.* 3d ed. The Foothills Trail Conference.

Great Smoky Mountains Natural History Association. *Hiking Trails of the Smokies.* 2d ed. Gatlinburg, Tenn.: Great Smoky Mountains Natural History Association. 2001.

Houk, R. *Great Smoky Mountains: A Natural History Guide.* Houghton Mifflin CO. New York 1993.

Kephart, Horace. *Our Southern Highlanders: A Narrative of Adventure in the Southern Appalachians and a Study of Life Among the Mountaineers.* Knoxville: University of Tennessee Press. 1976.

Weber, Walt. *Trail Profiles, the mountains-to-sea trail: from Beech Gap to Black Mountain Campground.* Alexander, NC: WorldComm. 1999.

Index

About the Authors

A resident of Asheville, North Carolina, Jack Igelman has explored the southern Appalachian Mountains by foot, bike, rope, and boat for more than fifteen years. A former Outward Bound instructor, Jack's writing has appeared in many outdoor publications.

Jack Igelman (Photo by Elizabeth Pendleton)

Corey Hadden first discovered the outdoors exploring the forests and trails near his childhood home in New Jersey. Since then, he has climbed, paddled, and carried a pack throughout the Americas—from Canada to the Andes. A graduate of Earlham College, and an avid birder, Corey lives in North Carolina and is an instructor for the North Carolina Outward Bound School.

Corey Hadden (Photo courtesy of NCOBS Archives)